ROUTLEDGE LIBRARY EDITIONS: TOURISM

BUILDING A NEW HERITAGE

T0300186

BUILDING A NEW HERITAGE

Tourism, Culture and Identity in the New Europe

Edited by
G. J. ASHWORTH AND
P. J. LARKHAM

Volume 3

Routledge
Taylor & Francis Group

LONDON AND NEW YORK

First published in 1994

This edition first published in 2013
by Routledge
2 Park Square, Milton Park, Abingdon, Oxfordshire OX14 4RN

Simultaneously published in the USA and Canada
by Routledge
711 Third Avenue, New York, NY 10017

First issued in paperback 2014

Routledge is an imprint of the Taylor and Francis Group, an informa company

British Library Cataloguing in Publication Data
A catalogue record for this book is available from the British Library

ISBN 13: 978-0-415-81233-7 (Volume 3)
ISBN 13: 978-0-415-75148-3 (pbk)

Publisher's Note
The publisher has gone to great lengths to ensure the quality of this reprint but points out that some imperfections in the original copies may be apparent.

Disclaimer
The publisher has made every effort to trace copyright holders and would welcome correspondence from those they have been unable to trace.

BUILDING A NEW HERITAGE

Tourism, Culture and Identity in the New Europe

Edited by *G.J. Ashworth* and *P.J. Larkham*

London and New York

First published 1994
by Routledge
11 New Fetter Lane, London EC4P 4EE

Simultaneously published in the USA and Canada
by Routledge
29 West 35th Street, New York, NY 10001

Typeset in Times by
J&L Composition Ltd, Filey, North Yorkshire
Printed and bound in Great Britain by
Biddles Ltd, Guildford and King's Lynn

British Library Cataloguing in Publication Data
A catalogue record for this book is available from the British Library

Library of Congress Cataloging in Publication Data
Building a new heritage: tourism, culture, and identity/edited by
G.J. Ashworth and P.J. Larkham.
p.   cm.
Substantially rev. papers from a conference organized by the Urban
Geography Study Group of the Institute of British Geographers, held Jan.
1992, together with other essays.
Cover subtitle: Tourism, culture, and identity in the new Europe.
Includes bibliographical references.
ISBN 0–415–07931–4
1. Cultural property, Protection of—Europe—History—20th century—
Congresses.   2. Ethnicity—Europe—Congresses.   3. Nationalism—
Europe—History—20th century—Congresses.   4. Tourism—
Europe—History—20th century—Congresses.   I. Ashworth, G.J.
(Gregory John)   II. Larkham, P.J. (Peter J.), 1960–
D1055.B85 1994   93–43216
940.5—dc20   CIP
ISBN 0–415–07931–4

CONTENTS

FIGURES

FIGURES

TABLES

CONTRIBUTORS

G.J. Ashworth	Professor of Heritage Management and Tourism, Department of Physical Planning and Demography, University of Groningen (The Netherlands)
E.A.J. Carr	Chief Executive, Cadw, Cardiff (UK)
A.G.J. Dietvorst	Professor of Recreation Studies, Centre for Recreation Studies, Agricultural University, Wageningen (The Netherlands)
B.J. Graham	Senior Lecturer, Department of Environmental Studies, University of Ulster, Coleraine (UK)
R. Hammersley	Principal Lecturer in Planning, School of Planning, University of Central England in Birmingham (UK)
P.J. Larkham	Lecturer in Planning, School of Planning, University of Central England in Birmingham (UK)
D. Light	Lecturer, Department of Environmental and Biological Studies, Liverpool Institute of Higher Education (UK)
I. Masser	Professor, Department of Town and Regional Planning, University of Sheffield (UK)
E. Morris	Lecturer, Urban Design and Rural Studies, University of Edinburgh (UK)
P.T. Newby	Head of Educational Development, University of Middlesex, Enfield (UK)

CONTRIBUTORS

R.C. Prentice	Lecturer, Department of Hospitality Studies, Queen Margaret College, Edinburgh (UK)
J. Soane	Research Fellow, Department of Geography, University of Reading (UK)
O. Svidén	Department of Management and Economics, Linkoping University (Sweden)
J.E. Tunbridge	Associate Professor, Department of Geography, Carleton University, Ottawa (Canada)
M. Wegener	Institute of Spatial Planning, University of Dortmund (Germany)
T. Westlake	Senior Lecturer in Planning, School of Planning, University of Central England in Birmingham (UK)

PREFACE

The topic of European unity and identity versus individual state identities and nationalisms is crucial in the discussions, both at governmental and public levels, that have been taking place throughout the late 1980s and into the 1990s. Many of the problems seem intractable, and matters became rather worse with the entry into the picture of the former Soviet bloc countries seeking to reinforce their own statehood and identity, minimize the history and memory of Soviet/communist control, and take advantage of the perceived material benefits of West European capitalism. Throughout these discussions, there runs a significant thread of nationalism, state-identity and place-identity, which many have sought to invoke and strengthen by calls upon history. Is there to be a new European history for a new Europe – however wide its net is cast? Or will the fragmentary trend continue, with nationalistic interpretations of national heritages dividing the Community?

The upsurge of interest in these topics, and the rapidity of change within Europe, suggested to the Urban Geography Study Group of the Institute of British Geographers (IBG) that a special session on these themes should be convened during one of the Institute's Annual Conferences, and this took place during January 1992. Even during the organization of the session, the potential shape of Europe changed dramatically as the Soviet bloc began to fragment, and the Berlin Wall was breached. The session was well attended, the diversity of scholars presenting papers and others contributing to formal and informal discussions demonstrating the popularity and topicality of these themes. The primary concern of both speakers and audience was to explore the potentially significant positive contribution that the identification and awareness of heritage, and heritage planning, could make to this newly emerging supra-national body. Yet the conference was of value more in identifying the nature and scale of the problem than in identifying answers. We are at a very early stage in thinking of the totality of Europe, including the former east and west; and in forecasting likely socio-economic changes and consequent demands on heritage and tourism. The likely exploitation of heritage in creating identity in the emerging small states – and, indeed, in Europe as a whole – is under-researched. There is no single conservation/heritage ethic: many approaches have been tried throughout Europe, but there has been no drawing-together of ideas or experiences.

It was evident to the session conveners that many of the papers presented would form the basis of a volume of essays which would provide an introduction to this topic. However, this volume is considerably more than the proceedings of the conference, for each of the papers has been substantially revised following the conference discussion sessions and editorial suggestions, and other essays have been included to present a balanced book. This volume identifies certain lacunae: it is the necessary foundation on which further studies must build.

The organization of the conference, and preparation of this volume, were greatly aided by the facilities of the Department of Urban and Regional Planning, University of Groningen, the School of Geography, University of Birmingham, and the School of Planning, University of Central England in Birmingham. The Nuffield Foundation contributed generously towards the cost of travel and accommodation of a number of speakers, many of whose contributions have been rewritten to form chapters of this volume. Members of the IBG Urban Geography Study Group assisted with the smooth running of the conference session, and have commented on various of the chapters in draft form.

Greg Ashworth, University of Groningen
Peter Larkham, University of Central England

1

A HERITAGE FOR EUROPE
The need, the task, the contribution
G.J. Ashworth and P.J. Larkham

THE NEED AND THE ARGUMENT

The halting progress of the post-Second World War nation states of Europe towards some form of supra-national integration has focused principally on economic affairs, and has predominantly been expressed through the establishment of institutions and through legal and administrative measures (see, for example, the majority of the contributions in Hurwitz and Lequesne 1991). With the exception of the short-lived relief and euphoria immediately following the war's end in 1945, these administrative and bureaucratic changes have had little evident root in popular sentiment. The evolution of a trading cartel of nation states into a social, cultural or political entity would seem to require a consensus of popular support or, at the very least, acceptance. This, in turn, requires a reformulation of the mental map of Europeans to encompass a new place-identity at the continental scale.

The idea of the nation state was strongly reinforced by nationalist interpretations of the past, and it is no coincidence that the timing of the rise in interest in the conservation of relict artefacts of the built environment in the latter half of the nineteenth century in Europe coincided with the creation of the nation states of Germany, the Balkans and Italy. It has become clear, in the post-Maastricht discussions in Europe, that the obituaries of the nation state written by the supporters of a new post-nationalist Europe were, to say the least, premature. National identity based on an awareness of a national history is still a vital force in the countries of western Europe, where it had lain somewhat dormant in the years of the post-war settlement and cold war confrontation of the supra-national ideologies. In addition, the collapse of the Soviet hegemony

1

in central and eastern Europe is releasing sets of new, or at least previously suppressed, and conflicting nationalisms based upon a rediscovery of national histories. The shaping of a European place-identity to complement, if not replace, national identities has thus never been more urgent or more necessary. The political, economic and ultimately social goals of a European Community (however defined) cannot be achieved by summits, treaties and directives alone. These must receive an echo of consent from Europeans who identify with a supra-national entity. This, in turn, requires a reinterpretation of the past. The central assertion of this volume, contained implicitly or explicitly in all of its constituent Chapters, is thus that a new Europe requires a new past as a precondition for its emergence.

The enormity of this task is daunting. We are aware that history, in the sense of the remembered past, is not the only contributor to the broader concept of heritage, which also draws upon mythologies, folklores and the products of creative imaginations. The focus of this volume is principally upon the use of the surviving physical relics in the built environment, but new 'historic' monuments, or monuments to a new, reconstructed or reinterpreted history are also of relevance. This is partly because these relics and monuments have always been of major, and possibly disproportionate, importance in what can be termed 'public history'; that is, the financing, organization or encouragement by government agencies at various scales of relics, monuments and locations in a declared public interest. It is this public aspect that brings this activity into the arena of public scrutiny and public planning and intervention, even though we are aware that such public histories are only one element in the private histories that form the heritage of individuals. Similarly heritage, however composed, is only one aspect of the identity of places which is composed of much wider individual satisfactions with ways and qualities of life.

Against these limiting caveats, we would argue two fundamental points that render this volume's task not only possible, but in practice inevitable, in one form or another. First, heritage – as we define it – has a proven track record of outstanding success in formulating and reinforcing place-identities in support of particular state entities. We are, therefore, suggesting no more than the addition to, or redirection of, a portion of these efforts. Second, this is an activity in which governments have already assumed large responsibilities, for a variety of ostensible reasons. Major historical resources in most countries are already in official ownership or guardianship, as are many of the most important channels of interpretation. Selected aspects of the past are thus being, and will continue to be, interpreted by public agencies for public objectives, whether overtly stated or not. This has consequent impacts, whether stated or not, upon place-identities.

Finally, set against the daunting task of reformulating the place-identity of a continent by reinterpreting its past, we balance the imperatives of its necessity and its urgency. There is no consensus among the contributors to this volume about the nature of the new European entity that will, or should, emerge over the next decade or so. Authors include all shades of 'Eurofanaticism', 'Euroscepticism' and even 'Europhobia'. All, however, believe that Europe at the end of the twentieth century is faced with a choice of repeating the example of the nineteenth century as a fragmented and warring set of nations and regions powered by religious heritages, or of moving into the twenty-first century with a new identity based upon a common and distinctive European heritage. This diversity of views is a strength of the volume.

CHALLENGE AND PROGRESS

The growth and development of a public concern with the surviving relics of the past has a relatively short, but surprisingly volatile, history. A useful early survey of conservation in Europe is given by Brown (1905). Dellheim (1982) shows how the vogue for local archaeological and historical studies grew, particularly in early nineteenth-century Britain, and the consequences of this for the discovery and formulation of local and national interpretations of heritage artefacts. The manner in which the enthusiasm of such small groups of influential and knowledgeable amateurs, and powerful individuals, grew from the second half of the nineteenth century in Europe, and was recognized and formalized in national legislation a hundred years or so later, is related in, among others, Dobby (1978) and Kennett (1972). Concerns for monument identification and preservation have changed (see, for example, Thompson 1981). The shift towards concern for wider areas rather than individual monuments or buildings, and for conservation rather than preservation, with all the implications of this shift in focus for the management of land and building uses, occurred in the middle decades of the twentieth century in almost all European countries (see the comparative studies in Burtenshaw *et al.* 1991). The last twenty years have been characterized by attempts to manage the problems of success, as more designated buildings, more extensive conservation areas and whole towns have been included in the ever-inflating official lists (see, for example, Jones and Larkham 1993). Not only is the modern use of the past now an inescapable aspect of its preservation, but it is also clear that there now exists a 'conserver society' that creates its own landscapes (Relph 1982; Larkham 1992).

The choice of content of the distinctly European heritage, intended to reinforce popular identification with that scale of political entity, requires answers to two main questions. First, which of the many diverse European heritages is to be selected? The current European Community model favours institutional, bureaucratic, free-market, social-capitalist and liberal representative democratic elements. A review of the long history of attempts at achieving European unity, in its various possible forms, reveals many other models based upon quite different heritages, from medieval Christendom to communism. Second, what is to be done with 'dissonant heritage'? For there is much heritage that does not conform to these currently prevailing norms and objectives. Europe's long history of war, pogrom and persecution between nations, classes, races and religions has left its own legacies, which markedly contradict any theme of harmonious unity. Are these to be ignored, or somehow reinterpreted within the new European heritage product? Dissonance may equally be caused by shifts in population groups that leave behind cultural and material relics that no longer reflect contemporary place symbolisms. Similarly, shifts in dominant ideologies leave memorials of previously prevailing values to haunt and conflict with current interpretations, as can be seen throughout post-communist Europe.

BUILDING A NEW HERITAGE: STRUCTURE AND CONTRIBUTIONS

The contributions to this volume are as varied in their disciplinary approach and selection of regional application as are the expertise and experience of the authors. All, however, are attempting in various ways to bridge the two main gaps in the argument which have briefly been outlined above. The first is the gulf between the resources from the past, frequently in practice being conserved buildings and cities, and their modern uses, which include identity with specified spatial-jurisdictional entities, but which are by no means exclusively so. The past is used in many different ways, and the heritage industry has many customers. The second gap is between those producing heritage and those consuming it, either of which groups may or may not be conscious of their role in this relationship.

The various attempts to bridge these gaps are not always successfully completed, if only because frequently an individual Chapter or author is principally and inevitably concerned with only a part of the total construction. Nevertheless, in bringing together these contributions, this volume is preparing the ground for the summary and synthesis necessary if a new European heritage is to emerge.

Chapters 2 and 3 both attempt to state initial integrating positions. The first does so through the establishment of a simple process model, then deriving sets of concepts from this, hoping thereby to arrive at assumptions which can be used as common currency in the following, more detailed, sectoral analyses and empirical studies. The second examines the nature of the emerging new Europe in terms of broad trends likely to occur in various aspects of the European economy and society in the next three decades; a necessary scene-setting exercise. Although the research reported in this Chapter does not cover the former communist bloc, plausible scenarios are expressed for the rest of Europe, which are clearly applicable to much of eastern Europe in its apparent rush to embrace many elements of western capitalism.

Those agencies concerned with the care and maintenance of preserved artefacts, such as the Welsh Cadw (Chapter 4), clearly all have agendas that are both narrower, but more sharply focused, than 'heritage' as defined throughout this volume. Their focus of attention is on objects entrusted to their care, rather than to any actual or possible use of such objects and sites. Visitors often seem to be accepted as a necessary evil, or tolerated as a marginal extra function, to be managed in such a way that the exhibits remain intact. However, what is implied by 'intact' varies through time and from place to place, as the contrast between the English and Welsh preference for sanitized, manicured ruins to the French reconstruction shows (Thompson 1981). Similarly, although on a different scale, the German town planning, or more accurately town designing, which is the subject of Chapter 9, may have considerable implications for the shaping of the identities of the cities so treated by 'vernacularization'. Although these may include the types of political objectives central to this argument, they are equally a result of a much wider range of factors involving changing ideas about the functioning of cities.

The agencies and companies with an interest in the consumption of heritage are similarly concerned with only a part of the heritage process, but they are also responsible for wider functions or activities well beyond the topic of interest here. The visitor to historic sites, as described in Chapter 6, is evaluating heritage against other possible leisure pursuits. The relationship of historic resources and tourism, as analysed in Chapter 5, is very asymmetrical. Tourism may contribute substantially to the financial maintenance of monuments, be used as a justification for their continued existence by their managers, and help to create popular public support for conservation policies. It is, however, interested in actually using only a small proportion of extant historic resources in a limited area of a minority of selected cities. Above all, heritage tourism is only one form of tourism among many, and historical attractions but one set of easily substituted tourism facilities among many others. The current demand for heritage tourism may be high and growing, for all of the reasons described in Chapter 6, but the supply of possible products created from what is, after all, a ubiquitous resource (in so far as all places have a past) is larger and probably growing faster. Conservation may be becoming aware of its increasing dependence upon tourism, but the tourism industry is not so dependent upon the conserved built environment, as the growing number of 'authentic' reconstructions and theme parks suggests.

Several chapters that attempt to take a more comprehensive view of both the supply and demand sides do so at the expense of narrowing the types of relationships between producers and consumers considered. Chapter 7 has as its central interest the relationship of the producer and consumer of heritage interpretations, summarized in the insistent and recurring question of 'whose heritage is it?' An important contribution of this chapter in particular to the discussion is its consideration of non-participating individuals and groups. Chapter 8 takes the single national case of one small European country and confines itself to the single use of heritage interpretation in underpinning specific, but changing, conceptions to the nation state in at least partial response to the new international realities of European consciousness. Chapter 9 discusses the renaissance of cultural vernacularism in post-war Germany: important in its depiction of selective heritage interpretation and re-creation, particularly in the current phase of redeveloping the immediate post-war comprehensive redevelopments. But this new vernacular is almost a bowdlerization of medieval urban form, particularly in the tourist centres. Chapter 10 presents an overview of the use of urban heritage in the Czech Republic as it makes the transition from communism to post-communism. In this heartland of central European cultural heritage, many urban centres retain their historic form in a dilapidated state: crises occur as this heritage becomes exploited – for both heritage tourism and, in some cases, opencast mining. An interesting point in this case is what happens to the heritage of 'ethnic cleansing' half a century after the event, when survivors are few and their descendants widely dispersed?

Finally, the separate studies of producers and managers of resources and products, consumers whether engaged in tourism or other uses of the past, together with the case studies of national and local planning involving heritage, must be brought together so that the basis for policy can be constructed. The final three chapters differ in their attempts at synthesis, in that Chapter 11 can be categorized as pessimistic and minatory, arguing the limits of the use of heritage; Chapter 12 is practical, assessing the future capital city of a new Europe and the contribution of heritage and culture to the selection process; and Chapter 13 is more optimistic, assessing the degree of success in achieving the initial objectives of the argument.

THE WIDER CONTEXT

A volume written by European specialists on an aspect of Europe of such obvious topical importance almost inevitably slips into a Eurocentric myopic exclusivity. It is salutary, from time to time, when considering all the manifold difficulties and problems discussed by the authors in this volume, to consider that the deliberate fostering of a place-identity with a particular political unit through the reformulation and interpretation of the surviving relics of history is a task that has been quite routinely undertaken by almost every post-colonial successor state. If an answer is sought to the question 'can it actually be done?' then, in quantitative terms, the rewriting of history to create popular identity with a newly emerging political and governmental structure is more the norm than the exception among contemporary states. In the very different post-colonial cities of San Juan (Puerto Rico) and Zanzibar, McQuillan (1990) shows that conservation has been significant from the national and local perspectives, from the preservation of the Hispanic tradition important in the formation of a Puerto Rican sense of nationhood to the colonial heritage of Zanzibar, where no symbol of the indigenous Swahili culture remained. But, in both cases, preservation served nationalistic needs. In particular, the forging of identity on a continental or near-continental scale from disparate ethnic and social groups is a preoccupation of countries such as the United States, Australia or Canada. In Canada, for example, the first objective of the federal agency responsible for the selection, interpretation and management of historic parks (the National Historic Sites division of the Canadian Parks Service) is stated quite simply as the 'fostering of a sense of Canadian identity'. Similarly, the Canadian National Capital Commission deliberately used urban conservation in the federal capital, Ottawa, to create a distinctly Canadian federal identity (Ashworth and Sijtsma 1988).

Thus the simple and reassuring point is that the European case is not unique. It is only, given the continent's long and troubled history, more difficult to achieve. Most of the chapters that follow generate more questions than they provide answers, and are studded with caveats, warnings and the revelation of difficulties. This is inevitable at this stage in the consideration of such a vast topic, but it should not convey the impression that heritage planning cannot fulfil the various tasks assigned to it in the initial argument, and specifically be used for the political purposes suggested. Heritage has already proved to be demonstrably successful in the provision of an economic resource for a commercial activity of growing importance. The deliberate fostering of place-identities for political purposes is routinely assigned to heritage interpretation in countless nation states and, more relevant here, in some federal entities endeavouring to shape a new collective consciousness.

A continental-scale identification built upon the Berlaymont, Place Schumann or the naming of EC international express trains may seem poor competition for the strident nationalist interpretation of most European heritage. The EC has been notably slow to develop the symbolism and trappings of a popular state. A second-hand flag (borrowed from the Council of Europe) and a second-hand anthem (borrowed from Beethoven), let alone the second-hand politicians who fill the seats at Strasbourg and Brussels, are no substitute for the heroes and villains, battles and revolts, of most national founding mythologies. It is equally clear, however, that there is a need to forge a new continental identity to replace that inherited from the now-crumbling post-war territorial settlement, without which the new Europe has little relevant and popular meaning. Only with such identification, shaped through a reinterpretation of the heritage of a European past, can a truly European future be created. This volume is an attempt, if not actually to perform the tasks outlined, which are beyond the competence of academics, at least to make clear to those with such powers the dangers, difficulties and, above all, opportunities of this aspect of the European present.

REFERENCES

Ashworth, G.J. and Sijtsma, P. (1988) 'Planning in the Canadian city', *Veldstudies* 13, Groningen: GIRUG.

Brown, G.B. (1905) *The Care of Ancient Monuments*, Cambridge: Cambridge University Press.

Burtenshaw, D., Bateman, M. and Ashworth, G.J. (1991) *The European City: Western Perspectives*, London: Fulton.

Dellheim, C. (1982) *The Face of the Past: the Preservation of the Medieval Inheritance in Victorian England*, Cambridge: Cambridge University Press.

Dobby, A. (1978) *Conservation Planning*, London: Hutchinson.

Hurwitz, L. and Lequesne, C. (1991) *The State of the European Community: Policies, Institutions and Debates in the Transitional Years*, London: Longman.

Jones, A.N. and Larkham, P.J. (1993) *The Character of Conservation Areas*, London: Royal Town Planning Institute.

Kennett, W. (1972) *Preservation*, London: Temple Smith.

Larkham, P.J. (1992) 'Conservation and the changing urban landscape', *Progress in Planning* 37, 2: 83–181.

McQuillan, A. (1990) 'Preservation planning in post-colonial cities', in Slater, T.R. (ed.) *The Built Form of Western Cities*, Leicester: Leicester University Press.

Relph, E. (1982) 'The landscape of the consumer society', in Sadler, B. and Carlson, A. (eds) *Environmental Aesthetics: Essays in Interpretation*, Western Geographical Series 20, Victoria: Department of Geography, University of Victoria.

Thompson, M.W. (1981) *Ruins: Their Preservation and Display*, London: Colonnade.

Part I

Theories and contexts

2

FROM HISTORY TO HERITAGE – FROM HERITAGE TO IDENTITY

In search of concepts and models

G.J. Ashworth

THE ARGUMENT

The argument underlying this volume is simply stated. History, that is the occurrences of the past, is widely used to fulfil a number of major modern functions, one of which is shaping socio-cultural place-identities in support of particular state structures. Such deliberate use of aspects of the past is neither new nor confined to Europe, but the particular political situation in which Europe finds itself at the end of the twentieth century offers the unique challenge of using European history to support the shaping of a new continental political entity. If this opportunity is to be utilized, it is first necessary to move from practice to theory: what is occurring, and probably in one form or another has always occurred, must first be understood before such deliberate and goal-directed intervention in the use of the past is possible.

Undertaking this seemingly straightforward task immediately raises a number of complications. First, the use of the past as an expression of place-identity serving the creation and reinforcement of spatial political entities can occur at various spatial scales. The specific supra-national scale of state-building selected in this argument is in competition with other scales, whether local, regional or national, whose promotion is generally older-established and more powerfully advanced.

Second, there are many other modern functions of history. These

13

include satisfying the psychological needs of the individual, and by extension society as a whole, 'so that the comfort of the past may anchor the excitement of the future' (Lynch 1972), lest collective amnesia lead to social disorientation. Education, used by museums from their inception as a major justification for their existence, would be renamed by sociologists as 'socialization', that is the process whereby the norms and standards of a society are passed on to new generations. Political scientists would add the word 'legitimation' and argue that the events of the past are narrated to the present not only so that society's norms are continued but so that currently powerful political ideologies and groups can justify their dominance by an appeal to the continuity of the past and present. If these uses, or post-hoc justifications, have long been prevalent among those concerned with investigating, preserving and interpreting the past, purely economic arguments have more recently been added.

History provides the resources, not only for 'cultural' or 'heritage tourism' (itself a very major industry), but, more broadly, serves as an amenity resource base for a wide range of high-order economic activities.

Using the same resources to support a number of otherwise quite different needs of contemporary European society may offer profitable opportunities for satisfying a range of quite different objectives through a mutually reinforcing set of strategies. It may equally, however, lead to conflict, contradiction and therefore the need for choice.

Each of the propositions of this argument needs examination, definition and defence in depth. It is not history, as defined above, that is used for these modern purposes, but 'heritage', and the process through which the one is transformed into the other is obviously critical and must first be examined. From this process can be derived a series of intrinsic dilemmas, tensions and opportunities, all of which reinforce the necessity for choice, however difficult, and thus deliberate intervention to achieve specified objectives. The link between heritage and locality, and between locality and identity, must then be argued. Finally, it becomes possible to argue that strategies for the shaping of particular place-identities through the use of heritage can be devised. The necessary preconditions for developing such strategies specifically to shape a European identity will then be reviewed.

HISTORY INTO HERITAGE

From historical monument to heritage product

The concept of heritage has evolved from a concern for the preservation of the chance surviving relics from the past, but the process of this evolution has led to some important changes in its orientation. In summary (Figure 2.1), this evolutionary progress can be reduced to a number of distinct steps, each of which involves decisive shifts in the planning approach, its focus of objects of attention, the criteria for their selection, the instruments of operation, and even the composition and objectives of the decision makers. Preservation approaches dominated the first hundred years of European concern for the surviving artefacts and buildings from the past. These approaches focused upon buildings as monuments, selected according to sets of supposedly objective and obvious intrinsic criteria, such as age or beauty, preserved by legally protective designations, imposed by 'experts' in public taste who defined their role as being guardians of public cultural assets. The shift to conservation in the course of the 1960s widened the object of attention to ensembles and areas and thereby inevitably involved the modern functioning of such districts. The well-known definition of conservation, as 'preserving purposefully' (Burke 1976),

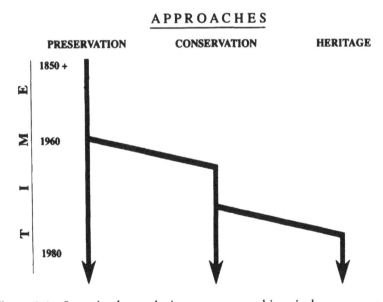

Figure 2.1 Steps in the evolutionary process: historical monument to heritage product

elevates qualities of function alongside those of form as selection criteria, and brings the planner and manager into the decision-making process alongside the architect and historian. The goals become widened to the regeneration or rehabilitation of areas to be achieved through the land-use management plan as much as protective designations. Finally, the more recent clear shift to a market orientation focuses upon the relics of history as a product, selected according to the criteria of consumer demand and managed through intervention in the market. This being the case, the search for a process model to explain what is occurring must be conducted within marketing science.

The commodification process

History is the remembered record of the past: heritage is a contemporary commodity purposefully created to satisfy contemporary consumption. One becomes the other through a process of commodification. Such a process is not unique to history but can, and has, been applied to other aspects of human activities and creativity, such as the arts or music (Whitt 1987). The use of marketing science as a method of analysis does not necessarily imply the existence of a market exchange mechanism in the same sense and calibrated in the same measurements as with many other traded commodities, only that a recognizable market exists, and choices are exercised by producers and consumers alike exercising specific strategies on the basis of some value exchange.

The initial and basic assumption is that heritage is an industry in the sense of a modern activity, deliberately controlled and organized with the aim of producing a marketable product. The process can be broken down into its components (Figure 2.2).

Resources

The raw materials from which the heritage product is assembled are a wide and varied mixture of historical events, personalities, folk memories, mythologies, literary associations and surviving physical relics, together with the places, whether sites or towns, with which they are symbolically associated. The past is thus best viewed as a quarry of possibilities, only a very small proportion of which will ever be utilized as heritage.

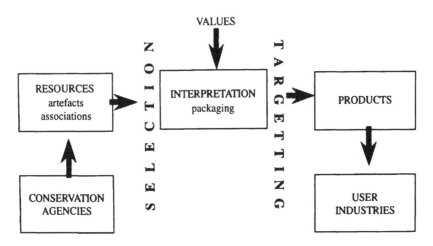

Figure 2.2 Components of the heritage industry

The interpretation process

Resources are converted into products through interpretation. This is a process involving both resource selection and packaging. It is not a marginal enhancement of a product but is, from the producer's viewpoint, the means by which the diverse elements are integrated: the interpretation, not the resource, is literally the product. Interpretation involves a conscious series of choices about which history-derived products are to be produced, and conversely which are not, and this in turn – as in all successful manufacturing – is a function of demand rather than supply. In marketing terminology, the product development is a consequence of market segment identification and targetting, rather than the reverse.

The heritage product

The end-product, heritage, has a quite specific meaning which is not the same as conserved relict historical resources. Heritage implies the existence of a legatee and is only definable in terms of that actual or latent user. More correctly, there is no national heritage product but an almost infinite variety of heritages, each created for the requirements of specific consumer groups; viewed from the side of the customer, each individual necessarily determines the constitution of each unique heritage product at the moment of consumption. The important point is that quite different products, for quite different markets, can be created from the same sets of raw materials by varying the interpretation process.

The heritage consumer

If heritage cannot logically exist without a consumer of that heritage, then it is a short step to argue that the answer to the question of 'whose heritage?' (Tunbridge 1984) determines what is heritage. If it is defined by the consumer, then the perceived problem of authenticity does not derive from any discrepancy between the interpreted heritage product and some objective historical truth. There is thus little purpose served by comparing the product with a supposed historical reality, whatever that might be and however it could be arrived at. The discrepancy, and its resulting problem, lie in the different versions of authenticity as defined by different customers. If heritage is consumer-defined, so also is its authenticity: the consumer authenticates the resource. From this stems both many of the difficulties for the producer, but also the possibilities for their solution.

Some implications of the model

Two implications of this model are relevant here. First, the nature of the heritage product is determined, as in all such market-driven models, by the requirements of the consumer, not by the existence of the resources. Although the range of possible products is neither limitless nor infinitely flexible, it is extremely broad and the nature of the final product is not determined by a fixed resource endowment, nor is it intended to reflect any supposedly accurate factual record of the past. No place is therefore inextricably locked into any particular past. Second, the necessity for deliberate selection is implicit at each stage in the process. In part, this is performed by the vagaries of time, which have determined what has survived either physically or in human memory, but deliberate choice from such survivals actually determines what is used: there is no question of a fortuitous endowment determining the nature of the resources employed. It is thus intrinsically a planned system; the question of who plans, for what purposes, remains open, not the necessity for intervention as such.

FROM HERITAGE TO PLACE IDENTITY

The central role of locality

To argue that there is a strong reciprocal link between heritage and places may be so obvious to many as to be self-evident, or even tautological. On the one side, places frequently are the heritage product, even if no single physical survival is present. The site, whether country, city or just point on the earth's surface, is 'sacralized' (to use the terminology of MacCannell 1976) by its ascribed associations. Equally, heritage is one of the main determinants of the individual character of places. Neither academic geographers nor tourists need persuading that heritage is one of the principal components of a real differentiation. Much heritage planning is, therefore, in practice place planning. Rather than labour this obvious point, it is more interesting to pursue the subsequent idea that if heritage, as defined above, can be used to shape the character of places, then who performs this important activity?

Although national governmental agencies have created the legislative and judicial frameworks for the conservation of the built environment, in most European countries this has generally been only a post-hoc recognition and consolidation of local and often non-governmental initiatives. Similarly, the easily appreciated visual dimension of architecture has endowed it with an international appeal and created a long-standing relationship between international tourism and conserved artefacts. However, the idea of a 'world heritage' and the resulting international agencies and programmes make a minimal contribution to actual conservation action compared with local policies.

Heritage planning in Europe is overwhelmingly a local activity, as heritage is specifically a local phenomenon, at least in the sense that it is most widely expressed through the heritage place (Ashworth and de Haan 1988). It is both created by, and in turn shapes, the sense of locality based on the uniqueness of local place-identities. Rarely, therefore, has local planning been presented with such ambitious, wide-ranging and fundamentally important objectives which, it might be argued, are far beyond its competence and responsibility. Not only is heritage intrinsically amenable to local planning action, but there is reason to believe that such intervention at the local scale in the creation and maintenance of heritage places has recently increased in importance. Economic success or failure was previously determined in the industrial city largely by external factors beyond the sphere of influence of local decisions. Local planning could only enhance the attractiveness of a place or purchase an amenity from the profits of other 'real' economic activities. The post-industrial production system, on the other hand, uses factors of local amenity, including historicity, instrumentally. They are important resources in a production system, and resources which by their nature are ubiquitous and amenable to local management. Heritage planning is thus a game anywhere can play, and local management, whether consciously engaged in it or not, will effectively determine the outcome.

The political uses of heritage place-identities

The commodification argument advanced earlier (p. 16) implies that not only may heritage contain a political component, but that it is very likely to do so. It is the interpretation that is traded, not its various physical resources. At one level the heritage product is a particular experience, such as a museum visit, but at a deeper level it is an intangible idea or feeling, whether fantasy, nostalgia, pleasure, pride and the like. The inescapable consequence of this is that both what is sold and what is bought contain messages. These messages stem from the conscious choices of resources, products and packaging, which are performed on the basis of sets of subjective values, consciously or not, of those exercising these choices.

The 'dominant ideology hypothesis' asserts that governments or ruling élites will project a message legitimating their position, as has been argued by Davies (1987) for British heritage in general, or by Bradbeer and Moon (1987) in the detailed case of maritime heritage at Portsmouth. Bourdieu (1977) took the argument further by assuming the existence of so-called 'cultural capital', which is composed of both the accumulated cultural productivity of society and also the criteria of taste for the selection and valuation of such products. Each governmental regime upon assuming power must capture this capital, which would include heritage, if it is to legitimate its exercise of such political power.

It is not necessary to accept uncritically the universal presence of this simple dominant ideology in all heritage interpretation. Producers are frequently conveying a multiplicity of quite different 'ideologies', even through the same heritage rather than a particular coherent political programme intended to support any distinctive prevailing view of society. Also, as Merriman (1991) has argued in the case of museums, visitors are not passive recipients but active participants in the heritage process. All that is argued here is that the assembly of the heritage product is indelibly linked to messages which are not marginal accretions to the process, or a rare perversion of it, but form the essential binding medium, without which the various components from the past could not be transformed into heritage products. Such messages are inevitably ideological only in the sense that sets of ideas are being conveyed and are no less ideological if it can be shown that there are many such possible messages, that producers are often insufficiently aware of their message-delivering role or that recipients, the consumers of the heritage product, receive a message quite different from that intended. Thus whether or not heritage is deliberately designed to achieve pre-set spatio-political goals, place-identities at various spatial scales are likely to be shaped or reinforced by heritage planning.

This has been most obvious in the phenomenon of the creation of the European nation state whose historical apogee coincided, not entirely accidentally, with the awakening of interest in the conservation of historical artefacts. Indeed, the relationship between nationalism and historic conservation has been particularly intimate. If the European nation state was forged by nationalist interpretations of the past (as Horne 1984 has exhaustively exemplified), then any reorientation to non-national place-identities will need to reformulate such interpretations. A new future for Europe can only be built upon a new post-nationalist interpretation of the past.

The argument that heritage planning plays a key role in such a reformulation receives support from both cultural/aesthetic arguments and from socio-political ones. The former stress the intrinsic internationalism of cultural movements and the permeability of political frontiers to aesthetic ideas, which has resulted in a cultural productivity that is both intrinsically international and, at least in the visual arts and architecture, essentially intelligible without linguistic intermediary. It is not by chance that international tourism and heritage conservation have historically evolved together. Meanwhile, the socio-political arguments stress that heritage planning can support the preservation and enhancement of ethnic and regional variety. The new Europe that will replace the Europe of the nation states will be a Europe of the cities and the regions, and thus the role of heritage planning in shaping local identity assumes a new importance.

The economic use of heritage place-identities

The planned heritage product can have a variety of different users but, for the purposes of this argument, can be described as being principally in the service of two sets of objectives. The first, and political objective, is the focus of this argument but can only be appreciated alongside a consideration of the other major objective, which is economic. The same resources may be employed in the shaping of two different heritage products for different markets. A consequence of this 'joint supply' is that reinforcement, coexistence or conflict between the two products is extremely likely, and provides both a necessity and an opportunity for intervention.

The economic objective is easier to understand, describe and measure than the political, and it is incontrovertible that historicity is being used instrumentally in the economic development policies of many, if not most, modern European cities. The conserved, enhanced or recreated events, personalities, associations, surviving objects and structures are treated as resources supporting the existence of a heritage industry. This industry, described graphically if sourly by Hewison (1987), is a varied collection of commercial activities, in both public and private sectors, that shape and market heritage products derived from these resources and intended for contemporary consumption.

Heritage tourism is the most obvious of such activities and its sustained spectacular growth, importance to local economies and planning implications have been widely discussed (see the work summarized in Ashworth 1988, and the many examples of local heritage planning in Ashworth and Tunbridge 1990). The sheer scale of the tourism dimension, however, has served to conceal until recently the importance of historicity as a factor underlying the more general economic competitive advantage of cities. The recent Datar studies (Datar 1989) of economic competition between European cities have reasserted the obvious but under-stressed importance of heritage planning in shaping quality environments capable of attracting high-order footloose economic activities.

A number of the following Chapters discuss in detail the nature, success and problems of the economic uses of heritage. Although heritage can be, and in practice is, used for both economic and political purposes, there are a number of tensions that are intrinsic to this dual use that will be raised here.

TENSIONS IN THE MULTI-USE OF HERITAGE

Tensions inherent in place products

Apart from the general dilemmas intrinsic to all product development, heritage as it is marketed is typically place-bound. It is not only located in a specific place, the place frequently is the product and often it is the place as a whole that is marketed in pursuit of either the economic or political identity objectives. Place products have certain distinctive characteristics (described at length in Ashworth and Voogd 1991), of which the most relevant here are as follows.

1 They are assemblages of many diverse elements: thus the same resources can be used in the production of a wide variety of place products serving an equally wide variety of consumer markets.
2 They are 'multi-sold', that is the same physical space can be sold simultaneously as different products to different users. In this context it can be added that they can also be 'multi-interpreted'.
3 They exist within nested spatial-scale hierarchies. This in turn raises questions of which spatial scale is being bought and which sold and these are rarely the same, as well as the reinforcement or contradiction that can occur between place products at different scales. This point has further implications which will be considered at length below.

Each of these characteristics raises particular tensions when the heritage city is used specifically for the promotion of political ideas but that of spatial scale can be considered in more detail.

The scale problem

If places cannot exist other than within a spatial hierarchy, then place products similarly exist on particular scales. This in turn creates the possibility for conflict in a number of different ways. The most obvious is that place products at different but related spatial scales will conflict by contradicting each other. The heritage interpretation used to sell a town may convey a different and contradictory message to that simultaneously being used to sell the region or country in which it is set. This is so common in tourism marketing as to be the rule rather than exception (see Goodall 1990), and can generally be discounted if the markets can be sufficiently segregated. The same phenomenon in the selling of political place-identities has been little researched but would appear to be as widespread, usually in terms of a regionalism/centralism divergence. Rather less obvious is the potential discrepancy between the place that is sold and that which is bought. Customers, or receivers of place products, are quite likely to be purchasing a different spatial scale from that which is being promoted generally because official promotion provides only a fraction, and the least credible fraction, of the information used by the customer to construct place-identities. Again, this difficulty has become apparent in tourism, where the mental geography of the visitor frequently bears no relationship to the jurisdictional structure of the places being sold. Finally, if heritage is to be marketed for both the economic and political purposes simultaneously, albeit to different markets, the question whether the spatial scale is the same for both sets of users arises.

From the many illustrations of the various ramifications of these potential difficulties, two have become particularly apparent. One manifestation of this problem emerges as the national or inter-national heritage product dilemma. Products made for sale on the international tourism market will, by the demand-led definition already given, be largely determined by that market. This has a myriad practical implications. The successful tourism product is, therefore, an interpretation of the local historical experience in so far as it can be related to, and incorporated in, the historical experience of the visitor. Thus a successful foreign heritage tourism industry is dependent not on the sale of the heritage of the destination country to visitors from the consumer country but, on the contrary, on the resale in a different guise of the consumers' own heritage in an unexpected context within the destination country.

TENSIONS IN THE HERITAGE CONTENT OF THE PLACE PRODUCT

The process of product creation and development, for whichever market, raises some fundamental dilemmas of content selection which are fundamental to this application to place-identity. The most relevant of these can be summarized in two pairs of dichotomies familiar in marketing.

Generalize or particularize the heritage product

The choice as to whether to stress the unique or the generic qualities of a product is fundamental to all marketing. Tourism will tend to favour generalization. On the product development side, tourism requires simplicity to the point of banality. A rich and complex past not only can, but must, be reduced to a set of characteristics easily recognizable by the visitor who has limited local knowledge, time and attention span and who is collecting a limited set of previously 'marked' experiences (MacCannell 1976). Success in the customer acceptability of the product will largely depend on it being incorporated into the existing experience, expectations and historical understanding of the visitor (Cohen 1979), which in this context can be taken as pre-existing and at this scale unchangeable by the immediate local tourism experience. Heritage products designed to shape or reinforce political place-identities on the other hand will tend strongly towards particularization. They will stress the uniqueness of the specific historical experience and attempt to differentiate it from other and contrasting experiences elsewhere.

The short answer to the question of whether it is possible, given these differences, for the same heritage product to serve both markets is that the possibility depends on the stages of product development reached within each market. In any event, there is a need for skilful and sensitive product management which avoids the conflict which is otherwise quite intrinsic.

Homogeneous or heterogeneous heritage product

The production of a largely homogeneous heritage product greatly simplifies many of the marketing problems. The brand image can be easily established and conflict between interpretations of different aspects of the product minimized. Such a homogeneous product at the national scale may satisfy both the main targeted consumer groups discussed here. A simple national identity can be shaped through a few selected national stereotyped qualities, representative personalities and supporting mythologies. Equally, a homogeneous national product may well be an ideal tourism product, at least in the early stages of tourism development on foreign markets, where potential visitors have a weakly developed consciousness of the destination. Of course, although both markets may favour homogeneity, it is unlikely to be the same homogeneous product that is required, as was argued earlier (p. 25).

However, a homogeneous heritage product development is likely to be unsatisfactory in the longer-term development of both primary markets considered here. A homogeneous national heritage disinherits non-participating social, ethnic and regional groups, as their distinctive historical experiences are ignored or distorted by the hijacking of history by the dominant groups. Whether this is sustainable or even desirable will depend on the value placed on national unity and the ability of the national image to compete with its rivals. At the very least, the result will be an impoverishment of the country's heritage resource potential. Equally, although the early stages of tourism development favour concentration in product line as well as spatial distribution, further expansion from these beginnings increasingly stresses deconcentration (Pearce 1987). This can be elaborated in many ways. In terms of tourism product development, for instance, the early necessity for a very limited product range, easily recognized and differentiated from other national products, gives way in later stages to the necessity for product differentiation, in order to extend the market by new products (i.e. aggressive strategies), and also to hold on to existing, and presumably increasingly sophisticated and experienced, markets in the face of anticipated competition from imitators (i.e. defensive strategies). Economically and spatially, the same shift from concentration to dispersal is likely to become increasingly necessary. In purely spatial terms, the early trends towards concentration in specific localities, where suitable facilities are clustered, leads in later stages to strategies for the spreading of benefits, and lowering apparent local congestion costs.

The result is likely to be an increasingly heterogeneous tourism product, within which ethnic and cultural variety, as well as regional and local differences play a larger role. The conflict with the necessarily homogeneous national identity heritage product is obvious. Tourism becomes if not an instrument encouraging political separatism, then at least a support to aspects of regionalism and multiculturalism.

In summary it is clear that the multi-selling of heritage places simultaneously for political and economic objectives raises problems of content and scale. The heritage product being marketed to tourists for economic reasons is just unlikely to be the same as that promoted to local markets for state-building objectives. Whether this matters or not will be determined not only by the degree of interference between the contents of the two interpretations but equally by the segmentation, and even spatial separation, that can be maintained between the markets.

Potential conflict, however, is likely not only between the two main sets of objectives but also within the political product. Ideology and place-identities may be strongly related, as they clearly are for example in much regional and ethnic separatism, but they are not identical and there is frequently little reason why a particular ideology should relate to particular place-identities. Similarly, the homogeneous/heterogeneous product dilemma can be reflected in conflicts between the levels in a spatial hierarchy. Local identity tends to stress the unique attributes of the heritage place associations, while international heritage tends to favour the replicable, easily identifiable standardized characteristics.

TOWARDS PLANNING STRATEGIES

Effective market intervention strategies for the resolution of these various conflicts depend upon four main preconditions.

The acceptance of the necessity for intervention

If heritage is a commodity produced for contemporary consumption, and not a chance collection of surviving relics or remembered events, then it is created by deliberate action for specific contemporary purposes. Implicit in many of the arguments outlined above is the necessity for strategic intervention in this process. Indeed, intervention is inevitable, the only questions at issue being who does it and for what purposes.

An additional argument for the acceptance of the necessity of planned intervention for collective objectives is the resolution of the potential conflicts discussed above, some of which are amenable to the conventional planning solutions for land-use conflict. For example, the dual use of the same resource in the same place creates the possibility or, as argued here, the probability, of conflict in a number of ways. The least important stems from the multi-use of the same limited resource. More important, and threatening to the achievement of both objectives, are the consequences of the multi-selling of conflicting products constructed from the same materials to different consumers for different purposes. So, simply expressed, the possibility of conflict would seem so clear as to be easily recognizable and thus avoidable. Unfortunately, the nature of the potential conflict is more complex than it appears, and there is frequently little evident awareness of it; and thus recognition of its existence appears in practice to be more difficult than the devising of strategies for its avoidance.

Acceptance of the process of heritage planning

Planning for the consequences of heritage creation requires a prior understanding of how it is created and thus the nature of the conceptual and philosophical shifts described above. This is not merely a question of the adoption of marketing terminology but, more fundamentally, an acceptance of this way of viewing the past and its association with places. The idea of the heritage place product, its creation, marketing and consumption for specific purposes, whether economic or political, implies new valuations of the past and its surviving artefacts, and thus a new philosophy for their management. It is clear, even from some of the following chapters in this book, that many of those involved in the preservation, care and presentation of aspects of heritage do not share such a philosophy but have quite different views of their objectives.

Choice of heritage product

The shaping of any heritage product by definition disinherits non-participating social, ethnic or regional groups, as their distinctive historical experiences are discounted. This is quite unavoidable, and is a direct consequence of the concept of heritage. All heritage involves choice from a wide range of pasts, many of which will not be selected. It is not the existence of this disinheritance, but the failure to recognize it that presents problems. Once accepted, then choices can be made and their consequences assessed.

Organization and implementation of successful intervention

A major weakness of the industrial assembly model used above is that, unlike many commercial products, the production of the place-bound heritage product is not managed by a single organization. On the contrary, each component of the process model is most usually managed by quite different organizations for quite different motives. Historic resources are preserved and maintained by quite different organizations from those responsible for shaping and marketing the heritage products from which they are constructed. Taken further, it is likely that the existing institutions responsible for the various phases of heritage production, in both the public and private sectors, are pursuing quite explicitly different objectives, often at quite different spatial scales. The most telling objection to the whole argument advanced here is not that local heritage planning cannot in principle be used for shaping new political identities, but quite simply that it is not being done in practice because there is no organization capable of doing it.

REFERENCES

Ashworth, G.J. (1988) 'Marketing the historic city for tourism', in Goodall, B. and Ashworth, G.J. (eds) *Marketing in the Tourism Industry*, Beckenham: Croom Helm.

Ashworth, G.J. (1990) 'Can places be sold for tourism?', in Ashworth, G.J. and Goodall, B. (eds) *Marketing Tourism Places*, London: Routledge.

Ashworth, G.J. and de Haan, T.Z. (1988) *Uses and Users of the Tourist-Historic City*, Field Studies 10, Groningen: GIRUG.

Ashworth, G.J. and Tunbridge, J.E. (1990) *The Tourist-Historic City*, London: Belhaven.

Ashworth, G.J. and Voogd, H. (1991) *Selling the City*, London: Belhaven.

Bourdieu, P. (1977) *Outline of a Theory of Practice*, Cambridge: Cambridge University Press.

Bradbeer, J.B. and Moon, G. (1987) 'The defence town in crisis: the paradox of the tourism strategy', in Bateman, M. and Riley, R.C. (eds) *A Geography of Defence*, Beckenham: Croom Helm.

Burke, G. (1976) *Townscapes*, Harmondsworth: Penguin.

Cohen, E. (1979) 'A phenomenology of the tourism experience', *Sociology* 13: 179–201.

Datar (1989) *Les Villes européenes*, Paris: Documentation Française.

Davies, G. (1987) 'Potted history', *Marxism Today* 47: 187–96.

Goodall, B. (1990) 'The dynamics of tourism place marketing', in Ashworth, G.J. and Goodall, B. (eds) *Marketing Tourism Places*, London: Routledge.

Hewison, R. (1987) *The Heritage Industry: Britain in a Climate of Decline*, London: Methuen.

Horne, D. (1984) *The Great Museum: the Re-presentation of History*, London: Pluto.

Lynch, K. (1972) *What Time is this Place?*, Cambridge, Mass.: MIT Press.

MacCannell, D. (1976) *The Tourist: a New Theory of the Leisure Class*, New York: Schocken Books.

Merriman, N. (1991) *Beyond the Glass Case: the Past, the Heritage and the Public in Britain*, Leicester: Leicester University Press.

Pearce, D.G. (1987) *Tourism Today: a Geographical Analysis*, London: Longman.

Tunbridge, J.E. (1984) 'Whose heritage to conserve? Cross-cultural reflections on political dominance and urban heritage conservation', *Canadian Geographer* 26: 171–80.

Whitt, J.A. (1987) 'Mozart in the metropolis: the arts coalition and the urban growth machine', *Urban Affairs Quarterly* 23, 1: 15–35.

3

WHAT NEW HERITAGE FOR WHICH NEW EUROPE?

Some contextual considerations

I. Masser, O. Svidén and M. Wegener

INTRODUCTION

Heritage, in the sense of a culture worth preserving for future generations, can never be regarded as a static concept. The extent to which heritage issues are highly volatile can be seen in many countries that are undergoing rapid political or social change. For example, huge statues of Lenin and monolithic Stalinist palaces of culture formed an important part of the heritage of most east European countries until their recent removal. There is nothing new about this phenomenon. What it illustrates, as argued in earlier chapters, is the degree to which we are highly selective about what constitutes heritage, and the extent to which the heritage of some periods of history, or some groups of participants, is seen as more important than the heritage of others.

There is also a marketing dimension to the presentation of heritage-related issues. Heritage is not only something we want to hand down to future generations, it is also something we want to appreciate and experience to the fullest extent. As a result, a whole range of new services has grown up to meet these needs. Some of these services are largely educational in character, while others are primarily directed towards entertainment; the distinction between the two may be difficult to draw. No discussion of what is likely to constitute the new heritage for the new Europe can ignore these issues, which are widely discussed in other chapters.

At the same time, however, it must be recognized that Europe is facing fundamental political, economic and social changes over the next generation. After the collapse of the socialist systems in eastern Europe, the west European model of a federation of democratic countries with market economies is becoming more and more attractive. During the coming decade, the European Community may grow to form the world's largest economic region with more than 500 million consumers. The completion of the Single European Market in 1993, and further steps towards a monetary union, has created new economic opportunities of a magnitude as yet unknown. At the same time, the European countries are facing the same long-term socio-economic developments as are other countries of the world; these include the globalization of the economy, the emerging information society, the deepening gap between north and south and the increasing risks of global environmental change.

The future of Europe is extremely uncertain in the face of these conflicting tendencies. It is necessary, therefore, to consider the creation of a new heritage for a new Europe in the context of a number of scenarios of possible developments. This chapter draws upon the findings of a scenario-writing project undertaken by the authors as part of the Network for European Communications and Transport Activities Research (NECTAR), which has been established under the auspices of the European Science Foundation. Long-term scenarios for transport and communications were developed for this project in order to identify relevant fields for future research from a European perspective. A comprehensive account of the development of these scenarios and their evaluation by a panel of sixty experts from the nineteen European Science Foundation member countries can be found in Masser et al. (1992).

This chapter makes use of some of the findings from this project to raise a number of contextual questions which need to be taken into account when discussing issues relating to the kind of new European heritage that may come into being over the next thirty years. After a brief summary of the methodology developed for the project, attention is focused on three key areas: population, lifestyles and economy. In each of these three key areas, current trends are evaluated first in general terms and then in relation to their likely consequences for the new European heritage. The final section of the chapter draws together the findings from the discussion, and considers some of the choices for those concerned with Europe's future heritage.

METHODOLOGY

Scenarios are descriptions of future developments based on explicit assumptions. As a method for exploring the future, scenarios are superior to more rigorous forecasting methods such as statistical extrapolation or mathematical models, if the number of factors to be considered and the degree of uncertainty about the future are high. This clearly applies in the case of transport and communications. Transport and communications are closely interrelated with almost all aspects of human life, are linked with social and economic developments, are influenced by technological developments and are subject to numerous political and institutional constraints.

In the face of this complexity, scenarios are perhaps the only method of identifying 'corridors' of relevant and feasible futures within a universe of possible ones. Moreover, scenarios have, in relative terms, only moderate data requirements, permit the incorporation of qualitative expert judgement and, in conjunction with appropriate techniques such as Delphi, facilitate the process of converging initially different expert views towards one or possibly a few dominant opinions. To add one further point, scenario-writing as a group exercise has the potential of generating awareness of factors and impacts which may not have been identified through more formal forecasting methods.

The year 2020 was chosen as the forecasting horizon. This may seem a rather long forecasting period if one considers the speed of socio-economic and technological change. However, on the other hand, transport and communications infrastructure changes only very slowly because of the heavy investment involved, and the introduction of fundamentally new transport or communications technologies such as high-speed train systems or ISDN may even require decades to complete. Conversely, if one looks at the impacts of new transport or communications systems on land use and location of households and firms, these changes become effective only with considerable time lags, and even more time is involved before the changes in travel behaviour induced by these land-use changes are felt in the transport system. Political changes are sometimes even slower, as the history of the adaptation of standards between national railway systems in Europe or the slow diffusion of pollution control for cars in some European countries demonstrates. For all these reasons, it was thought to be necessary to study the future of transport and communications in Europe within a thirty-year framework.

To stimulate thinking in terms of fundamental options for the organization of post-industrial society in time and space, seed scenarios covering all aspects of transport and communications in their social, economic, technological and political context were compiled and presented to the respondents. Before the scenarios could be formulated, however, it was necessary to ask which kind of Europe should be envisaged throughout all scenarios. After the rapid changes in eastern Europe during the last few years, few questions could be more difficult to answer. However, it was necessary to fix ideas. Therefore, without being too specific, a few general assumptions about the Europe of the year 2020 were made.

The first assumption is that in 2020, Europe will be larger than the current EC. Most likely, some or all of the east European countries and the countries now forming EFTA will have joined the European federation in some form. Altogether, the European federation will encompass between 400 and 500 million people, more than twice as many as either the USA or Japan.

Second, by 2020 there will be a European government. It is most likely that Europe will be a federation of more or less autonomous countries, each with its own legislation, jurisdiction and government. Nevertheless there will be a European president, a European cabinet, and a European parliament with significant powers over member states where European matters are concerned. International Trade and Industry, Research and Technology, Environment, and Transport and Communications will be the most prominent European ministries because in these fields the need for integrated European policy-making is most obvious.

Third, in 2020 there will be peace in Europe. Of course this is more a hope than a scientific hypothesis, but it is a necessary one in order to make any predictions about the future. In short, it is assumed that between now and the year 2020, there will be no major political or economic crises, climatic or nuclear catastrophes, civil wars or military aggressions that would substantially disrupt the peaceful process of European integration.

Beyond the assumptions stated above, everything else was left open. No assumptions were made about the forces that will shape policy-making in local, regional or European governments. However, by identifying a set of different political directions or paradigms a domain for the future evolution of Europe was opened up. In this top–down approach the point of departure is three major directions or global scenarios. Tentatively they are associated with the keywords: growth, equity and environment.

The growth scenario

The first scenario shows the most likely development of transport and communications in Europe if all policies emphasize economic growth as the primary objective. This would most probably also be a high-tech and market-economy scenario, with as little state intervention as possible. This scenario might be associated with the political ideas of many current Conservative governments in Europe.

The equity scenario

The second scenario shows the impacts of policies that primarily try to reduce inequalities in society both in terms of social and spatial disparities. Where these policies are in conflict with economic growth, considerations of equal access and equity are given priority. This scenario might be associated with the typical policy-making of social-democrat governments.

The environment scenario

The third scenario emphasizes quality of life and environmental aspects. There will be a restrained use of technology and some control of economic activity; in particular where economic activities are in conflict with environmental objectives, a lesser rate of economic growth will be accepted. This scenario might be associated with the views of the Green parties throughout Europe.

Transport and communications are secondary, or derived, human activities that cannot be seen in isolation from the social, economic and political development of a society. Therefore, in order to assess their future development it is necessary to take account of concurrent developments in other major fields of human activity with which transport and communications interact. For this study, the following nine fields were selected.

Population:	changes in fertility, mortality and migration and their impacts on the overall age structure of the population.
Lifestyles:	changes in household size and composition, labour force participation and activity patterns.
Economy:	economic structural change to a post-industrial society and its impacts on industrial organization and reorganization.
Environment:	the use of energy, air and land resources

	and factors governing human well-being, safety and protection from noise and physical disturbance.
Regional development:	growth and decline processes in central and peripheral regions of Europe and the spatial disparities resulting from them.
Urban and rural form:	changes in the internal structure of regions and the relationship between cities and their hinterlands.
Goods transport:	changes in the volume and directions of raw materials, bulk cargo, energy, food and industry production movements.
Passenger transport:	changes in personal mobility, the volume and intensity of trips and the use of different modes of travel.
Communications:	the emergence of the information society, restructuring of telecommunications and information handling.

These nine fields are not independent of each other. In the real world they overlap and are linked by an intricate cobweb of mutual interdependencies: population and economy interact on the labour market, consume environmental resources, determine regional development and urban/rural form and generate flows of goods, passengers and information which in turn co-determine the process of spatial development, affect the environment and give rise to new mobility patterns and lifestyles.

This chapter deals with the implications for the new European heritage that arise from the first three of these fields. Because of the interrelationships between these and the other six fields, however, reference is made where appropriate to developments in these fields that impinge upon population, lifestyles and economy (see Table 3.1).

SOME FACTORS WHICH WILL DETERMINE THE NEW HERITAGE

Population

The most important demographic trend in most European countries is the decline in fertility. If only natural change is considered, most European countries are likely to experience a fall in population in

Table 3.1 Socio-economic trends and their impact on the new
European heritage

Field	Socio-economic trends	Implications for the new European heritage
Population	Decline of birth rates; new cultural migration from eastern and southern Europe; ageing of the population	Increasingly multinational society: tensions between immigrants and 'native' Europeans: heritage as a political device
Lifestyles	Decreasing household size; higher labour force participation of women; new lifestyles; shorter working hours	Decline in family values; rise of the leisure class; tensions between leisure activities and heritage conservation; heritage as a marketing strategy
Economy	Decline in manufacturing and agriculture; growth of service industries; reorganization of production and distribution; internationalization	Destruction of traditional agricultural landscapes; heritage as an experience instead of heritage as a product

the next decades. The decline is likely to be most pronounced in countries such as Germany where the fertility rate has already reached a very low level. The most fundamental impact of declining birth rates – in conjunction with increasing life expectancy – is the progressive ageing of the population. It is estimated that in western Europe the proportion of persons over 65 years will increase from 13 per cent in 1985 to more than 20 per cent in 2020, with increasing proportions beyond that year. This is likely to be most evident in countries such as Sweden and Germany.

The ageing of the population throughout Europe is likely to have important impacts on social and economic life in the twenty-first century. A considerable increase will be required in health and social services in all countries to meet the demands of old people. There will also be relatively fewer children in schools and there will be a surplus of jobs for school leavers. As the proportion of elderly in the population rises, there will also be increased demands on public transport and a relative decline in private car usage especially in urban areas, unless new types of cars suited for elderly people are developed.

If only present trends are taken into account, it is unlikely that the population decline in most countries will be offset to any significant extent by international migration. The number of 'guest workers' in most European countries has declined over recent years and restrictions on Commonwealth immigration in the UK have reduced the flow of immigrants to that country. Nevertheless, work-related immigration into the major receiving countries is still substantial. Moreover, the impact of recent developments in eastern Europe is likely to spark a new wave of international population movements. Germany would be the most obvious destination for such migrants, but all western European countries may be affected.

In addition, there remains the more fundamental question of whether the affluent European countries will be able to shield themselves against immigration from their less affluent southern neighbours where the demographic transition has not yet started, i.e. where population growth is still high. It is hard to imagine that the countries of the European Community will be able to deny access completely to these people at a time of open borders and international co-operation.

The impact of developments such as these on the nature of the future European heritage is considerable. The ageing of the population may lead to a strengthening in traditional values. At the same time, these values are likely to be challenged because of the growing cultural diversity of Europe as a result of immigration from eastern Europe and north Africa. The tensions that this produces are already apparent in the recent emergence of extreme right-wing and neo-Fascist groups in a number of European countries. Under these circumstances, heritage may become a more intense political issue which is seen as reinforcing traditional values or, alternatively, as in the United States at the turn of the century, as a means of highlighting the shared values of new and old Europeans alike.

Lifestyles

The size of the average household has fallen substantially in all European countries. This trend reflects a number of demographic, social and economic factors such as the decline in overall fertility over this period and the increase in the proportion of old people in the population, the decline in three-generation families and the reduction in the proportion of married couples in the population, together with increasing overall affluence, the growing economic independence of women and young people and the decline of traditional peasant agriculture.

With households becoming smaller, more women tend to work. Up to 80 per cent of all households in inner cities are one- or two-person households: young workers, students, pensioners, yuppies ('young urban professionals'), dinkys ('double income no kids yet') or affluent 'senior citizens' of the 'silver generation'. The darker side of the demise of the large family is the fragmentation of the activity spheres of the individual. The liberation from the traditional bonds of family, neighbourhood or community may facilitate a richer set of transient attachments for the young and active at the same time as cultural diversity is increasing as a result of greater international mobility, but it can also mean isolation and loneliness for the old and sick, polarization of interests and discrimination against ethnic, cultural or social minorities. The ideal of the pluralist, multicultural, tolerant and co-operative society has yet to be put into practice.

A consequence of the ageing society, but more importantly of new technologies in manufacturing and services, is a marked increase in free time. If automation increases productivity faster than output grows, labour becomes redundant. This can lead to unemployment, but can also be turned into reductions of working hours per day, per week, per year or per lifetime. This has happened in all industrial countries since the abolition of Sunday work, and although there are still large differences between the work-time regimes in individual European countries, it is safe to say that by the year 2020 both the eight-hour working day and the five-day working week will be a thing of the past.

One of the effects will be an enormous increase in the amount of time devoted to leisure activities. To meet these demands, it is likely that there will be a massive expansion of the leisure industry. By 2020, leisure activities may account for as much as 40 per cent of all land transport (in terms of kilometres travelled) and 60 per cent of air transport. The growing diversity of lifestyles will be reflected in the emergence of new types of specialist tourist markets. A further boost to international tourism can be expected after 1992 with the removal of many of the existing institutional barriers to movement.

The consequences of these changes in lifestyles for the type of new European heritage that will emerge by 2020 are likely to be profound. In particular, the decline in traditional family values and the emergence of a new leisured class will substantially alter attitudes towards heritage matters. Nostalgia and popular culture, for example, are likely to feature much more prominently in future discussions about heritage than in the past. There are also likely to be increasing tensions between conservationists/preservationists and the leisure industry in the next thirty years. For example, the desire to prevent the further environmental degradation of many historic city centres as well as large parts of the Alps and the Mediterranean coast may make it increasingly necessary to manufacture heritage experiences in theme parks and other commercial leisure developments. Under these circumstances, many historic sites and artefacts may be protected by the restriction of mass access and by channelling visitors to replica developments operated as commercial operations.

Economy

Throughout Europe, the decline in traditional manufacturing industries has been compensated for by the expansion in service activities, while agricultural employment has also declined. This trend is likely to continue, in particular in the countries of southern Europe where agricultural employment is still relatively high.

However, behind the shifts in employment are more fundamental changes in the total organization of production and distribution. The introduction of computerization in manufacturing has brought a new flexibility of production. This has become possible by an increasing vertical integration of the production process from supply to delivery by computer control and telecommunications. Earlier steps in the assembly chain are contracted out to outside suppliers who have to synchronize their operations and delivery with the main production schedule ('just-in-time') over increasingly long distances.

This transition also changes the character of work. Ever more sophisticated machines take over more and more of the repetitious and monotonous tasks at the assembly line, so the role of people becomes more supervisory. Where manual work is still required, the traditional division of labour is replaced by more comprehensive work packages to increase job satisfaction and responsibility. The proportion of jobs requiring higher skills is growing, as is the number of staff employed in research and development and sales. Workers who are not able to adjust to the new skills are becoming redundant. For the remaining work force, individual working hours are decreasing with rising productivity, but continuous production jobs require more shift work or work on Saturdays and Sundays.

Another characteristic of the post-industrial economy is a polarization of firm sizes. On the one hand there are very large corporations which continue to become even larger. In addition to the vertical integration referred to above, they employ a strategy of horizontal integration by acquiring smaller companies to diversify into fast-growing high-tech products or services. Large companies increasingly become multinational or transnational in order to compete on the world market and to exploit labour cost differentials between individual countries. On the other hand, the number of small companies is increasing rapidly. Empirical studies have shown that much of the employment growth in recent years has been due to small and medium-sized firms with innovative product or service ideas. In many countries special subsidy programmes have been set up to promote the establishment of new, promising companies. Technology centres are set up as incubators for innovation-oriented enterprises, which later move out to new technology parks and enterprise zones to attract investors with relief from taxes and environmental regulations. Technopolis programmes imitating the Japanese example are other technology-oriented policies directed to small and medium-sized firms, although in most countries the bulk of high-tech promotion funds go to the big companies of the military-aerospace complex.

The growth in the service sector does not in all cases compensate for the industrial job losses. The surplus manufacturing workers do not have the skills required for the new high-level financial and consulting services, nor can they compete with cheap temporary unskilled labour hired by retail and fast-food outlets. Especially in the wealthier countries, skilled personal services are becoming less and less affordable for the majority of the population, with the effect that the alleged 'service society' is gradually turning into a 'self-service society'.

As was the case with population and lifestyles, the impact of these changes in economic activities on the new European heritage are likely to be considerable. The decline of agriculture and the disappearance of many elements of the traditional peasant culture are transforming the rural landscape that is such an important component of the heritage of the European countries. In the process, tensions are growing between those who wish to preserve parts of the traditional landscape, such as hedgerows or mixed cropping systems, and those involved in the development of agriculture as a food-producing industry.

Another important consequence of current trends is the extent to which values associated with manufacturing are being replaced by values associated with services. The essential difference between these two sets of values is that the former revolve around the sale of a physical product whereas the latter revolve around the sale of an experience. As a result, heritage products such as historic houses and antiques may give way to heritage experiences such as mock battles or 'medieval' banquets. If this is the case, the way in which heritage is perceived may change considerably over the next thirty years.

CHOICES FOR THE NEW EUROPE

The main lessons to be learnt from the above discussion of some of the findings of the scenario project is that heritage cannot be regarded as a static concept. For this reason it is essential to consider heritage from the standpoint of the future as well as the present or the past. In this process it is necessary to examine in some detail the implications of current trends in a variety of fields for the likely development of Europe's new heritage.

The findings of the scenario project also point to the impact that changes in technology as well as changes in social values are likely to have on views of heritage issues. Recent developments in transport and communications technology have made it possible for everyone to discover the heritage of other countries either by travel or by TV satellite communications. Once again, there is nothing new about this phenomenon. Developments in transport technology in the eighteenth and nineteenth centuries made it possible for the first tourists to undertake the Grand Tour of Europe. However, the combination of increased travel opportunities, and the emergence of new service industries to meet the demands of the leisure classes is giving rise to the globalization of the heritage phenomenon. For example, one of many such developments is the EPCOT centre at Orlando, Florida, where visitors can wander through a scaled-down version of St Mark's Square, Venice, to a replica of a London Georgian terrace street; and thus experience something of the respective heritages without the need to travel to Europe. Similarly, in Nagasaki the Japanese have carefully constructed their version of a Dutch town, with all the associated works of art, on a 150–hectare site for the benefit of Japanese tourists.

The question that has still to be resolved is the extent to which a common heritage will emerge out of the new Europe over the next thirty years and to what extent this will be an amalgam of the various national heritages. Some elements of the national heritage may suffer in the process while others may benefit. It is also important in this context to remember that what may be a vitally important difference to the residents of the different European countries may be barely discernible to non-Europeans, who may think about heritage on an intercontinental scale and see Europe as homogeneous from a competitive standpoint relative to the Middle or Far East. What, then, may be the consequences of an increasingly globalized experience-oriented and commercialized heritage culture for the new Europe? A possible sign of things to come is contained in an advertisement for a three-day all-in package deal vacation at the EuroDisney resort in France, which also offered an optional half-day side trip to Paris. In any event, such a heritage will be a response to much wider demographic, economic and social changes, and must be considered in that context.

REFERENCE

Masser, I., Svidén, O. and Wegener, M. (1992) *The Geography of Europe's Futures*, London: Belhaven.

Part II

Producers and consumers

INTRODUCTION: FROM
CONTEXTS TO ACTORS

The task of the previous section was to lay the essential groundwork for the argument developed in all the following chapters. Both of the initial chapters are ostensibly descriptive of what is happening in Europe today.

The initial assumptions upon which the general arguments advanced in the rest of the volume depend are stated in Chapter 2 by Ashworth. Heritage is defined as a 'commodified' product using a selection of the resources of the past for the construction of products to satisfy modern demands. It is a specific use of history, not a synonym for it. It is these assumptions about the nature of heritage that make possible its quite particular use in the shaping of a new Europe, which is the central theme of this volume. A reader who cannot accept this opening chapter's description of how the past is being treated will have difficulty with the logic of the remainder.

Heritage as a consumable commodity has been brought into existence in response to the needs of contemporary society. The important trends in that society must, therefore, be outlined. Quite obviously, the demands for heritage in Europe, as with the demands for any other product, will be strongly influenced by changes in the demographic structure, economic activities and evolving character of European society as a whole. Chapter 3, by Masser, Svidén and Wegener, is based upon a much wider research project which reviews such changes within the European Community as a whole. Here, they summarize each of the main trends identified, and indicate their possible implications for heritage demand. These trends may be extrapolated to the widening Europe, as countries of the former Soviet bloc strengthen their ties with western Europe.

Having described the theoretical and contextual framework, the following three chapters describe some of the most important actors operating within the heritage industry. Such actors may be viewed as either producers or consumers of the commodified past. The former are concerned with aspects of the selection, preservation, maintenance, interpretation and promotion of historical resources and the heritage products they become. Rarely is the same organization involved in all of these processes and, frequently, different producing agencies are involved at each of these stages. Public agencies such as Cadw in Wales (see Chapter 4 by Carr, Cadw's Director) have a long-standing responsibility for the care of the historical resources entrusted to them by the State; onto which has more recently been grafted, not entirely comfortably, its function as a provider of countryside recreation facilities. The study of the user of heritage as a willing customer or unwitting recipient of 'public history' involves a shift in focus. Both Chapter 5 (Dietvorst) and Chapter 6 (Light and Prentice) are concerned with the aspects of the behaviour of visitors to heritage sites and historic cities.

It is clear that such actors, from whichever side, are not only unaware but uninvolved in the total process of which they are a part. Similarly, many resource-maintaining agencies, especially in the public sector (as Carr in Chapter 4 implies), have a wider set of responsibilities than merely satisfying contemporary heritage visitors. The resulting developmental choices are evident in a number of perceived dilemmas raised in this chapter. For example, should Cadw preserve ruins as they are at present, or reconstruct the buildings as they were (or might have been)? The former means that the agency is little more than the guardian of some randomly scattered stones, which may by chance have acquired their own value as picturesque ensembles, but which have little to do with the original form or function of the structure. The latter option, however, practised in France since Viollet-le-Duc in the nineteenth century, begins a process of intervention that leads from reassembly of what is, through reconstruction of what was, to facsimile creation of what might have been. Similarly, such agencies agonize over the extent to which display and interpretation to visitors impinge visually or distract attention from the objects themselves. It is clear from this chapter that Cadw, and equally almost all similar public-sector agencies elsewhere, are uncertain as to whether they are in the business of preserving an 'authentic history' for an unspecified general public, or are serving an immediate customer demand for entertainment as part of a 'heritage industry'. Amongst the many ironies implicit in the description of work of Cadw is that almost the only aspect of the agency that relates to the indigenous inhabitants of its area of operation is its name: the bulk of the historic buildings in its care are the product of the Anglo-Norman conquest and subjugation of Wales, and its visitors are increasingly drawn from Europe as a whole. Its contribution to local place-identities is, therefore, complex, and its intrinsic political agenda remains unclear.

Similarly, the heritage visitor is part of a leisure activity or tourism industry that is far wider than heritage alone. In Dietvorst's study, for example, the time–space budgets of visitors involve heritage consumption in numerous trade-offs with other possible uses of time: the heritage attractions visited are only a part of the wider urban product that includes many other facilities, attractions and attributes. For the visitor, heritage is just one of many possible urban attractions while, for the city authorities, heritage tourism is but one possible means of economic regeneration. Equally, however, the historic resources of a town such as Enkhuizen are contributing to the civic consciousness of residents and are projecting the selected self-image of citizens and even the Dutch as a whole. Despite the growing importance of culture tourism for the reasons advanced in this chapter, it is interesting to pose the question 'how different would Enkhuizen's heritage selection and interpretation be if no single visitor crossed its boundary?' If that answer is 'much the same', then the market described by Dietvorst (Chapter 5) is merely supplementing a more important, but unmeasured, market; and Enkhuizen, like the monuments of Cadw, is in the business of multi-selling, as was argued in Chapter 2.

4

TOURISM AND HERITAGE
The pressures and challenges of the 1990s
E.A.J. Carr

INTRODUCTION

The removal of West European trade barriers, the dismantling of socialist political structures in Eastern Europe, and the ease of international travel have combined in the late twentieth century to produce the largest potential for tourism since wars and xenophobia shut down such freedoms some 70–100 years ago. Such radical changes have a marked effect on social and economic behaviour: witness the effect of the Napoleonic Wars, which put an end to the lengthy and uplifting Grand Tour. The curious energies of the educated and moneyed classes of Britain were, perforce, directed to the antiquities, arts and environment of their homelands. The Romantic Movement was born. Its legacy remains, forming part of the portmanteau concept of 'heritage'. Today, pieces of the Berlin Wall, whose thirty-year life has given it an importance beyond any architectural wonderment, are also cocooned in that concept. The degradation of landscapes and of people has led politicians, bureaucrats and entrepreneurs to rescue the remains of nineteenth-century industrial exploitation in the USA and Europe and to give them new life as leisure components. Former concentration camps in Poland and Germany are being considered for rehabilitation through conversion to time-shares or holiday chalets: not too wildly different from the Paradors of Spain. Warships of timber or steel are rescued and, with concrete foundations, moored in 'appropriate' locations for the interest of tourists and with the purpose of gleaning cash. Whole townships in Germany and France (St Malo, for example) are rebuilt in their former style and street patterns. All is done in the name of 'heritage', which has an ancient and honourable pedigree as a component of the long-established tourism industry dating from the time of the Colossus of Rhodes, through the side-trips branching from the main purpose of the Crusades, the eighteenth-century indulgence of the Grand Tours, the earliest picture postcards of such artists as the brothers Buck, to air-lifted visits to the Taj Mahal, the Pueblo villages of New Mexico, the glories of St Petersburg and the steep byways of Mont St Michel on the Normandy coast.

Every country and every society has its own inheritance, whether social, cultural, military or economic. Some of that inheritance, but by no means all, is discernible in tangible remains. In Cadw's terms, as the state organization responsible for the protection of the built heritage of Wales, those tangible remains are principally the structures designed by people for their own use to meet specific needs: hill-forts, burial chambers, Roman forts, towns and barracks, castles, abbeys, houses, remains of industrial processes and, most recently, townships: not excluding such twentieth-century curiosities as 1930s telephone boxes. Our job is to seek to ensure that these structures are preserved for the foreseeable future, and even in perpetuity. On the one hand, we expend much effort on scheduling and listing ancient monuments and historic buildings, seemingly without thought to their continued usefulness. On the other, we seek to prolong the useful life of individual buildings and townscapes and to conserve structures whose economic value is narrow, if not questionable. Our application of the law, itself an inheritance continually modified from one generation to the next, tends to be preventive of change, and thus of exploitation requiring change. Yet, paradoxically, we promote the larger, more complete ruins in state care as visitor attractions, but within the limitations of what has become the traditional technique of 'preserve as found', implying little or no reconstruction.

From the 1880s until the early 1980s, that policy gradually resulted in freezing or squeezing structures into particular time zones. It became exemplified in the way in which the state has developed preservation of what is called the 'estate in care': crew-cut lawns, minimum visual intrusion into the frozen remains, lip-service attention to meeting the interest of the public and an overwhelming leaning towards, perhaps even a fixation upon, the architectural merits of a structure, even to the extent of losing sight of those who built and lived in it. But, since the early to mid-1980s, state heritage protection bodies such as Cadw, Historic Scotland and English Heritage have been charged with the task of making each country's state-controlled monuments more accessible and more enjoyable to the public and, not least, seeking to ensure that they make a positive contribution towards their own running costs and conservation. Such a remit immediately aroused the fears and anger of the conservation lobbies. How could the application of feared commercial techniques fail to attack the integrity of this marvellous priceless inheritance? It would be destroyed for ever. Even a decade on, there are those still clinging to the Olympian academic heights who regret and resent the greater attendances by those they see as the uninitiated, the uneducated and the unappreciative: the general public, on whose behalf the monuments have been afforded state protection and management.

THE HERITAGE BUSINESS

Our search for an anchor in the past has created a massive, world-wide industry. Or did entrepreneurial awareness of potential create the ideal of such an anchor? Whichever came first, and evidence suggests that it has been people's curiosity in their roots which pointed to the potential for exploitation, it is a fact that heritage is now big business internationally. Indeed, the work of UNESCO in identifying natural sites and artefacts as being worthy of inscription on the World Heritage Lists has done much to bolster that business: perhaps unintentionally, but none the less effectively.

On a localized level, the heritage industry in Britain is huge. More than 90 million people pay to view about 650 historic properties, museums and galleries each year. Broadly speaking, another 40 million discover untold numbers of heritage attractions where no charges are made, such as local museums and galleries, field monuments, remote ruins, redundant canals and railways.

By 1994, it is predicted that 167 million visits to designated heritage sites in Britain will generate £24 billion of expenditure, directly from entry fees and retail sales, and indirectly via airlines, petrol stations, restaurants, hotels, car hire and so on, not including general retail sales. That, crudely, amounts to expenditure by the visiting public of some £44 per head in pursuit of heritage *per se*. In the context of total tourism expenditure in Britain by UK residents and overseas visitors of roughly £250 per head in 1989, the £44 per head spent on heritage amounted to nearly 28 per cent; a very handsome proportion, but one which will continue inevitably to bring its own pressures and problems (data extrapolated

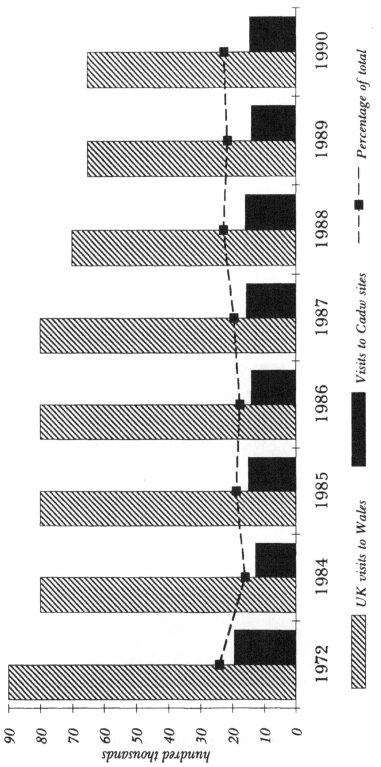

Figure 4.1 UK visits to Wales and visits to Cadw sites
Source: Cadw

UK visits to Wales   Visits to Cadw sites   Percentage of total

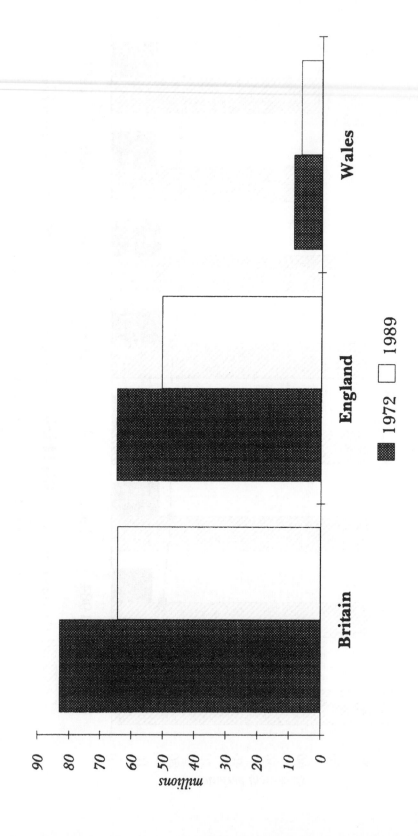

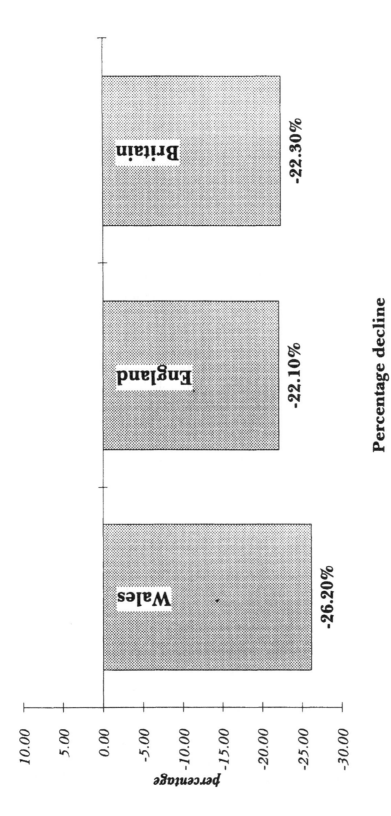

Figure 4.2 Estimated number of trips by British residents for holiday purposes
Source: British Tourist Authority

from British Tourist Authority (BTA) *Digest of Tourist Statistics* 12–14).

In 1989, Wales attracted 6.5 million holiday tourists from the UK, compared with 9 million in 1972. Add to those the 640,000 from overseas, and the Principality's resident population of 2.8 million increases by around 7 million during the year, with the peak inevitably being in the summer months of July and August.

From those 7 million, 4.3 million visits are recorded by paying visitors to some eighty historic properties, galleries and museums. That ignores the sundry other sites where no charges are made. In Cadw's case, research suggests a figure of 200,000 people to the balance of our ninety unmanned sites; there are no figures for other attractions, but the scale can be imagined and that pressure is set to grow to levels beyond previously recorded peaks. Figure 4.1 shows the decline over the past twenty years in numbers of UK visits to Wales, and the comparative fall in visitors to Cadw sites. While there have been reductions of 28 per cent in numbers of tourists to Wales, Cadw's hold on a declining market has strengthened since the organization was formed in 1984. Indeed, a modest renaissance in visits has occurred since then, although it has to be said that within the current economic climate and within the declining Welsh tourism market, the prospects for sustained growth beyond a mean of 1.45 million visitors, plus or minus 10 per cent, do not look rosy without some stimulating factors, whether from within Wales or from outside. How Wales has suffered to some significant degree compared with England and Britain as a whole is shown in Figure 4.2.

OVERSEAS VISITS BY UK RESIDENTS

The structural decline in British tourism by UK residents should be seen in the context of their overseas visits. In the twenty-four years between 1965 and 1989, Britons travelling overseas more than quadrupled from 5 million to 21 million. Indeed, in cash terms, Britain is a net exporter of currency: £9.36 billion going out compared with £7 billion coming in. In all, we temporarily exported 15.5 million people overseas in 1979; this doubled to 31 million in 1989. In holiday terms, the figures are lower at 25.3 million in 1989. By 1995, the British Tourist Authority (1991) forecasts that Britons will make 38 million visits overseas.

Such a growth rate clearly has a marked effect on home tourism and on heritage in Britain, as the bulk of overseas travel in both directions occurs in the peak months of June to August. Indeed, the BTA is gloomy about the prospects for UK tourism by UK residents, suggesting that the growth of 1.5 per cent per annum over the next three to four years will largely be in business and conference travel and in short stays of one to three nights duration (British Tourist Authority 1991).

OVERSEAS VISITS FROM OTHER COUNTRIES

While Britons spread their impact unevenly between North America (7 per cent), the EC (72 per cent), non-EC Europe (12 per cent) and the rest of the world (8.6 per cent), their homeland bore the full force of 17.3 million inward visitors in 1989. Of these, 3.7 per cent (some 640,000) came to Wales. Table 4.1 demonstrates dramatic growth in North American visitors over the ten-year period, both in terms of hard numbers and in that sector's position in the overall market. Western Europe and Australasia have varied to an insignificant degree over the ten years as proportions of the population as a whole. But, galloping along at a phenomenal pace, if not in huge numbers, are the Japanese who have nearly quadrupled in numbers and now take a good slice of the cake.

But, as Figure 4.3 shows, the dominant reason for visits to Britain is to view our heritage, whether in the form of historic structures or of galleries and museums. At present, and before the newly democratic Eastern Europe and former Soviet Union are taken into account, key visitor markets are Western Europe, North America, Australasia and Japan. Between them they accounted for 88.4 per cent of 1989 visitors, compared with 85.7 per cent in 1989 (Table 4.1), with 63.1 per cent and 61.6 per cent coming from western

Table 4.1 Overseas visitors: numbers in market sectors and proportion of those sectors to the total

	Number of visitors ('000)		%	Proportion of total (%)	
	1979	1989	Change	1979	1989
North America	2196	3481	+ 59	17.6	20.1
EC	6605	8960	+ 36	52.9	51.7
Non-EC	1268	1728	+ 36	10.2	9.9
Australasia	497	658	+ 32.4	4.0	3.8
Japan	140	505	+261	1.1	2.9
	10706	15332	+ 43		
World total	12486	17338	+ 38.9		

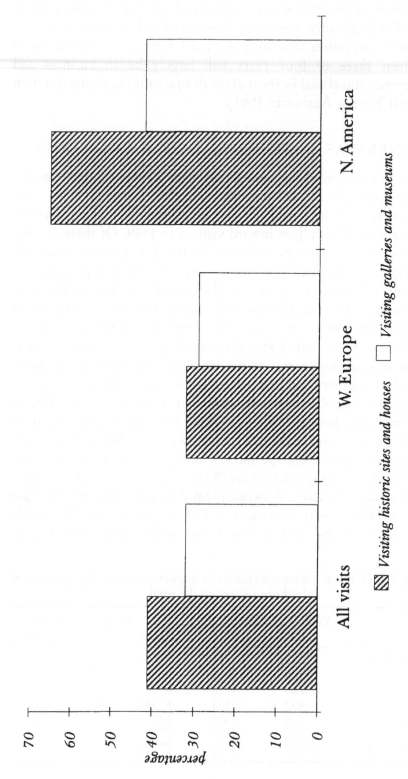

Figure 4.3 Reasons for visits to Britain
Source: British Tourist Authority

Europe in the respective years. Key growth markets were North America and Japan. For different reasons, both are exceptionally devoted to heritage visits: the Americans seek a stability in the past, perhaps adding to their own short history that of their perceived origins, while the Japanese may assuage their guilt about taking holidays by filling them with cultural pursuits, an acceptable means of justifying time taken from work.

UNESCO forecasts population growth in North America of 7 per cent from its 1989 level of 275.3 million to 295 million by the year 2000 (UNESCO 1990). Despite its insularity and, admittedly, the variety of home-present visitor attractions, the United States is gradually beginning to look outwards: for example, in 1979 only 6 per cent of US citizens held passports; by 1990 that had grown to 10 per cent or some 25 million people, according to the United States Embassy in London. In 1990, Britain attracted some 11.4 per cent of passport holders or 2.84 million US citizens (BTA 14). If the growth in visits between 1979 and 1989 is sustained and supported also by an increase in the population of passport holders, then we can expect 5.1 million US visitors to Britain by the end of the millennium (Figure 4.4). If, also, the numbers of visitors from other key markets increases at the same rate as it has over the past ten years then, as Table 4.2 shows, we can expect growth from 15.3 million to 26 million overall.

Table 4.2 Hypothetical forecast of overseas visits to Wales and to Cadw sites

Wales % overseas		Wales overseas ('000)	Cadw UK ('000)	Cadw overseas (at 55%)	Total Cadw ('000)
3.7	1991	640	1070	350	1420
4.0	1992	724	1086	398	1484
4.5	1993	888	1102	488	1590
4.7	1994	968	1119	532	1651
5.0	1995	1075	1136	591	1727
5.2	1996	1167	1153	642	1795
5.4	1997	1265	1170	696	1866
5.6	1998	1370	1187	754	1941
5.8	1999	1482	1206	815	2021
6.0	2000	1600	1223	880	2103

Source: Based on: (1) the BTA forecast of 1.5% per annum growth in the domestic UK market (*Tourism Intelligence Quarterly*, August 1991); and (ii) proportions of the overseas market in Britain which Wales might attract

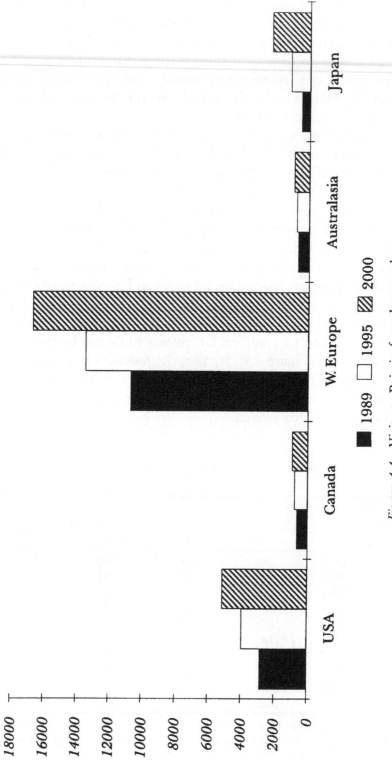

Figure 4.4 Visits to Britain from key markets
Source: Cadw

This prediction, admittedly lacking in statistical rigour, postulates a 69 per cent increase in overseas visits to Britain by the end of the present decade. That sounds unlikely. However, the British Tourist Authority (1991) forecasts 24 per cent growth overall to 22.3 million by 1995. Taking that 4.4 per cent cumulative yearly growth up to the year 2000, a figure of 27.7 million for all overseas visitors emerges: up 60 per cent in a decade.

In 1989, Wales welcomed 3.7 per cent of the British total. Given maintenance of that level, by the year 2000, the Principality could expect more than one million visits from overseas. But the Wales Tourist Board is now able to market directly overseas, so a greater proportion might reasonably be expected. Forecasting is difficult, yet on the basis that Scotland has for some years had the powers to market overseas and gains 8.5 per cent of overseas visitors to Britain, it is conceivable that Wales could gradually achieve the levels shown in Figure 4.5.

The impact on the Principality's tourism infrastructure of an additional one million overseas visitors would present a huge challenge, even if it proved possible to spread the load from the traditional peak months of June to August. The demand for additional quality bed-spaces, for improved roads and for other services would put enormous pressures on the natural and physical environments.

The earlier statement that Cadw's heritage estate would be unlikely to vary much from 1.45 million visitors, plus or minus 10 per cent, given continuity of present factors, changes with the BTA's forecast of 1.5 per cent domestic growth per annum and the addition of the increased numbers of overseas visitors into Wales. Table 4.2 postulates a gradual increase in the proportion of overseas visitors to Wales and the maintenance of the proportion of overseas visits to Cadw sites. If Wales attracts 1.6 million overseas visitors from a 6 per cent share of the market into the UK by the year 2000, then Cadw might expect to receive 880,000, taking its visitor levels to about 2.1 million. This represents the total experienced in 1974, but from a much larger number of charging sites where numbers were recorded. As Cadw's own research suggests that 200,000 people visited unmanned sites in 1990, it is conceivable that some 300,000 would find them by the year 2000. While the manned sites tend to be more robust, the effect of an additional 100,000 people on the more environmentally delicate and remote field monuments will, inevitably, require careful management and planning of routing and maintenance.

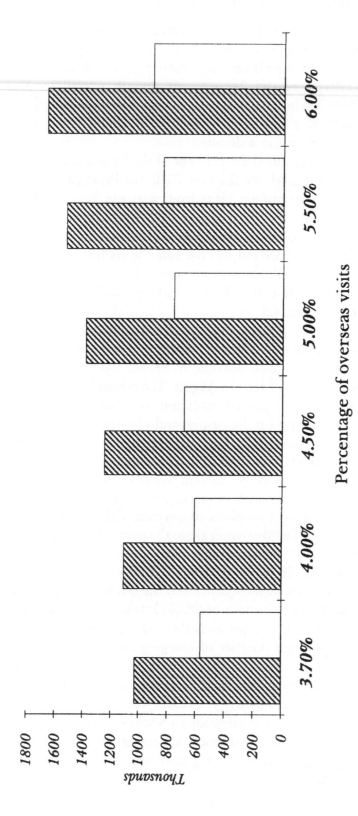

Figure 4.5   Overseas visitors to Wales and to Cadw sites
Source: Cadw

THE EUROPEAN MARKET

As shown in Table 4.1, Europe accounted for 10.7 million (or 61.6 per cent) of all visits to Britain in 1989, a slight decline proportionally over the ten years since 1979, but significantly lower in growth terms than the North American and Japanese markets. None the less, the numbers from the European Community countries, and their expenditure, demonstrate their relative value to the UK economy over the period 1979–89 (Table 4.3). From BTA data available for overseas visitors staying in Wales for the years 1986–9, it is clear that the valuable growth markets for Wales are (Western) Germany, France and the Netherlands, with Italy coming along

Table 4.3 Overseas visitors to Britain: numbers and expenditure by market countries 1979–1989

	Numbers ('000) 1979	Numbers ('000) 1989	% Difference	Expenditure (£ million) 1979	Expenditure (£ million) 1989	% Difference
Belgium/ Luxembourg	629	618	− 2	73	105	+ 44
France	1377	2261	+ 64	139	424	+205
W Germany	1547	2027	+ 31	226	410	+ 81
Italy	408	708	+ 74	79	291	+268
Netherlands	976	940	− 4	121	178	+ 47
Denmark	292	259	− 11	43	68	+ 58
Irish Republic	923	1302	+ 41	112	345	+208
Greece	97	128	+ 32	38	91	+139
Spain	312	622	+ 99	77	279	+263
Portugal	44	95	+116	10	39	+292
Total EC	6605	8960	+ 36	918	2230	+240

Source: British Tourist Authority, *Digest of Tourist Statistics* 14

Table 4.4 Overseas staying visitors to Wales (thousands)

	1986	% of Total	1988	% of Total	1989	% of Total	% Change 1989 over 1986
France	42.1	25.7	31.5	18.6	49.7	22.7	+18.1
W Germany	73.6	44.9	67.7	40.0	103.4	47.3	+40.5
Netherlands	26.9	16.4	43.2	25.5	33.9	15.5	+26.0
Belgium/ Luxembourg	15.9	9.7	12.3	7.3	16.1	7.4	+ 1.3
Italy	5.4		14.5		15.6		
	163.9		169.2		218.7		

Source: British Tourist Authority, *Digest of Tourist Statistics* 12–14

nicely (Table 4.4). But none is as important as the USA, and only Germany exceeds the contributions of Canada and Australasia.

It is argued by the CBI in Wales that the Channel Tunnel will add to the attractiveness of Wales (particularly the south) as an economic centre for European investment. As Cadw's research shows that more than 93 per cent of visitors to its sites are car-borne, it is also arguable that Britain, and Wales, can expect an influx of tourists from at least those countries with relatively easy access to the Tunnel – which happen to be the existing markets of Germany, France and the Netherlands. As the economy of the former East Germany picks up, Wales can look forward to welcoming more, not least because of the marked difference in terrain between the plains of northern Europe and the lush mountain greenery of Wales.

As, and if and when, the economies of the states emerging from the fractured former USSR and other eastern bloc countries improve, new market elements will appear. From a union of some 280 million people, forecast by UNESCO to grow to 294 million by the year 2000 (UNESCO 1990), we can expect a steadily growing stream of stable middle-class visitors into Wales. When, and how many, it is impossible to foretell, but the industrial and social connections between Wales and many eastern bloc countries remain strong, at least in folk memory. Perhaps the greatest interest initially will be in the Principality's industrial past, such of it as physically remains or will remain by the time stability allows confidence for foreign travel.

THE HERITAGE PRODUCT OF WALES

Traditionally, Wales is seen as the land of castles: not surprisingly, as there are more than 500 officially identified medieval fortifications in the Principality's 21,000 square kilometres. The majority fall into the period from roughly 1070 to 1500, with the greater proportion built in the Norman and post-Norman early and mid-medieval period (to c. 1350). The relative stability of the Norman era also encouraged the burgeoning of ecclesiastical buildings, mostly abbeys and priories – daughter houses of Cistercian, Benedictine and Premonstratensian foundations in France – but also more modest churches which complemented the already existing Celtic Christian settlements. Yet the dominance of the medieval period should not be allowed to overshadow the equally significant remains of the prehistoric burial chambers, Bronze and Iron Age settlements and fortifications, of Roman influence seen in the remarkable survivals at Caerleon, Caerwent, Caersws, Carmarthen, Dolaucothi and Segontium near Caernarfon, of late medieval industrial workings of lead, gold and iron, and of the relics of the Industrial Revolution.

As important as the unoccupied ruins in the panoply of Welsh heritage are the surviving examples of the country houses and estates – with which Wales was perhaps surprisingly well blessed, although not often on a scale to match those in England – and, of course, the historic townscapes. Wales may not be able to boast the glories of Bath, York or Chester, but the towns of Monmouth, Chepstow, Llandudno and Conwy are only examples of what survives in some richness in the Principality, and which the state actively seeks to enhance with grant aid via Cadw.

RECONSTRUCTION AND INTERPRETATION

It is Cadw's policy to preserve as found the ancient and unoccupiable monuments on the one hand, and to encourage retention and continued use of viable structures on the other. Taken together, they reflect the social, military, religious and economic past of a country whose culture has arguably survived in a more complete form than elsewhere in Europe, even Brittany, but perhaps no more than the Basque region. Ruins simply preserved as found may present the visitor with difficulties of interpretation; but there is a possible risk of diluting the essence of a place if it is reconstructed by modern methods and in materials crafted in the twentieth century. That is not to deny that the ministrations of William Burges (aided by the fabulous wealth of the Marquess of Bute) at Cardiff Castle and Castell Coch have produced anything other than structures to marvel at. They are, and should continue to be, unique. Burges has added a nineteenth-century genius, but has created things that never existed in the periods in which they originated. Even Caernarfon Castle, reconstructed in the late nineteenth and early twentieth centuries, has arguably lost some of the awe and majesty that survive at Harlech, Conwy and Beaumaris. While all four are inscribed on the World Heritage List as examples of the genius of Edward I's master builder, the Savoyard Master James of St George, Caernarfon alone among them has lost some of its magic through reconstruction. Paradoxically, those monuments in Wales which have been in continued occupation – Powis, Picton, Gwydyr and Chirk castles – provide insight into the evolution of human involvement, but their purity of origin (their integrity) is blurred by comparison with those whose viable use ceased at the time of the Civil War or, in the case of monasteries, at the Reformation.

Reconstruction may have its attractiveness as a means of generating revenue through introducing economically productive space, but any pastiche lacks conviction, unless it benefits from the genius of men like Burges. Even at Castell Coch it is Cadw's philosophy and policy to conserve as now found. It would be foolish arrogance to seek to emulate such a unique style: the monument's statement should be left to emerge as intended. (As an aside, I wonder how we would react today to an application to convert the medieval ruins of this previously obscure castle on Cardiff's outskirts. Cadw's present conservation philosophy could not cope with such a proposal.)

None the less, there is scope – even within so rigid a philosophy – to create modern spaces within an ancient fabric, provided that they do not encroach upon or irretrievably damage the visual or physical fabric. For example, the reflooring of the great hall at Conwy or the reroofing of towers can be acceptable, so long as the materials and techniques do not pretend to be other than modern insertions, do not damage the original fabric and do not seek to restore the whole structure to its original form. Quite apart from the prohibitive cost, it is not within Cadw's policy to emulate the Paradors of Spain in recreating spaces for domestic or tourist habitation in medieval monuments. The integrity of the original, with its garderobes (lavatories) and kitchens carefully sited away from the living quarters, for fire safety and hygiene reasons, would be destroyed with the introduction of soil pipes and sewers, bathrooms and electricity, washing machines, refrigerators, double glazing and fitted units veneered with plastic. It may appeal to the romantic to spend a night in a castle, but it would certainly be unreal, unless occupation had evolved continuously from first build.

Yet such enterprises make money, which helps to boost the economy. Is there harm in them if they do not damage the physical fabric? I believe that the real danger is the potential for the present generation to be programmed to expect unchallenging images of our inheritance, so that the stimulus of intellectual curiosity is blunted.

In a less obvious way, the interpretation industry is faced with similar pressures and challenges. When curators are determined to seek to maintain the historic integrity of their sites, interpretation presents another set of pitfalls.

There is continuing pressure to attract more people and, therefore, money. The balance sheet becomes the driving force. The results of this are the development of gimmickry: talking heads, 'smellies', the 'blood and guts' of re-enactment, the technical marvels of holographs. Let us by all means move on from the incomprehensible Ministry of Works labels still encountered at many sites, such as 'reredorter', 'piscina' or 'machicolation'; but let us also be conscious that the introduction of electronic wizardry may excite, in this computer age, more interest in 'how' material is being presented than in the pursuit of the 'who, what, why, when and where' of the structures themselves.

The threat comes from superficiality; from bolting modernity onto antiquity with no concern for the evolutionary nature of the use of structures. Worse, capitalizing in this way on people's interest in their past may serve not to sharpen that interest, but actually to blunt it by subsuming innate curiosity through spoon-feeding impressions. On the one side, we encounter exploitation of historic sites by the introduction of attractions alien to their intended ambience and selected history, which could equally well and more appropriately be developed in Kenya or Florida. On the other, we can encounter a pastiche of unrelated elements. How comfortably do the great cats of the world sit in the ambience of Longleat alongside the Butterfly House? Or the white-knuckle rides at Alton Towers? Or, less blatantly, the medieval banquets served up in some castles?

With increasing intercontinental mobility for the heritage seekers, the industry will expand, but will encounter challenges in interpretation and exploitation, not least from the fantasy worlds of Disney in California, Florida and, since 1992, near Paris.

SUSTAINABILITY OF HERITAGE

The UK government's White Paper *This Common Inheritance: Britain's Environmental Strategy* (1990) defines sustainable tourism as meaning 'living on the earth's income rather than eroding its capital'. That capital surely includes our inherited culture, as well as the physical resources. With an estate in care whose fabric is constantly subject to the vagaries of wind and weather, gradual deterioration is inevitable but can be stemmed by continuous conservation. Even Cadw's field monuments, which have withstood robbery and erosion for six millennia, will continue to stand mystically on their carefully chosen sites, and only the pathways to them and their surrounds require twentieth-century intervention, and this more for aesthetic than preservation reasons. More vulnerable are such delicacies as Burges's decorations and the softer sandstone corbels and decorative stonework of the medieval period, but it is wind-borne chemicals and weather which threaten them more than the tramp and touch of tourist feet and fingers.

The capital of heritage is the knowledge of the reasons for its survival as a record, however incomplete and selective, of the past. For successive millennia, since the retreat of the ice barriers, the concept of 'Europe' has moved westward and eastward, pushing evolving cultures as overlays one upon the other to the extremes of the land masses. The people of Wales have suffered the physical hurt of conquest many times, as have many other peoples in Europe, but the additions to their experience have resulted in a rich and varied culture, which finds echoes and inspiration in the descendants of those whose homeland has contributed to it. No wonder, then, that Europe finds a microcosm in Wales. Failure to sustain the quality of the Welsh inheritance will be to damage that which is most attractive to the outside world. We must not compromise the future of our past. This heritage is not for squandering.

REFERENCES

British Tourist Authority (annual) *Digest of Tourist Statistics*, London.
British Tourist Authority (1991) *Tourism Intelligence Quarterly*, August.
UNESCO (1990) *Statistical Yearbook*, Paris.
Great Britain (1990) *This Common Inheritance: Britain's Environmental Strategy*, Cm 1200, London: HMSO.

5

CULTURAL TOURISM AND TIME–SPACE BEHAVIOUR

A.G.J. Dietvorst

INTRODUCTION: A DIFFERENT VIEW OF THE CITY

Any survey of the past twenty years of urban development in Europe would reveal considerable change. Not only has there been a substantial expansion of the built-up area but, more importantly, attitudes towards the city have drastically altered. The city is being rediscovered for purposes of tourism and recreation. In the 1970s, little attention was paid to the potential for tourism and recreation in the city centre. In the 1980s, however, radical changes took place. Since then, the potential of tourism and recreation has been positively emphasized in a never-ending flow of plans to renew city centres and waterfronts. Shopping as a form of leisure activity is being discovered, and more attention is being paid to the cultural function of the city centre. Any wider conception of European heritage and its planning should be based on detailed local knowledge of tourism and recreation patterns and demands.

THE GROWING INTEREST IN CULTURE

The interest in culture has grown to such an extent that it has become a factor of economic significance. Furthermore, an identifiable culture has become crucially important to a country. Knulst (1989) has attempted to discover why there appears to be growing interest in only certain forms of entertainment outside the home. During the past thirty years, theatre, cinema and concert attendance has been decreasing, while visits to museums, amusement parks and restaurants have not. Moreover, cinemas and theatres have lost more public than concert performances. Knulst provides some explanations for these differences.

69

First, there is a difference in the degree to which amusement can be substituted in the home. Modern mass media have brought music, sport, theatre and film into the living room. Unique experiences, however, cannot be substituted. Television can replace an evening at the cinema, but it cannot satisfactorily provide the sensation of a tourist excursion to a museum.

Second, there is a difference in the extent to which the consumer can influence the development of public entertainment. Many manifestations have scarcely any flexibility in satisfying individual needs. However, the opening hours of museums and restaurants, as well as individual services, are more responsive to the requirements of the consumer.

Third, there is a difference in opportunity costs. Watching television at home costs far less, and requires less effort, than the preparation of a meal.

Fourth, alternative possibilities for stimulating experiences may be expanded. The media did indeed bring a large variety of experiences into the home, but not the feeling of going, or being, out. Tourism, however, could easily compete with the live spectacle.

Fifth, there is a decrease in social gain from cultural performances and other forms of entertainment outside the home. Knulst (1989: 217) states that puritanism and the introduction of informal dress and forms of away-from-home entertainment have accelerated the decline of the entertainment-seeking public. 'Since the arrival of television, those who go out really do something special. Compared to the many who stay at home, great sacrifices are needed in preparation (time and effort) and money. For this reason one not only wants to see something out of the ordinary, but also in an environment that is at least as 'luxurious' as home.'

Sixth, the decreasing safety of city centres is a deterrent on going out. Evening entertainment in particular has lost ground. Apart from a few localities, city centres are deserted in the evenings. Consequently, not only is there an increase in the measurable risk but, more importantly, a negative image of the city centre is also created.

THE GROWING IMPORTANCE OF CULTURE IN EUROPE

Culture, according to Urry, has 'come to occupy a more central position in the organization of present-day societies, whose contemporary culture can be at least in part characterized as 'post-modern" (Urry 1990: 82). This post-modern character involves a de-differentiation, a fading of former distinctions between culture and life, between high and low culture, between professional art and popular pleasures and between élite and mass forms of consumptions (Urry 1990: 84). Bianchini (1992), referring to an analysis of the cultural policies developed by the Rome City Council and the Greater London Council, underlines the innovative and high-profile initiatives undertaken in Italy, France, West Germany and Britain to put forward cultural policies as part of a strategy to establish a connection between the distinctive style and substance of their government and the citizens' identification with the city. This revival of cultural policy is not restricted to the arts or media. Much attention is paid to the cultural heritage of European cities as reflected in monuments, urban design and urban symbols. The trend to transform public space into representations of the cultural identity of the cities is noteworthy in this respect. Numerous European cities, including Amsterdam, Nijmegen, Barcelona, London, Hamburg and Liverpool, have been producing waterfront development schemes with all kinds of cultural entertainment. No doubt the cultural quality of our cities is reflected in the urban design: 'without the right design, no amount of local state involvement will attract tourists. It will be seen that much of the architecture of these developments is in different senses postmodern' (Urry 1990: 120).

CITY, CULTURE AND ECONOMICS

Interest in the city and in certain cultural manifestations has grown since the early 1980s because cultural tourism has had a significant influence on the development of tourism and recreation as a whole. Better still, culture has become a significant economic factor. In Amsterdam, culture generates a direct turnover of 500 million guilders, and provides employment to 12,000 people. The City of Amsterdam annually invests approximately 120 million guilders in the arts. This is, however, a very modest sum compared to the amounts which comparable cities in Germany invest, Frankfurt being the indisputable leader with some DM 450 million per year.

Van Beetz (1988) mentions three factors which show that culture, like any other product, is an economic activity. First, culture is an important determining factor of location along with convenient transport, good employment prospects and a good living environment.

A good example is the radiating effect of the Stopera (an acronym for the combination of Town Hall and Opera) in Amsterdam (Meulenbelt 1991). The neighbourhood in which the Stopera was built was in a state of decline. The Music Theatre was opened in 1986, followed by the Town Hall in 1988. This signified the beginning of drastic changes in this part of Amsterdam. In the daytime, 1,300 people work in the Town Hall and 600 in the Music Theatre. On about 250 days of the year, 80–85 per cent of the 1,600 seats of the Music Theatre are occupied in the evenings. The number of shops has increased by 40 per cent, half of which confirm that their choice of location was influenced by the presence of the Stopera (particularly book, record, magazine and food shops). There is a noticeable increase in new passers-by, including tourists. The Stopera has become a special attraction in the eastern part of the city, and generates a continuous bustle of activity. There is a marked clustering of catering establishments: clusters attract more visitors than solitary establishments; a cluster is clearly recognizable and offers the client a choice. Consequently, an upward spiral is created in the entire neighbourhood, together with a simultaneous improvement of the buildings in the area. Furthermore, the area has also become an attractive location for firms from the non-artistic sector.

Second, a flourishing cultural life gives a city or a region a positive image, attracting visitors from far beyond the borders of a country. In Amsterdam, for example, 800,000 visitors are attracted annually, with a spending power of 350 million guilders. For companies, a good image also acts as a sales lubricant for products and services abroad; it adds an invisible extra dimension to the quality of the product for sale.

Third, although not easily empirically demonstrable, many experts believe that a dynamic cultural climate is a pre-condition for innovation: 'the rich diversity of cultural events with its mutual interdependence creates the environment in which innovation takes place and where advertising, marketing, design, fashion and media feel at home' (Van Beetz 1988: 14).

TOURISM AND RECREATION COMPLEXES AS PREREQUISITES FOR SOUND CULTURAL TOURISM

It has already been shown that culture can obviously play a dominant role in developing tourism and recreation in a city or a region. This focus of attention from the tourist and recreational sector could also lead to a greater appreciation of the cultural-historic heritage. A sound development of cultural tourism cannot succeed solely by allowing an autonomous development to take its course. To make effective use of the cultural-historic potential of a city, many questions must be answered. These may include:

1 Is there a coherence among the attractive facilities offered? Are the various demands of tourism related to one another?
2 What is the cultural-historic relationship between the city and its surroundings? Do the cultural-historic cities in a particular area form islands or are they part of a recognizable cultural-historic regional identity?
3 How can cultural history be 'marketed' in a responsible manner? Is there a possibility of including a coherent cultural policy for the city in the revitalizing of the city centre? Does this include the provision of culture in its totality, from bookshops, design studios, cafes with live music, galleries and street furniture, to museums and monuments?

We are dealing with cohesion and a recognizable identity if positive answers are made to these questions. Cohesion implies that the interests of the user are paramount. The criterion for cohesion must, therefore, be derived from the interrelationship between the various and spatially separate facilities brought about by the visitors themselves. By identity, we mean the recognizable identity of the leisure environment. Uniformity and levelling have eroded local and regional identities. When the cohesion of tourism and recreation is no longer solely determined by those supplying the product, but also determined by the visitors themselves, a variety of relevant research methods must be employed. To create or maintain a recognizable cohesion of tourism and recreation in a city, research and planning must be focused on identification of the tourist and recreation complexes, analysis of their strong and weak links, and the formulation of a strategy for the development of the product.

IDENTIFICATION OF THE TOURIST AND RECREATION COMPLEX

Following a stage of inventory and survey, the product elements can be amalgamated in clusters, following a specific criterion of spatial association. To a certain extent, this clustering is intuitive, demanding much local or regional knowledge. A detailed analysis of the tourist recreation product in a specific region generally reveals spatial concentrations of various product elements. If research merely describes the spatial concentration of the existing product elements, and much tourist recreation planning goes no further, then the concept of the 'cluster' is preferred in the determination of the concentration of elements. The concept of the 'complex' is reserved for sets of tourist recreation product elements with a specific coherence (Ashworth and Jansen-Verbeke 1989; Dietvorst 1989). In determining the presence of this coherence, this functional association, two different procedures can be followed.

First, the complexes can be determined by consideration of the organizational, legal and financial aspects. A number of questions are important in this respect, including the extent of the relationship between the product elements in terms of competition, complementarity or dependency; the relation between product elements of the public and private sectors; the existence or otherwise of co-operation in marketing and promotion; the extent of control exercised in the local tourist economy by 'foreign' enterprises (such as hotel chains or multinational leisure companies); and the existence of networks as driving forces for economic growth in regional or local tourist economies. These are not the only relevant questions, but a client-oriented procedure is preferred.

Second, and of considerable importance for the planning process proposed here, is the identification of tourism and recreation complexes as experienced by potential and existing visitors. It is essential to determine the relationship between the complexity of the spatial context and the more individual leisure experiences. Thus tourist recreation complexes must be created or identified when analysing the coherence within and between clusters of product elements from the visitor's point of view. It is the visitor, the tourist and/or recreationalist who creates the tourist recreation complex through a specific time–space behaviour. Different target groups (based upon different recreation or leisure styles) form different tourist recreation complexes. It is obvious that spatial scale plays an important role in determining the different complexes.

Two different strategies can be put forward, each resulting in a specific research methodology. The first is desk research to set up a typology of target groups. This can be done by matching the product elements supposed to be used by a specific target group with the product elements present in a region. This procedure will give a first global impression of the tourism and recreation complexes present in a city or a region.

The second is empirical research to explore the time–space behaviour of tourist and/or recreationists. Such empirical research is effective, although difficult to execute. The theoretical concepts developed by Hägerstrand and others are of use. At present, however, there is a considerable lack of empirical data on the time–space behaviour of visitors. Some experience has been gained in measuring the multiplier effects of visiting local museums in the Dutch cities of Amsterdam and Nijmegen (Dietvorst *et al.* 1987; ten Tuynte and Dietvorst 1988). The following section gives a short introduction to the conceptualization of time–space relationships, then discusses the results of empirical research carried out in several parts of the Netherlands.

TIME–SPACE ANALYSIS

Analysis of the dynamics of tourist recreation complexes as defined earlier necessitates the use of time–space analysis of tourist behaviour. The ideas put forward by Hägerstrand are fundamental in this respect and can be considered as a physicalist approach to society (Thrift 1977), an appreciation of the biological, ecological and locational realities which impose constraints on human activities. Other researchers have subsequently complemented this constraint-oriented approach with a more choice-oriented one (Floor 1990: 3–6). In addition to capability, coupling and authority constraints, the way in which people make their choices depends upon: (1) their motives, preferences and experiences; (2) their images and opportunity estimations; and (3) their material resources. The view that human beings are indivisible is essential, and a used location not only has co-ordinates in space but also in time, and neither an escape from time nor its storage is possible: 'jumps of non-existence are not permitted' (Blaas 1989). The different time–space paths of tourists, and hence the different assemblages made out of the supply of attractions and activities, can be illustrated by hypothesized models of time–space paths of different tourists in a city environment. The models are situated in Enkhuizen, one of the historic cities around the former Zuiderzee (now Lake IJssel). The city has many notable historic buildings, and is known as a watersports centre. Figure 5.1 shows a simplified impression of the city, although not all of the product elements are represented.

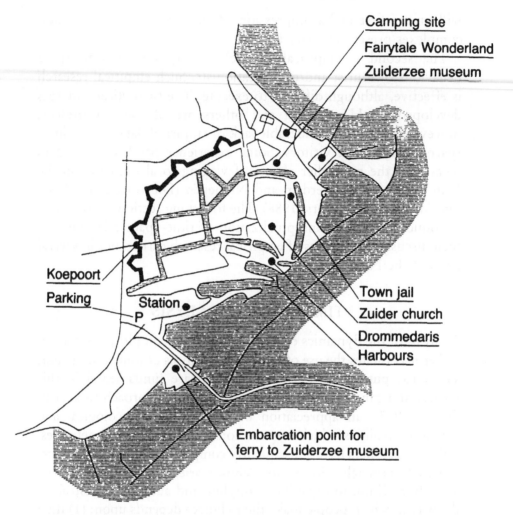

Camping site
Fairytale Wonderland
Zuiderzee museum

Koepoort
Parking
Station
P

Town jail
Zuider church
Drommedaris
Harbours

Embarcation point for
ferry to Zuiderzee museum

Figure 5.1 The Enkhuizen tourism/recreation cluster

Hypothesized models of tourist time–space behaviour

Figures 5.2 and 5.3 give hypothesized models of time–space behaviour
for two tourist types. The first considers the 'water-sport tourist'
as a potential customer for a tourism and recreation complex. A
well-educated, well-off childless German couple are represented.
Their hypothesized daily time-path begins in Enkhuizen harbour
(in 1989 some 10 per cent of tourists came to the city by boat). They
take the small ferry from near the railway station to visit the
Zuiderzee museum. This museum is a primary element in the
Enkhuizen tourism and recreation cluster, having about 300,000
visitors per year to its reconstructed village showing the lifestyle of

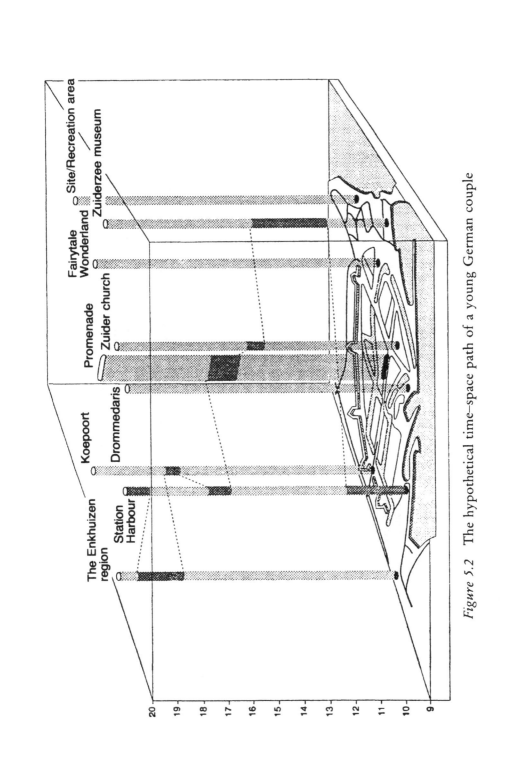

Figure 5.2 The hypothetical time–space path of a young German couple

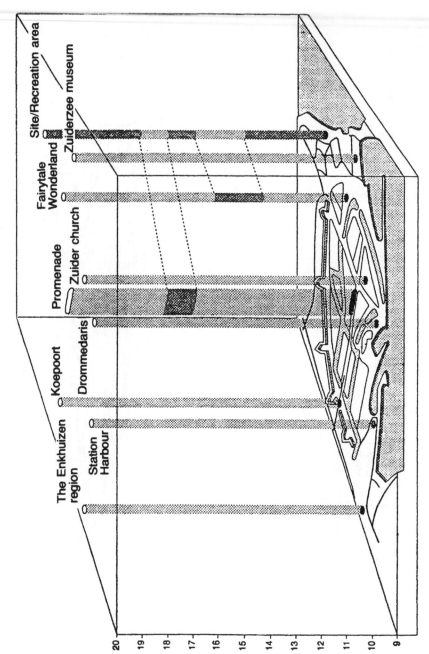

Figure 5.3 The hypothetical time–space path of a young couple with two children

the 'fisherfolk' around the Zuiderzee at the turn of the century. On the basis of a 1989 study it can be assumed that the visit will last about three hours. After visiting this museum, the German couple decide to go for a walk in the town. They combine this sight-seeing walk with a meal in one of the restaurants. Back on their cruiser in the afternoon, they decide to hire bicycles and go on a short cycle tour, returning in the early evening. The daily time–space path ends with a walk along the harbour front.

To reflect the impact of a quite different tourist behaviour, Figure 5.3 shows the hypothesized time–space path of a young, low-income couple with children. Their path begins at the camping-site near Lake IJssel. They plan to visit the Fairytale Wonderland with their children, and this visit takes about two hours. Before going to the town, they return to the campsite for lunch to save money. Then they walk to the town centre to do some shopping. Sight-seeing is not a favourite activity for young children, and so they return to the campsite immediately after the shopping, and stay there for the rest of the day.

Methods of analysing flow patterns and time–space behaviour

Several methods can be used for analysing the time–space behaviour of visitors, of which the following are the most significant. First, principal component analysis can explore patterns to reveal 'visitor preference spaces'.

Second, network planning can be used in combination with Geographic Information Systems. The INTRANET programme (Jurgens 1991) has been developed for solving planning questions related to land use and infrastructure. It is possible to grade the network in terms of accessibility, the type of land use it has to serve and the economic qualities; grading of a more psychological nature (for instance whether the route offers enough variety) can even be added. INTRANET thus gives the opportunity of calculating several solutions to optimize the coherence of a tourist recreation complex.

Third, apart from the application of operations research, networks can also be analysed using mathematical graph theory (Nystuen and Dacey 1961). This method is suitable for analysing flows of tourists in order to discover underlying hierarchical structures within tourist recreation complexes. The origin-destination matrix representing the network reflects the prevailing structure of linkages and dominance.

Fourth, if the researcher has access to flow data for a sequence of periods, Markov chain analysis is very appropriate for describing the process of change within a tourist recreation complex (Dietvorst and Wever 1977). The comparison of several calculated so-called transition matrices is extremely suitable for tracing the tendencies of change in the system under observation.

A case study of Arnhem

Time–space analysis of tourist behaviour can be extremely relevant for the development of a sound cultural events policy. Cultural events such as large exhibitions are expected to have an important multiplier effect, but a critical evaluation of the real impact is seldom carried out. In 1986, the city of Arnhem was selected for an exhaustive survey of the visitors to the Sonsbeek Exhibition, the Municipal Museum, the Netherlands Open Air Museum and the Burgers Zoo. The first two attractions are located within the city centre. The Sonsbeek Exhibition in the Sonsbeek Park is an international sculpture exhibition, and the Municipal Museum is known for its fine collection of Dutch Magic Realism. The Burgers Zoo and the Netherlands Open Air Museum lie at a distance of about 5 kilometres from the city centre, in the urban fringe of Arnhem.

For the multiplier impact of the attractions on the city itself, the distance to the city centre and the character of the attractions are crucial. Time–space analysis of Sonsbeek and Municipal Museum visitors revealed a strong relationship with 'city-centre activities' such as shopping, restaurant and terrace visits. But the visitors to the Burgers Zoo and the Netherlands Open Air Museum did not wish to extend their day-trips by a visit to the city centre, which is unsurprising as spending a day in a large attraction park with children is an energy-absorbing activity in itself. Thus these visitors spend their time and money in the attraction parks, whereas the Sonsbeek and Municipal Museum visitors can be considered as a reinforcement of the city's own economy.

If a city wishes to make socio-cultural and financial profits from cultural attractions and events, they have to be embedded in a spatially accessible, but differentiated, complex of attractions and facilities in the city centre. Differentiation and time–space association are key concepts for tourist recreation complexes.

Preliminary results of the Enkhuizen research

The city is a tourist attraction owing to the historic nature of its urban environment and its water-sport facilities. The Zuiderzee Museum is an important attraction, but its poor relationship with the city stimulated research into the presence and dynamics of tourist recreation complexes. This poor relationship is caused by the specific access policy of the city authorities. Visitors to the open-air section of the Zuiderzee Museum only have access to the museum via the ferry and, although they can leave the museum for a walk in the city, they usually take the ferry back to the car parks outside the city. Thus the multiplier impact of the museum for the city is under developed.

The data were collected in 1990 over six days at Easter and three days during the summer. The total samples were respectively 735 and 212. However, only 57 per cent of questionnaire returns were in a form that could be processed for this time–space analysis. A map of Enkhuizen was included in the questionnaire, showing the most important attractions and monuments. Visitors were asked to mark on the map the route followed during their visit, the start and finishing points, and to note the names and times of all points visited. From respondents' comments afterwards, it was clear that some of them had difficulty in tracing their exact route on the map. There are, obviously, differences in the way people make use of maps. There were problems with spatial awareness and the capacity to orientate. Further, some were unaware of exact routes and times, and were unable to reconstruct their own time–space patterns. Hence 43 per cent of the questionnaires were unreliable, and the remainder also have interpretation problems. In addition to visitors, a 400-strong sample of the local population were also asked to register their daily leisure activities, their use of cultural facilities and their opinion of the impact of tourism on their life world.

Owing to these problems, real origin-destination matrices could not be established. A real graph analysis of the data was not possible, and the analysis therefore proceeded differently. The map of Enkhuizen was overlaid with a grid, each cell representing a tourist recreation attraction or element. These elements built up the behaviour space for the Enkhuizen visitor. The number of visitors at a certain point in time and a certain element is represented by the height of the column. The time element was introduced through a sequence of maps (of which Figures 5.4–5.7 are samples) (Sijbrandij 1990).

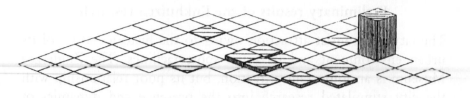

Figure 5.4   Behaviour space of visitors to Enkhuizen: 10.30–10.45

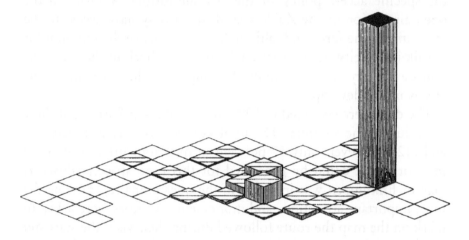

Figure 5.5   Behaviour space of visitors to Enkhuizen: 12.30–12.45

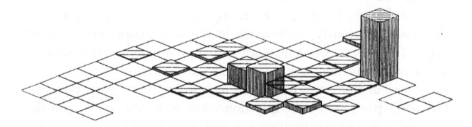

Figure 5.6   Behaviour space of visitors to Enkhuizen: 16.30–16.45

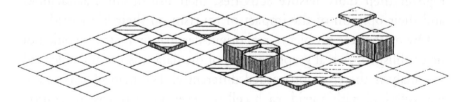

Figure 5.7   Behaviour space of visitors to Enkhuizen: 17.30–17.45

Key to Figures 5.4–5.7
Number of tourists

200–250	50–99
150–199	1–49
100–149	None

The interpretation of the time–space analysis can be summarized thus. In the period 10.30–10.45 (Figure 5.4) the city resembles a more or less flat plane, as there are not many visitors at this time. Only along the marina and in the shopping centre can visitors be seen. The Zuiderzee Museum (ZZM) already has the first significant groups of visitors. In the period 11.30–11.45, visitor numbers are still increasing at the ZZM. The centre of the town now attracts more visitors. A few are to be found in the Boerenhoek (Farmers' Quarter). This pattern changes little in the periods 12.30–12.45 (Figure 5.5) and 14.30–14.45. The visitor intensity for the main elements is increasing, with the inner city and ZZM being busiest, but the marina and Drommedaris both more crowded than before. By 16.30–16.45 (Figure 5.6) the marina attendance is already fading away. The Boerenhoek still has some tourists, but the numbers remain very low. Although the ZZM's numbers are already declining, the inner city remains busy. By 17.30–17.45 (Figure 5.7), ZZM numbers are declining very quickly. Not all of the ZZM's visitors can pay a visit to the inner city, as they go back via the ferry to the car parks outside Enkhuizen. The influence of the 'authority constraint' – the closing time of the shops – is remarkable. After 18.00 the city is dead.

These figures reveal a series of cross-sections through time and space, but do not give insight into the relationships between the different product elements. On the basis of an interaction matrix, the relations between the different elements were also analysed. Table 5.1 shows the relationships between the Horeca-Marina-inner-city shopping-Drommedaris-ZZM. (Horeca is an acronym indicating the economic sector composed of hotels, restaurants and cafes, that is the catering and hospitality services.) The strongest relationships are between the city elements. The position of the ZZM is remarkably weak in this complex.

Table 5.1 Interaction matrix of visitor movements in Enkhuizen

Origin of visitors (percentage of all visitors per attraction)				
	Horeca	*Marina*	*Inner city*	*Drommedaris*	*ZZM*
Horeca	–	22	20	19.7	24.3
Marina	18.7	–	17.5	17.2	13.4
Inner city	16.8	17	–	14	15.3
Drommedaris	16	16.5	13.9	–	13.7
ZZM	19	9.9	11.5	10.5	–

TOURIST RECREATION COMPLEXES IN ENKHUIZEN

The time–space analysis was completed with the determination of the so-called visitor-preference spaces using principal components analysis. The combination of the time–space analyses and the results of various principal components analyses on data sets obtained from both visitors and local inhabitants revealed different types of tourist recreation complexes. These differences are due to the different ways in which time and space are used. Visitors coming to Enkhuizen for just one day make their tourist recreation complex by combining the various attractions and facilities. Local inhabitants, however, assemble their complexes during a much longer period through their use of facilities and their participation in activities. The preliminary results of the Enkhuizen research project demonstrate these different types of complexes.

Tourist recreation complexes of visitors

The first complex is made up of the time–space paths of visitors arriving in Enkhuizen by yacht. They patronize several facilities in the harbour area, preferring restaurants and cafes. A second complex is assembled by visitors with cultural interests. In fact, there are several possibilities or sub-complexes. Some visitors combine the Zuiderzee Museum with a walk in the city – sight-seeing or restaurant visiting. Others can be typified as being interested in the historical or architectural aspects of the city. For them, the visit to Enkhuizen is often part of a series of visits to famous tourist-historic cities in the Netherlands. Enkhuizen is thus part of a regional, or even national, tourist recreation complex. Finally, there is a large group of cultural tourists who come to Enkhuizen solely to visit the Zuiderzee Museum. The third complex is assembled by visitors attending events (such as Sailing Enkhuizen) or specific activities (such as the Fish Auction) in the city, in combination with the use of restaurants and cafes.

Recreation complexes of local inhabitants

Events organized for tourists also attract the attention of local inhabitants. Thus the first recreation complex consists of events, the Summer Garden and the Zuiderzee Museum. The second complex can be labelled as 'entertainment', including sports facilities, cinemas and jazz events. The third is oriented to the preferences of children, the fourth to water recreation and, finally, a complex can be reconstructed for those interested in fun shopping and city visits in general.

THE SWOT ANALYSIS

Having ascertained the significant tourism and recreation complexes in a specific region, their qualitative strengths or weaknesses must be discovered. One of the main objectives in managing tourism and recreation complexes at a regional level is to ensure the continuity of the tourist and/or recreation region as an attractive area for potential visitors. Ensuring continuity in terms of maintaining the market position, or even improving the relative market share, is an essential issue in the process of strategic planning. A well-known procedure for this is the SWOT analysis (Strengths-Weaknesses-Opportunities-Threats).

Many methods are available for examining the SWOT elements of tourism and recreation complexes. Most originated in the context of marketing management at the levels of the company, factory or corporation. Economic geographers have attempted to transpose the typical management and/or marketing methods for corporate strategic planning (see, for example, Kotler 1988) to more spatially relevant methods (De Smidt and Wever 1984; Ashworth and Voogd 1987). The concepts of the 'portfolio analysis' can be of use in developing more spatially oriented analytical tools.

The original portfolio model, as developed by the Boston Consulting Group, shows a growth-share matrix, divided into four cells (Kotler 1988). More sophisticated portfolio matrices consist of nine or more cells, making a balanced judgement possible. The original factors, such as market growth and market share, are replaced by competitiveness and attractiveness. Figure 5.8 is an illustration of a portfolio analysis of the product elements in the Enkhuizen area. The portfolio is related to the primary product elements in Enkhuizen and is based upon visitor figures and personal observations. Owing to a lack of detailed data, for example on visitor expenditure at each product element, a more sophisticated portfolio of Enkhuizen for a series of tourist recreation complexes cannot be developed at present.

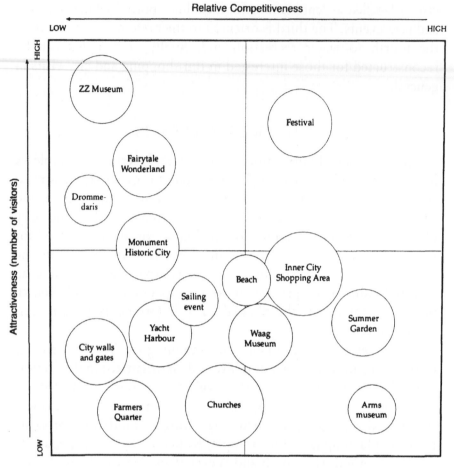

Figure 5.8 Portfolio of primary product elements in Enkhuizen

PRODUCT DEVELOPMENT STRATEGIES

The final phase in the planning process for tourism and recreation complexes in a specific region is the selection of product development strategies. Of course, these strategies have to be created for different spatial levels, and ultimately each should be matched with the results of the portfolio analysis of the different tourism and recreation complexes.

At a regional level, the general direction of future development is chosen from a set of alternatives. Roughly speaking, it is possible to start from two essential types of global strategy, as follows.

A *Strategies determining the direction of future development*
   expansion strategy, leading to a larger number of recreationists and/or tourists, but also to greater pressure on scarce resources;

86

consolidation strategy, directed only at a qualitative improvement and at maintaining the market share;
restrictive strategy, where existing conservational claims for the
preservation of cultural heritage make a dissuasive, or even a
demarketing, policy desirable.

B *Strategies focusing on the character of the tourism and recreation
product itself*
choices for strengthening the particular regional identity of the
tourism and recreation product.

It is important to realize that it is not necessary to select only one
strategy for the whole city or region in question. The goals and the
restrictive conditions may make a spatially differentiated policy
desirable. The basic assumption should be the maintenance and
improvement of the spatial quality.

CONCLUSION

Many cities have sought to develop their cultural heritage after the
collapse of local economies previously dominated by primary and
secondary industries. City marketing is launched as an important
aspect of restructuring policy. The increasing trend to take second
and third holidays, often as short breaks in western Europe,
stimulates city trips and, more importantly, spending during such
short breaks is on average higher than spending during longer
holidays. Promoting cities as interesting places for cultural heritage
is more than just selling an inviting cultural and physical infrastructure. Just as private companies have to develop a well-balanced mix
of products to hold their position in the market, cities have to base
a sound development of cultural tourism upon integrative policies
for what is called existing tourist recreation complexes. As a result
of the variety in types of tourist behaviour, tourists assemble the
essential elements of a day-trip in quite different ways. The time–
space behaviour of visitors is crucial in determining the weaknesses
and strengths of a cultural tourist product and, therefore, an
adequate monitoring system is an absolute prerequisite for a
balanced development. It is also a necessary means to avoid
undesirable exploitation and degradation of irreplaceable heritage
resources in providing the tools for effective city and heritage
management.

REFERENCES

Ashworth, G.J. and Voogd, H. (1987) 'Geografische marketing, een bruikbare invalshoek voor onderzoek en planning', *Stedebouw en Volkshuisvesting*, May: 85–90.

Ashworth, G.J. and Jansen-Verbeke, M.C. (1989) 'Functional association and spatial clustering: preconditions for the use of leisure in urban economic revitalization', *Proceedings*, WLRA Congress, Cities for the Future, World Leisure and Recreation Association, Rotterdam.

Bianchini, F. (1992) 'Cultural policy and the development of citizenship', unpublished paper presented at the VIII ELRA Conference: Leisure and the new citizenship, Bilbao.

Blaas, W. (1989) 'Theorie en toegepaste theorie van het tyd-ruimte onderzoek', *Amsterdamse Social - Geografische Studies* 23.

de Smidt, M. and Wever, E. (1984) *A Profile of Dutch Economic Geography*, Assen: Van Gorcum.

Dietvorst, A.G.J. (1989) 'Complexen en netwerken: hun betekenis voor de toeristisch-recreatieve sector', inaugural address, Agricultural University, Wageningen.

Dietvorst, A.G.J. and Wever, E. (1977) 'Changes in the pattern of information exchange in the Netherlands, 1967–1974', *Tijdschrift voor Economische en Sociale Geografie* 68, 2: 72–82.

Dietvorst, A.G.J., Poelhekke, W. and Roffelsen, J. (1987) 'Hoe meer verscheidenheid aan attracties, des te aantrekkelijker de stad', *Recreatie en Toerisme* 11: 441–5.

Floor, J. (1990) 'Aktiviteitensystemen en bereikbaarheid', in Floor, J., Goethals, A.L.J. and de Koning, J.C. (eds) *Aktiviteitensystemen en bereikbaarheid*, Amsterdam: SISWO.

Hägerstrand, T. (1970) 'What about people in regional science', *Papers of the Regional Science Association* xxiv: 7–21.

Jurgens, C.R. (1991) *Introduction to GIS-Applications in Land Use Planning*, Wageningen: Department of Physical Planning and Rural Development, Agricultural University.

Knulst, W.P. (1989) 'Van vaudeville tot video. Empirisch-theoretische studie naar verschuivingen in het uitgaan en het gebruik van media sinds de jaren vijftig', *Sociale en Culturele Studies* 12.

Kotler, Ph. (1988) *Marketing Management. Analysis, Planning, Implementation and Control*, Englewood Cliffs: Prentice Hall.

Meulenbelt, K. (1991) *De uitstralingseffecten van het Stadthuis-Muziktheater (STOPERA)*, Amsterdam: Rooilijn.

Nystuen, J.D. and Dacey, M.F. (1961) 'A graph theory interpretation of nodal regions', *Papers and Proceedings of the Regional Science Association* 7: 29–42.

Sijbrandij, J. (1990) *In de Loop der Tijd. Een Methode om Tijdruimtegedrag van Bezoekers van Enkhuizen te Analyseren*, Wageningen: Werkgroep Recreatie Landbouwuniversiteit.

Thrift, N.J. (1977) *An Introduction to Time Geography*, Catmog 13, Norwich: GeoBooks.

ten Tuynte, J. and Dietvorst, A. (1988) *Musea anders Bekeken. Vier Nijmeegse Musea Bekeken naar Uitstralingseffecten en Complexvorming*, Nijmegen: Werkgroep Recreatie en Toerisme, Katholieke Universiteit.

Urry, J. (1990) *The Tourist Gaze: Leisure and Travel in Contemporary Societies*, London: Sage.

Van Beetz, F. (1988) 'Cultuur en steden', *Raimtalijke Verkenningen*, The Hague: RPD.

6

WHO CONSUMES THE HERITAGE PRODUCT?

Implications for European heritage tourism

D. Light and R. C. Prentice

INTRODUCTION

One of the central arguments of this book is that the exploitation of historic resources is a major economic activity which is widespread throughout Europe, that it is most developed in the states of Western Europe, but that it is likely to be of increasing importance to the emerging states of Central and Eastern Europe. Heritage involves the conversion of history into a modern commodity – the heritage 'product' – for contemporary consumption (Ashworth, Chapter 2 of this volume). It is closely linked to the leisure industry; indeed, in marketing terms, heritage represents nothing more than 'a specific aspect of tourism supply to be marketed to an identified tourism demand' (Ashworth 1988: 164). Put another way, heritage is 'historical tourism' (West 1988; Light 1991a).

This chapter is concerned with one aspect of heritage tourism, namely the nature of demand for – or consumption of – the heritage product. Although the heritage phenomenon has generated a vigorous academic debate, there has been surprisingly little investigation of its consumers, and relatively little is known of their characteristics, motives and expectations. Yet arguably such research is essential for effective heritage planning. This chapter aims to consider the character of demand for heritage tourism with particular reference to Wales, and as such forms a natural complement to Chapter 4 by Carr which considers supply (or production). This discussion is structured in two parts. The first considers the characteristics of heritage consumers in terms of a number of conventional socio-demographic variables. The second part focuses on motives for visiting heritage attractions, attitudes towards the past, and expectations from the heritage product itself. As such, it is concerned with what is being consumed, and why.

This discussion presents evidence to demonstrate patterns of consumption for heritage tourism. Although the findings presented are, by their very nature, specific to Wales, we seek both to place them in a broader context and also to draw out the wider implications for European heritage tourism. The evidence we present pertains to a limited range of historic buildings and monuments, which constitute one component of the spectrum of heritage resources (Hewison 1988; Light 1991a; Prentice 1993).

The collection of the information presented in this discussion merits brief technical consideration. The data are derived from three surveys at historic buildings and monuments. Surveys 1 and 2 (SEREN 1986a, 1986b) were conducted in 1986; Survey 3 (Light 1991a) was undertaken in 1987/8. The database comprises responses from 3,887 visitors at fifteen sites. The sites can be allocated to three groups – castles (ten sites); ecclesiastical monuments (two sites); and industrial buildings/monuments (three sites). The location of the study sites is shown in Figure 6.1. Our concern in this chapter is primarily to identify general patterns of consumption; thus the data presented are aggregated within each category for the three surveys. However, where pertinent, site-specific variations are identified and discussed. Some variables were not common to all three surveys, and in such instances the figures presented refer only to those surveys where those variables were collected.

SOCIO-DEMOGRAPHIC CHARACTERISTICS OF VISITORS

Social class/age of completing education

Professional and managerial workers are clearly dominant (see Table 6.1), accounting for around half of visitors sampled. Skilled and unskilled workers are all present in smaller numbers. Figure 6.2 places this in a wider context by showing the representation of each social group with respect to the British population as a whole (after Prince 1983). Those bars above the line indicate over-representation; those below indicate under-representation. Thus a representation ratio of 2 means that a particular social group is present at double

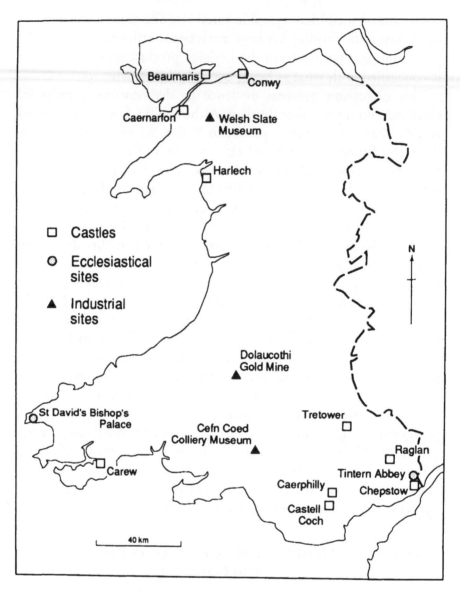

Figure 6.1 Location of the study sites

its representation in the British population; a ratio of 0.5 means that it is present at only half its representation in the population. A startling pattern emerges: the professional/managerial group is over-represented at heritage sites by between three and four times. With the exception of the skilled manual group at industrial sites, all other social groups, especially semi/unskilled and retired people, are under-represented. This pattern varies between sites. The over-representation of professional/managerial workers is smaller at

Table 6.1 Social class of visitors to heritage sites

	Castles (10 sites) %	Ecclesiastical sites (2 sites) %	Industrial sites (3 sites) %	British population* %
Professional/managerial	51	64	45	16
Skilled non-manual	13	9	13	25
Skilled manual	19	12	27	25
Semi/unskilled/retired	17	15	15	34

Source: Surveys 1, 2 and 3 (SEREN 1986a, 1986b; Light 1991a)
* English Tourist Board/Wales Tourist Board (ETB/WTB) (1989)

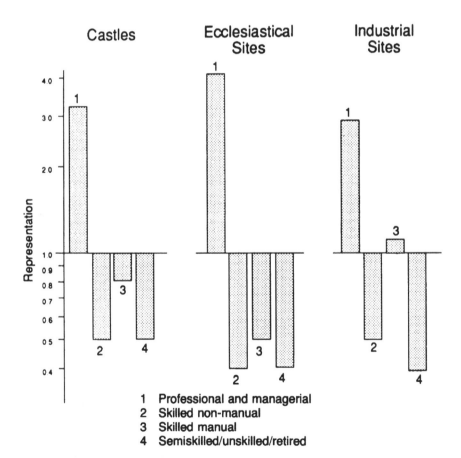

1 Professional and managerial
2 Skilled non-manual
3 Skilled manual
4 Semiskilled/unskilled/retired

Figure 6.2 Representation of different social groups
       Source: SEREN 1986a, 1986b; Light 1991a

industrial sites, where skilled manual workers are also slightly over-represented; thus different types of heritage site vary in their appeal. However, the general pattern remains: the consumption of heritage is highly selective and is undertaken disproportionately by the middle classes.

This finding may be developed by considering the age at which heritage consumers completed their education. This is presented in Table 6.2 for four sites considered in Survey 3, along with figures for the British population as a whole. At both types of resource, people educated beyond the age of 18 (that is, frequently to degree level) form over half the visitors. Once again, this information is placed in a wider context (see Figure 6.3) by considering the representation of the different educational groups with respect to the British population. A clear pattern is again apparent: those who completed their education after 18 are present at heritage sites at over three times their representation in the British population. Conversely, those who completed education at or before 16 (who account for almost three-quarters of the population) are most under-represented. The extent of education is related to social class. The consumers of heritage thus constitute a well-educated minority; this has important implications for their leisure needs and activities, and expectations from the visit to a heritage site.

The data presented here are not exceptional: there is a growing body of evidence that indicates that the consumption of many forms of built heritage is highly selective. Other surveys have noted that professional/managerial workers form the largest group at historic buildings and monuments (British Tourist Authority and Countryside Commission 1968; Mass Observation 1978; Public Attitude Surveys 1985; Prentice 1989a), and also at museums (English Tourist Board 1982; Prince 1983; Hooper-Greenhill 1988). The 1987 *General*

Table 6.2 Age at which visitors to heritage sites completed education

	Castles (3 sites) %	Ecclesiastical sites (1 site) %	British population* %
Before 16	26	28	72
17	8	4	8
18	13	10	6
After 18	54	57	15

Source: Survey 3 (Light 1991a)
* Figures derived from Office of Population Censuses and Surveys (OPCS 1990)

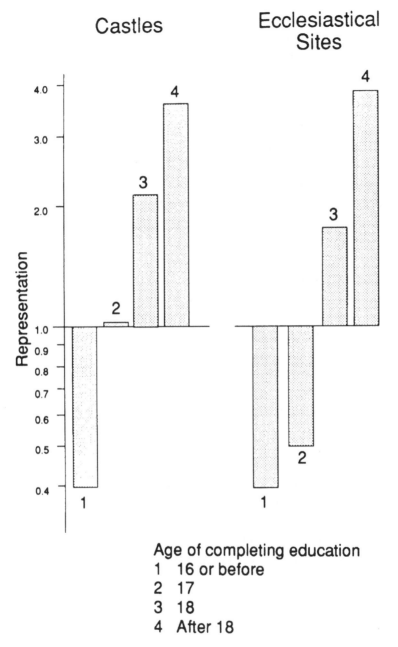

Figure 6.3 Representation of different educational groups
Source: SEREN 1986a, 1986b; Light 1991a

Household Survey (OPCS 1989a) noted that 15 per cent of professionals had visited an art gallery or museum, and 14 per cent some sort of historic building, within the four weeks prior to interview; for unskilled workers the figures for both activities were only 4 per cent. Moreover, the appeal of natural heritage places is similarly selective. The National Countryside Recreation Survey (Countryside Commission 1985) observed that managerial households were almost three times more likely to visit the countryside than unskilled workers. Similar findings are noted by OPCS (1989a). Both the Dartington Amenity Research Trust (DART and Department of Psychology, University of Surrey 1978) and Prince (1983) observed an over-representation of professional/managerial workers at visitor centres in the countryside.

Although sources are limited, there is also evidence that the consumption of the heritage product is similarly selective in other European countries. Bord Fáilte (1974) (Irish Tourist Board) recorded a large attendance of professional/managerial workers at monuments in Ireland. Hooper-Greenhill (1988) cites a study in Sweden which indicated that the extent of education was an important influence on museum attendance. Heinich (1988) observes that visitors to the Pompidou Centre in Paris are unrepresentative of the French population, being disproportionately drawn from the executive and professional classes. Moreover, if we consider the social class of European visitors at our Welsh study sites, a similar pattern is apparent. Almost two-thirds of European visitors are professional/managerial workers, while only 11 per cent are manual workers. This evidence, although patchy, does at least give an indication that the patterns of consumption of heritage in Britain are replicated throughout Europe; namely that continent-wide, the leisure use of the past is predominantly undertaken by a minority of the population, of similar social-class characteristics.

What, then, are the reasons for the highly selective appeal of heritage sites to the middle class? What processes of choice or constraint can be identified? A first constraint is access to transport (Patmore 1983; Prince 1983; Prentice 1989a). The private car is the most common means of transport (SEREN 1986a) to heritage sites and, since many sites are located in rural areas, opportunities to visit will be limited for those without cars. Department of Transport statistics (1988) indicate that car ownership is strongly related to social class: 94 per cent of professional households own a car, compared with 35 per cent of unskilled households. If access to transport is the sole constraint on visiting among manual workers, we would expect their representation at urban heritage sites, where access to a car is less important, to be higher. Yet this is not the case. There is no significant difference in the social-class profile between rural and urban sites. Transport constraints undoubtedly apply to those manual workers who do not own cars (Prince 1983), but do not adequately explain why those who do have access to a car do not visit in large numbers.

A second constraint will be cost, but this will operate at two scales. At one level, in order to experience the heritage of other countries, a traveller must have the necessary disposable income for foreign travel. In Britain, the tendency to take overseas holidays is closely related to social class and income; the professional/managerial classes are more likely to take overseas holidays (ETB/WTB 1989), and a similar situation is likely to exist among European visitors to Britain. Inevitably, then, the consumption of British heritage by Europeans (and conversely the consumption of European heritage by Britons) will be undertaken by the middle classes. However, on a domestic leisure/tourism scale there is far less evidence of cost (in the form of admission charges) acting as a deterrent to visiting among manual workers. Prentice (1989b) noted that admission charges were the most frequently given reason for not entering (as distinct from visiting) monuments in Wales, but that this response was not related to social class. Manual workers were not being deterred at the gates of heritage sites by high admission charges: instead they were not arriving at the sites in the first instance. Heinich (1988) reports a similar situation in France where, in an effort to democratize culture, no charge was made for admission to the Pompidou Centre. Yet manual workers do not visit the site in significant numbers. Heinich suggests that an entrance charge has little impact on visitor numbers since the barriers to culture are themselves cultural rather than economic.

Is it possible, then, that factors of choice rather than constraint account for the disproportionate appeal of heritage places to the middle classes? This notion may be further developed with reference to a socio-psychological understanding of leisure (Driver and Tocher 1979; Iso-Ahola 1983; Prince 1983, 1985a). Such an understanding sees leisure – which in this case will include the activities undertaken by tourists – as comprising goal-oriented activities satisfying perceived needs, whether or not these needs are articulated as such. An important requirement of leisure may be the successful completion of an activity which leads to a sense of competence and an enhancement of self-esteem. Motivations for leisure activity derive from learning based on past experience: those activities which an individual has previously experienced as rewarding are more likely to be repeated, and so behavioural consistency is maintained. Important influences on this process will be the activities with which an individual has been socialized – here the family is a key agent – and also the need to maintain a self-image which is acceptable to peer groups (Prince 1983).

In this context, the selective appeal of heritage places may be explained by considering the leisure needs and motivations of those people who visit, or do not visit, such places. An important motive for visiting heritage attractions is a prior interest in the past (this is discussed in more detail on pp. 106–10). A consequence of this interest may be the desire for discovery, learning and understanding about the past. Roggenbuck *et al.* (1990: 120) contend that 'learning is a high priority motivator for engaging in leisure activities'. Moreover, both Prentice and Prentice (1989) and Thomas (1989) suggest that an interest in learning about the site has increased among visitors to heritage attractions over the past two decades. The extent to which different social groups require learning from their leisure time varies considerably. Patmore (1983) noted that those with more skilled and responsible occupations, and with a longer period in education, tend to lead a more varied and active leisure life. This group is also more likely to see leisure time as something to be used constructively (Prince 1983).

There is evidence that learning is important to those visiting heritage attractions. Hood (1983) recorded that regular visitors to museums valued having an opportunity to learn, the challenge of new experience, and worthwhile use of leisure time. Thomas (1989) also noted that professional and managerial workers were more likely to visit monuments to be informed, whereas manual workers were more likely to visit for relaxation and entertainment. Similarly, Prince (1985b) noted that non-visitors (largely manual workers) regarded museums as being educational rather than entertaining, suggesting that such people did not regard education as a legitimate use of their leisure time. These findings strongly imply that heritage places are associated by both visitors and non-visitors with learning, and that these two groups have different requirements from their leisure time. Thus, although social class is correlated with leisure needs, social class *per se* does not determine such needs (Hood 1983).

The findings reported here add a further dimension to the 'whose heritage?' and 'whose benefit?' debate (Tunbridge 1984, Ashworth and Tunbridge 1990). This issue, usually discussed with reference to ethnic or cultural groups, may also be applied to social class. The working classes constitute another group (albeit not a minority one) which does not appear to empathize with the heritage values at these sites. The benefits of 'official' heritage are, to a very large extent, appropriated by the middle classes. Moreover, a socio-psychological understanding of leisure suggests that this situation will be perpetuated, since individuals will tend towards behavioural consistency (Prince 1983). It is, however, exacerbated by the fact that the production or supply of heritage is similarly, and traditionally, in the hands of the middle classes: middle-class producers define, present and interpret heritage for middle-class consumers. The presentation of heritage resources inevitably reflects the values and philosophies of their producers. It is hardly surprising, then, that many heritage sites present a 'professional-managerial view of the significance of history', as West (1988: 40) has forcefully argued for the Ironbridge Gorge museum. The result is that heritage interpretation concentrates on objects rather than processes (West 1988); the history thus presented is frequently devoid of political and economic tension. However, this situation will also arise from the perception among the producers of heritage of what their customers want. Given that heritage is an important commercial activity, the product presented must not be mismatched with the prior expectations and experiences of the consumers: middle-class visitors will expect something which accords with their experience. The heritage product is thus inevitably, as Ashworth (Chapter 2, this volume) identifies, consumer-defined; equally inevitably, what the consumers are not interested in or do not want to see will be omitted.

These findings also introduce a whole range of questions regarding the ways in which manual workers who do not visit heritage sites appropriate their past. Does this group in fact have a need to experience the past in their leisure time? And, if so, what form and activities does this take? Given that manual workers do not make much use of developed heritage products, they may not appropriate their past in the form of 'heritage' at all, but instead in a way which is not amenable to commodification and mass consumption. We also know little of where manual workers experience their past, beyond that such places appear to be spatially distinct from those visited by the middle classes. These issues represent important research questions which need to be addressed if we are to have more than just a partial understanding of the heritage phenomenon.

What are the implications of these findings extrapolated to the new Europe? First, attempts to create a common or integrated heritage for Europe will inevitably reflect middle-class values. Indeed, to judge from the popular press, support for an integrated Europe may itself be a middle-class phenomenon. Thus, given that its consumers tend to be drawn from one social group, the extent to which heritage in its current forms can integrate Europe is questionable.

Second, with regard to the future for central and eastern Europe, looking to generate western revenue from cultural and heritage tourism, these findings are encouraging. The consumers of heritage are exactly those high-spending groups which Hall (1992) identifies as target markets for this region. Furthermore, these people are likely to have an inclination for exploration and discovery as part of their holiday/leisure activities. The western middle classes are, therefore, likely to represent the major market for the cultural heritage of eastern Europe in coming years, and this heritage is increasingly likely to be presented in accordance with the requirements and expectations of middle-class westerners.

Third, given that demand for heritage is so highly selective, issues of public subsidy for heritage may come under increasing scrutiny. The 1980s were a decade during which redistributive financial policies in western Europe took second place, unlike the 1960s. The 1990s may be different, particularly as the international redistribution of both wealth and economic development becomes an issue within the European Community. If heritage is largely consumed by a minority of the population, its subsidy from public funds may be seen as regressive in a new era of redistribution. Alternatively, even if the 1980s policies of reducing the redistributive impacts of public policies in Europe continue into the 1990s, the future for heritage tourism is not certain. Such policies emphasize tax reductions, and bring with them an emphasis on commercialization in public services. The users of public-sector heritage resources may then be expected to pay progressively more for the consumption of these resources.

Age and group composition

Table 6.3 indicates that around three-quarters of visitors are aged between 20 and 49; over half are aged between 30 and 49. Heritage

Table 6.3 Age groups of visitors to heritage sites

	Castles (10 sites) %	Ecclesiastical sites (2 sites) %	Industrial sites (3 sites) %	Population of England and Wales* %
16–19	4	3	2	9
20–29	22	19	14	20
30–39	32	29	41	17
40–49	24	26	25	16
50–59	11	13	11	13
60+	8	10	8	26

Source: Surveys 1, 2 and 3 (SEREN 1986a, 1986b; Light 1991a)
* Derived from OPCS (1989b)

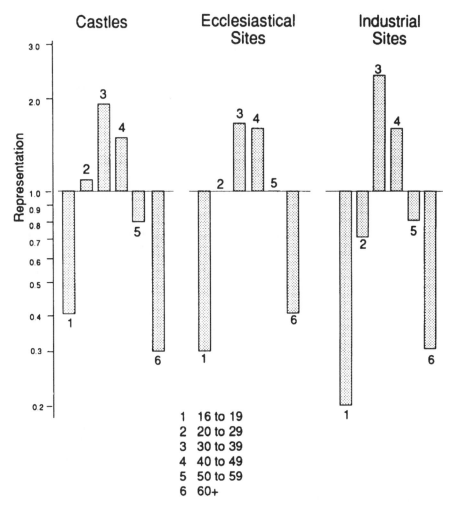

Figure 6.4 Representation of different age groups
Source: SEREN 1986a, 1986b; Light 1991a

101

sites have particular appeal to those of 'middle' age. Figure 6.4 confirms the disproportionate appeal of heritage attractions to the 30–49 age group at all three types of site. Conversely, the under-20 and over-60 groups are most under-represented, while the 20–29 and 50–59 groups are intermediate: their representation at heritage sites is closer or equal to that of the population as a whole. The age of respondents differs significantly between the types of resource. Industrial sites attract fewer younger visitors and more in the 30–39 group.

These findings are broadly supported by other research. The OPCS (1989a) indicated that the highest level of visiting historic buildings and museums/art galleries was among the 30–44 age group. Thus 10 per cent of this group had, in the four weeks prior to interview, visited a historic building, and 11 per cent a museum/gallery. For both the 20–24 and 60–69 groups, these figures were 7 per cent and 8 per cent respectively.

These findings clearly indicate that the tendency to visit heritage sites changes with age. This suggests that leisure needs are dynamic and change over time, depending on the stage of the life cycle (Prince 1983). Parker (1979) identifies three stages of the life cycle: adolescence, adult (between ages 20 and 65) and elderly. For adolescents, leisure needs are unlikely to encompass visiting and learning about a heritage site, while elderly people are more likely to suffer constraints of health. Thus visiting heritage sites is disproportionately undertaken by those in the middle stage. This middle (or establishment) stage is characterized by establishing and raising a family and, during this stage, family-centred activities assume particular importance (Rapoport and Rapoport 1975). The disproportionate attendance of the 30–49 age group at heritage sites may thus result from their importance as destinations for family outings. This notion may be investigated by considering the composition of visitor groups, which is presented in Table 6.4.

Table 6.4 Group composition of visitors to heritage sites

	Castles (4 sites) %	Ecclesiastical sites (1 site) %	Industrial sites (2 sites) %
Groups with children	48	31	60
Groups without children	52	69	40

Source: Survey 3 (Light 1991a)

However, Table 6.4 suggests that visiting heritage sites is not predominantly a family activity (cf. Prentice 1989a). The pattern differs significantly between different types of site, and industrial sites have a broader appeal to family groups but, even there, children are present in only 60 per cent of groups. At castles and ecclesiastical sites, groups with children are not in the majority, and religious sites appear to have considerably less appeal to family groups than do castles (cf. Thomas 1989). Thus, many parents do not appear to be socializing their children into visiting heritage sites, and this will probably perpetuate their existing selective appeal. Groups containing adults only are more numerous at castles and religious monuments than family parties, perhaps indicating an important social dimension to visiting a heritage site. A third of visitor groups comprised two adults only (Prentice 1989a; Light 1991a): this suggests that visiting heritage sites is important for couples without children, or those at a stage in their life cycle when their children have left home.

If replicated in Europe, the findings reported here again indicate that the consumption of heritage will be highly selective. Furthermore, efforts to attract younger and older people will meet with limited success. The population of Europe is getting older, thus there is an increasing number of people in the age group which does not visit heritage sites, while the number in the age groups which do so is declining. This suggests that the consumption of heritage in tourism may decline as the continent's demographic structure changes. European Community ideals of cultural integration through heritage promotion are equally likely to appeal to certain groups of the population, namely those in the establishment age group. Initiatives to promote travel and cultural exchanges among the young people of Europe may, it would seem from these findings, be of limited relevance to promoting a common European heritage.

Visit status

A conventional differentiation of visitors at tourist attractions is between tourists – those staying away from their home area – and local residents visiting from their home. The proportion of visitors in these two segments in Wales is presented in Table 6.5. At all three categories of site, around three-quarters of visitors are tourists staying away from their home area (predominantly England). At this level of analysis the pattern does not differ between the three

Table 6.5 Visit status of visitors to heritage sites

	Castles (10 sites) %	Ecclesiastical sites (2 sites) %	Industrial sites (3 sites) %
Tourists	77	80	75
Local residents	23	20	25

Source: Surveys 1, 2 and 3 (SEREN 1986a, 1986b; Light 1991a)

types of resource. Thus local residents are not the main consumers of heritage. There is, however, considerable variation in the proportions of tourists/local residents at individual sites throughout Wales, and distinct regional markets can be identified (Light 1991a; Prentice 1989a). At sites close to the main centres of population in south Wales (Swansea/Cardiff/Newport), the proportion of local residents is higher (30–40 per cent), and is largest at Castell Coch (49 per cent): however, at all but this site, local residents remain in a clear minority. At a given location, different types of heritage sites vary in their appeal to local people, and ecclesiastical sites are less popular. Thus 38 per cent of visitors at Chepstow Castle were local residents, compared with 24 per cent at Tintern Abbey: the sites are only 6 miles apart.

Why, then, are local people a minority group at heritage sites, even at those sites close to the south Wales conurbation? One explanation may be that this pattern simply reflects the numerical dominance of tourists during the summer months. Around 9 million people visit the Principality annually (figure supplied by the Wales Tourist Board), outnumbering Welsh residents who total around 2.5 million. A second explanation may be that local people do not visit heritage sites because they have already done so. At the study sites, local residents tended to have socio-demographic characteristics similar (with a few exceptions) to tourists: it is, therefore, probable that their leisure needs and behaviour are similar. However, local people were both more likely to have paid a previous visit to the sites, and to have approached a site but not entered, suggesting that heritage sites are not sufficiently attractive to justify a further visit (cf. Prentice 1989b). Certainly, a majority of people are on their first visit, and rates of repeat visiting are low (Prentice 1989a). This may indicate that visiting heritage sites is something undertaken more when on holiday in new areas, rather than in the area of permanent residence. Alternatively, local people may experience and consume their past in different ways and in different places to tourists, ways perhaps which are inaccessible to the latter group.

If extrapolated to Europe, these findings – that tourists are numerically the largest consumers of heritage in a country which receives tourists in large numbers – highlight the potential for conflict if the same heritage resources are used to fulfil simultaneously two functions – political and economic. The same resource must satisfy the demands and expectations of two very different groups of consumers: the tourists who are external to the country, and the indigenous population who are internal. In such situations, pragmatism and the demand for tourist revenue may lead to heritage being oriented for external, rather than internal, consumption. This dilemma will be greatest in eastern Europe, where tourism is a vital earner of western currency. The problem is compounded where the circumstances of history have resulted in the heritage of one country being now bound within the borders of a second country: the issue of 'whose heritage?' again comes to the fore. Examples include the Germanic heritage of the former Sudetenland in Czechoslovakia, or that of the former East Prussia in Poland. In both instances, the largest group of modern consumers will be German tourists (cf. Ashworth and Tunbridge 1990) to whom Poland and Czechoslovakia are now very accessible. For these countries the dilemma is, as Tunbridge (Chapter 7, this volume) observes, 'identity versus economy'. Ultimately, a stage may be reached where the same heritage resource cannot be used for both state-building and tourism purposes; one function – most likely the economic – will become dominant, and so local residents will have to find something else with which to consolidate their identity.

Such a situation arguably already exists in Wales. The use of the same heritage resource for political and economic purposes is frustrated where the resources are those of a former dominating power, and the consumers may be identified as the descendants of that power. In Wales, many of the castles (notably the Marcher castles in the south, and the mighty fortresses of Edward I in the north) represent repeated attempts by Norman and English monarchs to conquer and subdue the Welsh. To many English tourists, castles are an integral component of 'Welshness'. Unsurprisingly, they are not seen in this light today by many Welsh people: they represent instead the extinguishing of Welsh independence, and have little contribution to national identity. This role has instead been assumed by the Welsh language, particularly in west and north Wales. The castles of Wales thus represent English heritage, located in Wales, but largely sold to and consumed by the English.

The examples given here highlight the innate difficulties in using the same resource for different purposes, and emphasize the potential identified by Ashworth (Chapter 2, this volume) for conflict and tension inherent within the dual role of heritage, and the consequent need for intervention and heritage planning. However, in the struggling economies of eastern Europe, such intervention may be an unaffordable luxury, and the likelihood of conflict is high.

BEHAVIOURAL CHARACTERISTICS OF VISITORS

This discussion has thus far presented an overview of some of the most significant patterns of consumption of heritage tourism in terms of socio-demographic variables. The focus of attention now shifts to the behavioural characteristics of consumers, in particular their motivations, attitudes and expectations, and we are concerned not with who is consuming the heritage, but why they are consuming it.

Motives for visiting

Table 6.6 presents data from Surveys 1 and 2 about reasons for visiting heritage sites in Wales. Respondents were given a list of reasons, and for each they were asked to indicate whether or not it was important for their decision to visit. Two reasons for visiting are dominant: first an interest in castles/historic sites, and second a general interest/sight-seeing intent. All other reasons are of secondary importance. This evidence would suggest that both a historic interest and a general interest are equally important in the decision to visit. However, there is a strong tendency for the two reasons to be mutually exclusive: thus only 38 per cent of visitors who indicated a historic interest motive also declared a general interest. There is thus evidence of two broad segments of visitors as defined by their reasons for visiting. The pattern does, however, differ significantly between types of site: at industrial sites such a duality of reasons is not evident. Instead, far fewer visit from an interest in historic sites. This may reflect the wording of the questions, parts

Table 6.6 The proportion of visitors mentioning a reason as important for their decision to visit a heritage site

	Castles (8 sites) %	Ecclesiastical sites (2 sites) %	Industrial sites (1 site) %
Interest in castles/historic sites	59.4	72.5	16.7
Interest in Welsh culture/ history	17.2	23.1	22.0
General interest/sight-seeing	47.5	50.6	56.8
Part of day out in country	12.4	18.4	2.3
Somewhere to take children	19.2	13.7	4.5
Unable to go where planned	2.6	1.5	14.4

Source: Surveys 1 and 2 (SEREN 1986a, 1986b)

of which are not fully appropriate to industrial sites, but may also indicate that industrial sites are not strongly perceived by their visitors as being historic.

An alternative approach to eliciting reasons for visiting is to ask visitors to select from a list the single reason which was most important in their decision to visit. This convention was adopted in Survey 3 and the responses of visitors are presented in Table 6.7. A duality of reasons is again apparent at castles and ecclesiastical sites. The most commonly given reason was a specific interest in castles/ abbeys/historic sites, followed by general interest/sight-seeing.

Table 6.7 The single reason selected by visitors as most important in their decision to visit

	Castles (4 sites) %	Ecclesiastical sites (1 site) %	Industrial sites (2 sites) %
Interest in castles(*)/abbeys(*)/ monuments(*)/historic sites	52.7	42.9	17.6
Interest in Welsh culture/ history	4.5	4.1	11.2
Educational interest	2.4	2.0	13.2
General interest/sight-seeing/ part of a day in country	24.5	38.8	44.4
Brought friends/children	8.5	6.6	8.8
Saw in passing/unable to go where planned	7.3	5.6	4.7

Source: Survey 3 (Light 1991a)
Note: Similar reasons have been combined into categories.
* Only asked at appropriate sites

Once again, all other reasons are of secondary importance. Responses differ significantly between sites, with fewer people visiting industrial sites from historic interest, but more from interest in Welsh culture and history and educational interest. This affirms that industrial sites are perceived by their potential visitors in a different way to castles and religious sites. Overall, the findings of Tables 6.6 and 6.7 indicate that among at least half the visitors there is some prior interest in history and historic sites, and this influences the decision to visit. Thomas (1989: 78) describes it well: 'visits are not exclusively recreational but include a substantial ... historical-educational dimension. The latter dimension however probably comprises general rather than specialist heritage interests.'

Motives for visiting show some variation among different sub-groups of visitors. First, different social classes tend to visit heritage sites for different purposes: thus 64 per cent of professional workers declared a historic interest, compared to 47 per cent of skilled manual workers. Conversely, 55 per cent of manual workers indicated a general interest or sight-seeing motive, compared to 43 per cent of professionals. These findings indicate that middle-class visitors tend to display more specific and purposeful behaviour when visiting heritage sites, and also suggest that this group has a stronger prior interest in history. This lends support to the earlier discussion which suggested that the middle classes were more likely to use their leisure time in a constructive manner, which in this context may include learning about, and appreciating, the past. Manual workers seem more inclined to use a historic site as a setting or 'backdrop' for a more general recreational visit. Heritage sites are not, then, visited by a homogeneous public: instead the motives, and consequently the benefits, of visiting will vary among visitors.

Second, motives for visiting differ between tourists and local residents. Local people appear to be less specific in their reasons for visiting. This group was more likely than tourists to give its reason for visiting as 'part of a day in the country' or 'somewhere to take the children'. For example, 25 per cent of local residents gave the latter reason, compared to 16 per cent of tourists. For local people also the heritage sites serve more as a setting for general recreational visits (cf. Thomas 1989). Conversely, there is some evidence of more purposeful behaviour by tourists: 60 per cent of this group indicated a historic sites interest, compared with 50 per cent of local residents. This also lends support to the earlier suggestion that the specific desire to visit historic sites is most strongly manifest when on holiday in an unfamiliar environment.

Attitudes to the past

We can get a further indication of the prior interest in history of visitors to heritage sites by considering their responses to two statements. Responses to the first statement (Table 6.8) confirm a high degree of prior interest in history. Over 90 per cent of visitors agreed with the statement and, although not shown in the Table, around 25 per cent strongly agreed. This is a good indicator of a prior interest in history among the majority of consumers, including those who did not give a specific historic-interest reason for visiting, and who, as the earlier discussion suggested, use a historic site as the setting for a general visit. However, there is no reason to suppose that this disposition to history is shared by a wider public. Once again, consumption of heritage is seen to be selective: in addition to being undertaken by certain socio-demographic groups, it is also largely undertaken by those with an existing interest in history.

Responses to the second statement further qualify this prior interest. The statement was designed to establish whether visiting heritage sites is perceived as a retreat from the unpleasant realities of the present, as critics of the heritage 'industry' (e.g. Hewison 1987) claim. Between 30 per cent and 40 per cent of respondents agreed with the statement. This confirms a prior interest in the past, but may also indicate that it is seen in romanticized and escapist terms by some visitors. However, around two-thirds of visitors did not agree with the statement: the responses to the first statement

Table 6.8 Visitors' dispositions to the past

	Statement 1		Statement 2	
	Castles (3 sites) %	Ecclesiastical sites (1 site) %	Castles (3 sites) %	Ecclesiastical sites (1 site) %
Agree	90.8	91.4	38.6	30.7
No opinion	3.8	2.0	30.0	28.3
Disagree	5.4	6.5	31.4	40.9

Statement 1: History is an exciting subject.
Statement 2: The past is more interesting than the present.

Source: Survey 3 (Light 1991a)

suggest that these people still have an interest in history but that they do not see the past in more favourable terms than the present. Responses differ between sites, and visitors to religious sites were less likely to find the past more interesting than the present. Responses also differ among visitor groups. Those people who completed education earlier (and who hold a manual occupation) were more likely to consider the past more interesting. This suggests that this group may be more likely to hold what can be termed mythical or escapist views of the past, which may be an important influence on the decision to visit. Those holding a professional/managerial occupation and with a longer period in education were less likely to agree with the statement. Visitors to heritage sites can again be seen not to be a homogeneous group in terms of dispositions to the past. Most visitors have some interest in history, although not all indicate a specific historic interest as their main reason for visiting. Visitors are, however, divided in the extent to which they think the attraction of the past exceeds that of the present.

The evidence reported here about both motives for visiting and attitudes to the past have implications for heritage interpretation. This aims to present and explain a site to its visitors using a range of media, and has attained considerable significance within the heritage industry (see Herbert 1989; Light 1991b). Given that a large proportion of visitors have a prior interest in history, and that over half visit as a result of a specific historic interest, we would expect informal learning and appreciation of the past to be important for many visitors, and so we would expect them to be amenable to site interpretation. Recent studies have indicated that this is the case. For example, Light (1991a) noted that large proportions of visitors encounter interpretative media: most read at least part of the written material presented, and a majority learnt something new from their visit. Furthermore, large proportions of visitors considered that the interpretation had enhanced their visit. The motivation of visitors was an important influence on the effectiveness of interpretation, and those who visited from a specific historic interest displayed more interest in, and attention to, interpretation. Similarly, Prentice (1991) demonstrates the importance of both general and specific historic interests in terms of learning from information displays provided at sites of this kind.

EXPECTATIONS FROM THE HERITAGE PRODUCT

Finally, we can consider the expectations of visitors from the heritage product. In this chapter we have largely considered one type of heritage resource – ancient monuments – and a major characteristic of such sites is that they are usually in a ruined state. Is this experience what people require when visiting them, or would they prefer more development and provision of visitor and interpretative services? Part of Survey 2 included a series of questions concerning improvements to the sites, and visitors were asked which such improvements they wished to see (Table 6.9).

Few visitors seem to consider that 'improvements' are necessary. Even those visitor services which received most support (teashops, toilets) were mentioned by only one-third of visitors. These findings indicate a high degree of satisfaction with the product as currently presented, and visitors see little need for enhanced product development. This is confirmed if we consider satisfaction with the visit: 98 per cent of visitors agreed or strongly agreed that they had enjoyed their visit.

Table 6.9 also indicates that current visitors to the type of heritage site which we are considering may be broadly described as conservative, or even in one sense purist, in their views of how such sites should be presented. Certainly they favour presenting them as largely undeveloped ruins, and are suspicious of the sort of innovative developments (for example, rebuilding and people in costume) which would alter the nature of the historic resource. This suggests that visitors to monuments value highly what they perceive as the 'authentic' presentation of the historic relics. This is most apparent at ecclesiastical sites, where support for all types of innovation listed in Table 6.9 is consistently less than that at castles. Such 'authenticity'

Table 6.9 Improvements sought by visitors

	Castles (3 sites) %	Ecclesiastical sites (1 site) %	Industrial sites (1 site) %
Teashop	34.8	17.1	12.1
Toilets	32.7	10.5	25.8
Seats	15.3	10.5	7.6
Gardens	7.2	2.9	0.0
Restoration	13.0	11.4	3.0
Period demonstrations	21.0	17.1	21.2

Source: Survey 2 (SEREN 1986b)

should in practice be seen as largely consumer defined (as argued earlier) since most monuments have, at the very least, been preserved, maintained and consolidated, while others have been partially rebuilt for tourists. Somewhat surprisingly, visitor reactions to innovative developments vary little among different sub-groups of visitors, with the exception of stronger support for gardens among younger people and those visiting from home.

These attitudes of visitors highlight a dilemma facing heritage managers. One way of reducing the selectivity of consumption may be to develop and enhance the product on offer to give it broader appeal. However, since satisfaction with the current manner of presentation is so high, any development aimed at attracting wider attendance at monuments may effectively alienate the current clientele.

CONCLUSIONS

No understanding of modern heritage tourism is complete without a consideration of the people who appropriate – or consume – developed heritage products. The evidence presented here has indicated that the consumption of heritage – or at least of 'official' heritage – is highly selective. Heritage consumers tend to be from the middle classes, well educated, middle-aged, in a group without children, on holiday away from home, and with a prior interest in history. These people were identified as those whose leisure needs and requirements encompassed experiencing and learning about the past. Although the evidence we have presented is specific to certain sites in Wales, there are good grounds for arguing that these trends will, perhaps with some local exceptions, be replicated throughout Europe.

Our discussion has consistently highlighted aspects of the 'whose heritage?' debate. With respect to a range of socio-demographic variables, a group of visitors – the less educated, manual workers, the young, local residents – can be identified who choose not to appropriate their heritage. We have to consider why these people who have the opportunity to visit heritage sites choose not to do so. We also have to consider whether there are ways of broadening the market for heritage attractions, perhaps by altering or developing the product so as to give it a broader appeal. Can the consumption of heritage be turned into a majority pursuit, or is it destined to remain the preserve of a minority group? These findings have implications for the role of heritage in European identity and integration. Current integrative cultural policy is implicitly to create a common European heritage. If such a policy is to be successful, it must match the requirements of the communities of Europe. Our analysis for Wales would imply that existing heritage products cannot be a sole source of cultural integration for the simple reason that present consumption of them is highly selective, excluding certain groups of the population. If, as we believe, our analysis may be extrapolated beyond Wales, we suggest that any attempt to forge a common European identity through the creation of a pan-European heritage (dare we say Euro-heritage?) will have little impact on those groups currently under-represented at heritage sites. We must then question the extent to which heritage can ever effect European integration, and the extent to which it is possible to forge a common European heritage.

This discussion has also highlighted the dilemmas of using the same heritage resource for both economic (usually tourism) and political (in this case, state-building) purposes. Indeed, both the conceptualization and practice of a dual role for heritage may need to be revised. At the root of this problem is the existence of two segments of demand for heritage – domestic and foreign. These groups will differ in expectations and requirements: ultimately there will be tensions between the two groups. This problem will be most acute in central and eastern Europe, where heritage resources are important in establishing post-communist market-economy identities. However, the need for western currency and the current existence of abundant external demand for such heritage means that the pressures to develop heritage resources for external consumption are considerable. Eastern Europeans may have to look elsewhere for identity; their heritage is wanted by other people.

Investigation of the nature of demand for heritage tourism is at a comparatively early stage. Although there is a long tradition of visitor surveys at tourist attractions, much of this research has been oriented to site management goals, and is undertaken with little reference to the current heritage debate. We would emphasize the need for further research into why people visit heritage sites and the relationship between this behaviour and leisure needs. We need to know more about what expectations visitors have, and the benefits they gain from heritage sites (Prentice 1993). However, there is also a strong case for investigating why people do not visit heritage places, and how instead they experience and appropriate their past, if indeed they do so. Such research is a prerequisite if the heritage phenomenon throughout Europe is to be understood and effectively planned.

ACKNOWLEDGEMENT

We would like to thank Mr Guy Lewis for drawing the figures.

REFERENCES

Ashworth, G.J. (1988) 'Marketing the historic city for tourism', in Goodall, B. and Ashworth, G.J. (eds) *Marketing in the Tourism Industry: the Promotion of Destination Regions*, London: Routledge.

Ashworth, G.J. and Tunbridge J.E. (1990) *The Tourist-Historic City*, London: Belhaven.

Bord Fáilte (research section) (1974) *National Monuments Survey*, Dublin: Bord Fáilte.

British Tourist Authority and the Countryside Commission (1968) *Historic Houses Survey*, London: British Tourist Authority.

Countryside Commission (1985) *National Countryside Recreation Survey: 1984*, CCP 201, Cheltenham: Countryside Commission.

Dartington Amenity Research Trust and Department of Psychology, University of Surrey (1978) *Interpretation in Visitor Centres*, Countryside Commission Occasional Paper 10, CCP 115, Cheltenham: Countryside Commission.

Department of Transport (1988) *Transport Statistics in Great Britain 1977–1987*, London: HMSO.

Driver, B.L. and Tocher, S.R. (1979) 'Toward a behavioral interpretation of recreational engagements with implications for planning', in Van Doren, C.S., Priddle, G.B. and Lewis, J.E. (eds) *Land and Leisure: Concepts and Methods in Outdoor Recreation* (second edition), London: Methuen.

English Tourist Board (1982) *Visitors to Museums Survey of 1982*, London: English Tourist Board Market Research Department and N.O.P. Market Research Ltd.

English Tourist Board and Wales Tourist Board (ETB/WTB) (1989) *The British Tourism Market 1988*, London: British Tourist Authority and English Tourist Board Research Services.

Hall, D.R. (1992) 'The challenge of international tourism in Eastern Europe', *Tourism Management* 13: 41–4.

Heinich, N. (1988) 'The Pompidou Centre and its public: the limits of an utopian site', in Lumley, R. (ed.) *The Museum Time Machine: Putting Cultures on Display*, London: Routledge.

Herbert, D.T. (1989) 'Does interpretation help?', in Herbert, D.T., Prentice, R.C. and Thomas, C.J. (eds) *Heritage Sites: Strategies for Marketing and Development*, Aldershot: Avebury.

Hewison, R. (1987) *The Heritage Industry: Britain in a Climate of Decline*, London: Methuen.

Hewison, R. (1988) 'Making history: manufacturing heritage?', in Iddon, J. (ed.) *The Dodo Strikes Back*, Proceedings of a one-day conference held at St Mary's College, Strawberry Hill, London: St Mary's College.

Hood, M.G. (1983) 'Staying away: why people choose not to visit museums', *Museum News* 61: 50–7.

Hooper-Greenhill, E. (1988) 'Counting visitors or visitors who count', in Lumley, R. (ed.) *The Museum Time Machine: Putting Cultures on Display*, London: Routledge.

Iso-Ahola, S.E. (1983) 'Towards a social psychology of recreational travel', *Leisure Studies* 2: 45–56.

Light, D. (1991a) 'Heritage places in Wales and their interpretation: a study in applied recreational geography', Unpublished PhD thesis, University of Wales.

Light, D. (1991b) 'The development of heritage interpretation in Britain', *Swansea Geographer* 28: 1–13.

Mass Observation (UK) Ltd (1978) *National Trust Visitors' Survey 1978. Part 1: Report of Principal Findings. Part 2: Appendix of Tables and Comments on Properties*, London: Mass Observation (UK) Ltd.

Office of Population Censuses and Surveys (OPCS) (1989a) *General Household Survey 1987*, London: HMSO.

Office of Population Censuses and Surveys (OPCS) (1989b) *O.P.C.S. Monitor PP1 89/1 (Revised)*, London: HMSO.

Office of Population Censuses and Surveys (OPCS) (1990) *General Household Survey 1988*, London: HMSO.

Parker, S. (1979) 'Leisure in the life cycle', in Van Doren, C.S., Priddle, G.B. and Lewis, J.E. (eds) *Land and Leisure: Concepts and Methods in Outdoor Recreation* (second edition), London: Methuen.

Patmore, J.A. (1983) *Recreation and Resources: Leisure Patterns and Leisure Places*, Oxford: Blackwell.

Prentice, M.M. and Prentice, R.C. (1989) 'The heritage market of historic sites as educational resources', in Herbert, D.T., Prentice, R.C. and Thomas, C.J. (eds) *Heritage Sites: Strategies for Marketing and Development*, Aldershot: Avebury.

Prentice, R.C. (1989a) 'Visitors to heritage sites: a market segmentation by visitor characteristics', in Herbert, D.T., Prentice, R.C. and Thomas, C.J. (eds) *Heritage Sites: Strategies for Marketing and Development*, Aldershot: Avebury.

Prentice, R.C. (1989b) 'Pricing policy at heritage sites. How much should visitors pay?', in Herbert, D.T., Prentice, R.C. and Thomas, C.J. (eds) *Heritage Sites: Strategies for Marketing and Development*, Aldershot: Avebury.

Prentice, R.C. (1991) 'Measuring the educational effectiveness of on-site interpretation designed for tourists', *Area* 23, 297–308.

Prentice, R.C. (1993) *Tourism and Heritage Attractions*, London: Routledge.

Prince, D.R. (1983) 'Behavioural consistency and visitor attraction', *The International Journal of Museum Management and Curatorship* 2: 235–47.

Prince, D.R. (1985a) 'Museum visiting and unemployment', *Museums Journal* 85: 85–90.

Prince, D.R. (1985b) 'The museum as dreamland', *The International Journal of Museum Management and Curatorship* 4: 243–50.

Public Attitude Surveys (1985) *Historic Buildings Survey 1984. Volume I – Core Questions*, High Wycombe: P.A.S. Research Ltd.

Rapoport, R. and Rapoport, R.N. (1975) *Leisure and the Family Life Cycle*, London: Routledge.

Roggenbuck, J.W., Loomis, R.J. and Dagostino, J. (1990) 'The learning benefits of leisure', *Journal of Leisure Research* 22: 112–24.

SEREN (1986a) Herbert, D.T., Prentice, R.C., Thomas, C.J. and Prentice, M.M. (1986a) *Summer 1986 General Survey at Cadw's Sites*, Swansea: Department of Geography, University College of Swansea.

SEREN (1986b) Herbert, D.T., Prentice, R.C., Thomas C.J. and Prentice, M.M. (1986b) *Pricing Policy and Visitor Satisfaction at Cadw's Sites*, Swansea: Department of Geography, University College of Swansea.

Thomas, C.J. (1989) 'The roles of historic sites and reasons for visiting', in Herbert, D.T., Prentice, R.C. and Thomas, C.J. (eds) *Heritage Sites: Strategies for Marketing and Development*, Aldershot: Avebury.

Tunbridge, J.E. (1984) 'Whose heritage to conserve? Cross-cultural reflections upon political dominance and urban heritage conservation', *Canadian Geographer* 28, 171–80.

West, B. (1988) 'The making of the English working past: a critical review of the Ironbridge Gorge Museum', in Lumley, R. (ed.) *The Museum Time Machine: Putting Cultures on Display*, London: Routledge.

Part III

Choice: whose heritage, which heritage?

INTRODUCTION: FROM ACTORS TO CHOICES

Part II introduced the range of actors within what has been described as the 'heritage production-consumption system'. It was clear, however, from the accounts of both the visitors to historic sites and the policies of the agencies managing these sites that there are many contradictions implicit in such a system. Part III aims to identify and describe the most important of these.

If heritage is a selection and interpretation of the past then, clearly, many heritages can be constructed and the question of 'which heritage?' becomes pertinent. Similarly, the idea of inheritance leads to the idea of the content being determined by the legatee. Each individual ultimately constructs his or her own heritage from a unique personal selection from an equally unique personal past. Thus the question of 'whose heritage' becomes a central determinant of what is regarded as heritage. Each of the contributions to Part III poses these two central questions in a different context: each is concerned with choice, with the choice of histories being a result of the choice of contemporary objectives.

Chapter 7 (Tunbridge) poses questions about the content and purpose of heritage, but on the macro rather than the micro scale. He poses the questions 'which heritage?' and, therefore, 'whose heritage?' in a wide variety of situations, allusions and briefly mentioned cases. Almost all of these focus upon two problems of content. The first can be labelled 'disinheritance', that is quite simply that the selection of someone's heritage automatically disinherits someone else. This can be recognized in the case of various groups of individuals, whether definable in terms of ethnic origin, social class, cultural characteristics, gender or many other distinguishing features. The second problem of content can be labelled 'nastiness'. Perhaps it is salutary that it is a Canadian resident who points out to Europeans that our history is a chronicle of war, pogrom, revolt, discrimination and general unpleasantness between nations, religions, races, ideologies and classes. In contrast, the heritage of the theme park is usually a mixture of a return to a simpler golden age of harmony, whether or not it actually existed, together with the story of the steady progress of a perfectible humanity, culminating in the best of all possible presents.

The result of Tunbridge's insistent and international barrage is the conclusion that both disinheritance and nastiness are not exceptional conditions, but rather form the central themes of a European heritage. This is not the 'authenticity' dilemma raised by Carr (Chapter 4), nor the 'integrity' problem raised by Newby in Chapter 11. To Tunbridge, all heritage will inescapably confront these dilemmas of the choice of content, but such choices still have to be made.

Chapter 8 (Graham) poses similar questions through his examination of the use of heritage for the reinforcing of a particular political ideology and for the justification of the existence of a particular spatial/political entity. The case of the small European state selected could be duplicated across this and other continents and is itself unremarkable. However, this chapter is able to argue, with supporting evidence, that there has been detectable and radical change in the selected content of a national heritage in response to changes in the international position and objectives of the country concerned. The choice of types of historical site, the periods of history highlighted, and the interpretation of events can all be shown to have changed, or at least to be currently in the process of change. The national self-image shaped by the national historical mythology of the late nineteenth and early twentieth centuries was created to support political separatism from a larger governmental entity. This political objective was successful, but the separatist heritage created necessarily resulted in the disinheritance of a section of the population, and a distancing of this nation state from others in a wider Europe. The new political agenda of the late twentieth century has rendered one heritage effectively obsolete and is encouraging the shaping of another. This chapter therefore presents a microcosm of the larger problem tackled by this volume as a whole.

Chapter 9 (Soane) returns to the national scale, but focuses upon architecture and urban design. A dichotomy is set up between 'modernist' and 'vernacular' styles. Both are initially described as aesthetic styles, but both are strongly associated with the economic and social functioning of cities. The historical argument is that the post-war German city was fundamentally transformed by its rebuilding in the last forty years to accommodate new commercial and transport functions, and in response to new patterns of residential choice. More recently, in reaction to this reshaping, there has been a return to an architectural style that draws upon local identities and local histories. This 'vernacularism' is thus in part a reaction to the perceived problems of the modernist city, and in part an attempt to respond to new economic and social demands being made on the city.

There is a strong, although not always explicitly stated, political motivation behind what appears to be a dispute of architectural aesthetics. Soane's largely implicit argument is that 'Modernism' or the 'international style' can be seen as a symbol of the Anglo-American world which dominated West Germany economically, culturally and politically in the forty years following its defeat in the Second World War. Vernacularism appeals to a reassertion of German self-confidence and a search for a new German identity based on a rediscovery of a distinctive local past. The pre-war cities, and by association the societies and cultures that inhabited them, can be reconstructed as heritage. An added twist to this political reconstruction through architecture and town planning is given by the cities of the former East Germany. Such cities are now in the throes of their second reconstruction in one generation, in response to shifts in the dominant ideology. Soane is, therefore, providing answers in detail to Tunbridge's question of 'whose heritage?', at least in the case of Germany.

Hammersley and Westlake, in Chapter 10, again address a national scale, in the context of Czechoslovakia emerging from half a century of communist rule, and almost immediately fragmenting into the Czech Lands and Slovakia. Although Czechoslovakia itself was a creation of the early twentieth century, they argue that its heritage is strongly representative of much of central Europe in its cultural influences and resulting urban forms. Many historic urban centres survived the communist era, albeit more through ignorance and neglect than by conscious design. The authors remind us of the heritage of the dispossessed Germans and Jews, querying the future results if the survivors of these groups again become interested in their disinherited heritage. There are clear parallels with current events in the former Yugoslavia. The future of the country's urban heritage is now in some danger from pressures of tourism and commerce: the rush to de-communize is leading to a rush to privatize. The questions of 'whose and which heritage?' are thus implicit throughout, and, as with Soane's German examples, the lessons for heritage of rapid ideological shifts are explicit.

7

WHOSE HERITAGE?

Global problem, European nightmare

J.E. Tunbridge

WHOSE HERITAGE?

The 'whose heritage?' problem, which appears to be universal, possesses two facets: (i) what we identify as heritage, and (ii) how we interpret what is so labelled. In the first case, people identify an inheritance; in the second, a recognized inheritance is appropriated. By either route, the selectivity involved may be based upon such variables as cultural affinity, political affiliation or social class (Tunbridge 1984; Ashworth and Tunbridge 1990). A striking illustration of class dissonance concerns both the identification and interpretation of Glasgow's heritage, pivotal to its role as the European City of Culture in 1990, and thereby to the many conferences held there during that year (Boyle and Hughes 1991).

The identity/interpretation problem is central to contemporary European heritage issues, and to this volume. The concern of the present chapter, however, is specifically with the cultural/ethnic dissonance which, in a rising cacophony from all quarters, is becoming a hallmark of the 1990s; and with the built (as against the natural and the 'portable' human) heritage which is so typically a landmark expression of culture. The message of the chapter is unequivocal: the political implications of culturally selective identification and interpretation, conservation and marketing of the inherited built environment are profound and potentially deadly.

GLOBAL PROBLEM

In 1992, the year of the Columbus quincentenary, the global nature of this issue has been painfully apparent, and it will briefly be illustrated with examples relating to Europeans overseas. This in no way dismisses the multitudinous issues between Third World ethnic groups, for example in the Indian subcontinent. Inter-European and European-indigene heritage conflicts strike a familiar chord in Europe, and the ubiquity of these can be illustrated by brief reference to South Africa and Canada.

In South Africa, the built heritage of Pietermaritzburg reflects its Boer origins (site, street grid, Church of the Vow) with a British Victorian overlay (most central buildings, connecting 'Lanes'); historical tension has subsided, and the city is marketed as a Victorian showpiece (Haswell 1990). Reconciliation between the European groups, however, largely reflects common awareness of a much larger problem: those who physically built the heritage – primarily Zulus – are scarcely reflected in it, other than as the losing side in various colonial war memorials. Yet these are the people who surround this comforting European outpost, deny its apparent serenity with their own apartheid-bred township violence, and will assume majority power over it in the foreseeable future. What relevance and prospects will Victorian 'Maritzburg have then? (Wills *et al.* 1987).

In Canada, Quebec City illustrates continuing tension regarding heritage identity/interpretation between European groups. Francophone power has led to the marginalization of the British contribution to the city's heritage, except where controlled by the federal national parks authority; in an extreme case, the Wolfe memorial on the Plains of Abraham was blown up, albeit rebuilt (Ashworth and Tunbridge 1990). Preoccupation with the French identity of Quebec has latterly caused tensions with diverse 'New Canadians' in Montreal, and in 1990 exacerbated a heritage land conflict with native Indians at Oka into a crisis of international proportions. The Ottawa region poignantly reflects national capital symbolism in conflict with French Canadian nationalism, and tension with native peoples also surfaces there (Ashworth and Tunbridge 1990). So serious has the Canadian identity crisis become that the resolution of a comprehensive, multilateral concept of national heritage, in which the answer to 'whose?' is unequivocally 'everyone's', is now critical to national survival (Bayer 1991; Dalibard 1991; Nelson 1991).

Should Europeans question the relevance of these two examples, they would be wise to consider the origins of each case. Both result from cultural tensions inherited from Europe itself, and set in environments where tensions with further, non-European, cultural elements were inevitable. Such is the situation of contemporary Europe, albeit with different measures of like ingredients. In addition, the potential break-up of Canada, a country whose image is built upon traditions of social and cultural tolerance, should concentrate the mind of any country or region with a plural cultural inheritance.

EUROPEAN NIGHTMARE?

The potential for rival assertions or appropriations of heritage would appear to be greater in Europe than elsewhere, in light of the intensity of cultural/national struggles played out for so long on such a compact territorial base. Other chapters point to a variety of illustrations. Several distinctive manifestations are suggested here.

First, recent strangers: this apparent 'footnote' category may, in the long run, prove to be the most problematical to reconcile with host cultures and with a larger European identity. These are the *Gastarbeiter* and, of urgent current significance, the tide of refugees. We note these first because they link Europe not only to their global source areas, but also to advanced countries overseas which share the concern with cultural dissonance which they represent. Their numbers are still relatively small, but they are often very concentrated, very visible, and perceived as very alien. Majority acceptance will involve respect for the built environment they create, particularly difficult because only the passage of time will give it the patina we expect of 'heritage'. Europeans will probably need to recognize – and accept – the notion of 'adaptive heritage', a concept much discussed in Canada, as the newcomers find a cultural expression by pouring 'new wine into old bottles'; in addition to the redesign of existing housing, this could be manifested in the adaptive reuse of redundant commercial structures for places of worship or other cultural identification. But however long cultural acceptance takes, it assuredly will not come until Europe has reconciled its previously existing cultural discords.

Second, historical strangers: our cultural acceptance of present alien minorities is haunted by our failure to accept those of their predecessors who adhered to their identity. Outstanding among a number of historical oppressions of European minorities is the rejection of the Jews, in part so genocidal as to impel their survivors to re-establish a contentious extra-European homeland, a rejection which hangs like the proverbial Sword of Damocles over our dealings with recent newcomers. This is underlined by the inexplicable survival of antisemitism, even in the virtual absence of Jews, in Poland, Germany and elsewhere in contemporary Europe. A price we pay for that rejection is that we cannot simply 'Europeanize' our heritage – however difficult that may be – for one of its most powerful components is claimed by an externally based people. Contention over the exclusivity of that claim has been well demonstrated, but not resolved, by the case of the conflict over a Christian convent at Auschwitz.

Third, conflicting nationalisms: more familiar and 'comfortable' ground, although the most fundamental problem, is the age-long conflict between cultural/national identities within Europe. The power of the built heritage in national identity has been eloquently demonstrated by the detailed post-war reconstructions of some Polish and German cities (Diefendorf 1990). The power of disregard for someone else's built heritage has seemingly been demonstrated during the disintegration of Yugoslavia, notably perhaps by the Serbian-led attack upon Dubrovnik in November 1991; yet others see Dubrovnik as European, indeed not merely European but world heritage. Even within English-speaking areas, cultural tension exists over heritage identity, as Carter (1989) has indicated for Wales; while the Anglo/Ulster–southern Irish conflicts would suggest that one man's cherished heritage may well be another man's rejected past (Graham, Chapter 8, this volume).

Fourth, twentieth-century ideology and war: this painful century has compounded the devil's brew of national identity with extreme political ideologies, above all German Nazism and Soviet communism. Both have, in effect, been instruments of national aggrandizement, yet both have established heritage identities so monstrous as to take on a life of their own. This complication to heritage identity is particularly critical in the context of human suffering through war and persecution. This prominent European heritage type, often marked by monuments on forlorn sites rather than buildings, is beset by the highly emotive dual problem of who were the perpetrators and who the victims. In the case of Katyn, the choice of perpetrators for long lay between Germans, Nazis, Russians and communists, even if the Polish officer corps were clearly the victims; in the case of Babi Yar, how exclusively were the Jews the victims and how far were those who failed to help them co-perpetrators with the Germans/Nazis? The entire context of twentieth-century conflict, particularly that of the Second World War, which had such cataclysmic consequences and is still within widespread living memory, has left a Pandora's box of heritage interpretations. These are of immediate concern not only to tourist revenue, but also to the more profound issue of national/European identity (Uzell 1989).

The above thoughts are less a definitive categorization of heritage identity problems in Europe (though they are a step in that direction) than an indication that the problem of defining a 'new heritage for a new Europe' is daunting indeed.

NORTH-EAST EUROPE: GERMAN-POLISH-RUSSIAN AND RELATED QUESTIONS

The issue of rival cultural appropriations of heritage, and the daunting problem of European reinterpretation, can be most graphically illustrated from this part of the continent; the weight of allusions already made implies as much. In particular, the heritage identity/interpretation problem in Europe should logically climax in those regions of central and eastern Europe which formerly contained German minorities, were formerly part of Germany, or remained German under alien occupation after 1945. This core problem resolves itself into two parts: pre-twentieth-century heritage and twentieth-century conflict in terms of interactions between Germans and other peoples. The following observations primarily reflect conditions in 1990.

The case of Poland appears to present an acute heritage dilemma: identity versus economy. The country needs to market its heritage to tourists as a matter of economic urgency; the overwhelming market in terms of proximity, numbers and wealth is Germany; yet much of the heritage so marketed is of German origin and the subject of a German claim only recently relinquished. It is apparent in Szczecin and Wrocław that there is much interest on the part of German tourists in visiting their birthplaces in what were Stettin and Breslau. Wrocław is in fact completing a painstaking reconstruction of its war-devastated inner core, but whose heritage has it reconstructed? The problem is moderated by the existence of both regional and international elements in architectural style and historic association; with regard to the latter, the Hanseatic heritage is strong on the Baltic coast (especially in Gdansk) and the

Habsburg heritage in Silesia. But this still leaves considerable scope for tension over heritage identity, in which Polish emphasis upon the pre-eighteenth-century legacy is naturally apparent. An interesting problem is the castle of the Teutonic Knights at Malbork (Marienburg), obviously Germanic but symbolizing unjust colonization in Polish eyes.

The heritage of the Second World War, however, is both of great intrinsic tourist interest and unquestioned national relevance to Poland, albeit particularly to Poland-as-victim in the areas that were Polish before 1939. The memorial at Westerplatte, near Gdansk, which marks the starting point of the war, possesses important national and European symbolism, as was demonstrated by the fiftieth anniversary commemoration in 1989. Hitler's headquarters at the former Rastenburg, East Prussia, has no obvious Polish symbolism, but great European significance as the nerve centre of the Eastern Front. The heritage significance of Soviet monuments, such as the Red Army cemetery outside Wrocław, is more equivocal and perhaps subject to reinterpretation in the light of the recent reordering of both Europe and the Soviet Union. The significance of the extermination of the Jews is likewise equivocal, if one may judge by tensions over the interpretation of Auschwitz and less-than-consistent regard for Jewish heritage more generally (Gruber 1992). But that all these issues drastically affected the destiny of Poland, and are in that critical sense its heritage, can scarcely be queried. Beyond this, of course, is the question of their status as the heritage of Europe.

In eastern Germany, the heritage identity problem shifts from conflicting nationalisms to national culture versus ideology, in which interpretation of the Second World War legacy is of pervasive concern. The former East German regime did not deny its German heritage identity, at least in its later years; rather, it projected itself as the true custodian of what was best in German culture, a rivalry with the ideologically opposed West Germany made credible by its possession of central Berlin, Potsdam, Dresden and, above all, Weimar. The presentation of avowedly German heritage provided much scope for ideological interpretation, however, concerning both who built it, who knocked it down and who rebuilt it. These latter opportunities arose because the value of the heritage and the scale of its wartime destruction create overtones of atrocity. Thus at the Bach House in Eisenach we read that the Americans bombed it but that the Soviets, portrayed as benefactors of German culture, were responsible for its restoration. Likewise, at the Zwinger Palace in Dresden we read of Anglo-American bombing outrages, while the theme of Soviet benefaction recurs frequently, as in the discerning preservation of Sans Souci and other monuments at Potsdam. The theme of ultimate Nazi responsibility for heritage destruction, being indisputable, was an ideological gift to the subsequent communist regime, whose allegedly contrasting concern for heritage restoration certainly is a matter of dispute, at least among the citizens of Weimar. More subtle than the interpretation of recent heritage trauma is that of who built or was associated with it in the first place: thus socialist leaders such as Ernst Thälmann, or early figures who can be thus labelled such as Thomas Müntzer (who led a medieval peasants' revolt) and even Martin Luther, are frequently emphasized. In the overall process of heritage interpretation, the identification of socialism with the best humanistic traditions of German culture is a recurrent, pervasive message. Nowhere is this more so than in Weimar-Buchenwald which, if not the supreme expression of German heritage identity, could very well claim this distinction in terms of its ideological interpretation.

The heritage of Weimar projects a jarring discordance which is persuasively marketed as expressing the essential contradiction of German heritage. The city itself is a monument to German culture, particularly of the Renaissance period, for it was a 'Residenz' town in which the local nobility were outstanding patrons of the arts; Goethe was the principal among many luminaries (including Schiller, Herder and Liszt) and was the chief proponent and catalyst of Weimar as the intellectual focus of Germany. Its association with the founding of German democracy in 1919 both reflected and augmented its stature as a centre of enlightenment. The East German government not only recognized Weimar's outstanding heritage but co-opted it, creating a national research centre of classical German literature in Weimar Castle. The indifferent maintenance of the city by 1990 was claimed to result from means rather than ideology, appeals having been made for UNESCO support. On the Ettersberg overlooking Weimar, however, as if in cruel mockery, lies its nemesis: Buchenwald concentration camp. Here East Germany created an international memorial to those of many countries who had died there. What is striking about the interpretation of this lugubrious heritage, however, is the co-option of the Buchenwald resistance by the communists, and its identification with the tradition of humanism manifested by Weimar. Since

Buchenwald had been created for German political prisoners primarily, and since the communist leader Thälmann was murdered there, this interpretation is credible. Accordingly, one of the eighteen memorial columns to the victim nations of Nazism, which overlook Weimar from the Ettersberg, represents Germany. How the newly unified Germany handles these interpretations of Germany-as-victim and communists-as-resistance-leaders will be interesting to observe; clearly any tampering with the existing heritage interpretation at such an emotive site will be fraught with danger, particularly since the suffering of Poles and Russians there has been prominently represented, and united Germany now enjoys a delicate rapprochement with these peoples. A point of major difficulty will be the collaboration of German capitalists prominent then and now in the Buchenwald horror, which was highlighted there by East Germany in its own political interests. But whatever reinterpretation of detail may occur, the strongly international identity of the memorial, in which all Europe shares but in which the Jewish tragedy (though present) is not the overwhelming issue, should naturally make Buchenwald one of the central shrines of a 'new heritage for a new Europe'.

In central/eastern Europe generally, changing political ideology combined with resurgent nationalism are likely both to raise and to challenge the profile of heritage identity as never before. One of the most intriguing problems is Kaliningrad: how far will its Russian inhabitants, cut off by an independent Lithuania, acknowledge its ancient German heritage, encourage the German tourism which has been permitted again since 1990, and perhaps revert to its pre-Stalinist name of Königsberg? St Petersburg, newly reborn from Leningrad, is the most obvious precedent, but lacks the nationalist dissonance; however, as both the pinnacle of Tsarist Russian heritage and the birthplace of the October Revolution, it has a daunting ideological heritage identity problem of its own, which might be either reconciled or confused by its patriotic symbolism resulting from the German siege of 1941–3. With respect to other population transfers, what do the Poles make of Lvov in a newly independent Ukraine, and Vilnius as the capital, no less, of an independent Lithuania, when both have symbolic significance as lost Polish heritage (Martyn 1990)? The many examples of population heritage misfits dating from 1945 do not, however, conclude this issue: minorities continue to migrate, notably as economic refugees to Germany since 1989–90; some, such as the

Transylvanian Germans, are leaving seven centuries of heritage to an equivocal future.

The independence of the Ukraine alone would appear to open a Pandora's box of rival heritage appropriations, in which conflicting ideologies have been heavily entangled with nationalism in the main Ukrainian-Russian tension, and in which there have been abundant persecutions, well beyond and long before Babi Yar, to fuel conflict over perpetrators and victims. The openness of the newly democratic government of the Ukraine to heritage reinterpretation, and perhaps its commitment to particular directions therein, is a matter which transcends tourism; it reaches the heart of its relations with its Russian and other minority populations, with Russia itself, with Germany and with Europe as a whole.

In Europe overall, the heritage of nationalist and ideological conflict, and the opportunity for its redress in moulding a new European heritage, both reach their pinnacle in Berlin. The city's pre-Nazi heritage has been eclipsed by massive wartime destruction and by the sheer weight of Second World War and cold war symbolism which is focused there. Poignant ruins such as the Kaiser Wilhelm Memorial Church (symbolic focus of the former West Berlin), bullet-riddled buildings still standing, the enigmatic underground remains of Hitler's bunker, and the Soviet War Memorial speak eloquently of the Second World War; so also does the outlying Cecilienhof, site of the Potsdam Conference, which is marketed to tourists as the symbol of Germany's defeat and dismemberment (a breathtakingly unnationalist heritage identity fostered by East Germany). The Luftbrücke (Air Bridge) Memorial, Checkpoint Charlie Museum and, above all, the remnants of the Wall itself reflect the heritage of a recently vanished global ideological divide; in this regard the rededication of a chapel on Unter den Linden by the federal Chancellor in 1990 is particularly poignant, for with German unity it became a memorial to the victims of both Nazism and communism. Now, in ironic counterpoint to the Nazi plan to rebuild Berlin as the grandiose capital of Europe (Harris 1992), an unparalleled opportunity exists to create a new heritage not only of a democratic Germany but of the new Europe of which Berlin suddenly appears the destined focus. The Reichstag remains as a symbol of democratic continuity with a pre-Nazi past; but a huge swathe of redevelopment land exists along the line of the Wall, especially around the former Potsdamerplatz, in which the city can grasp or miss the chance to mould the focus of a democratic European identity. The construction of a centre for disarmament study on the site of Hitler's bunker, as proposed in 1990, is an interesting potential contribution.

CONCLUSION

The current heritage identity problem in Europe confronts us with a poignant and unexpected contradiction. On the one hand, the impending integration of the European Community which prompted this book gives hope for a Europeanization of heritage identity, and certainly underlines its necessity. One powerful illustration of its attainment is Verdun, which is now interpreted with a central message of Franco-German reconciliation. On the other hand, the integration of western Europe appears to be counter-balanced by disintegration in eastern Europe; the attrition of national-ism in the west, however gradual and halting, by its unbridled resurgence in the east. In the short term, at least, the question of 'whose heritage?' would appear to be a European nightmare, in at any rate that half of the continent which has experienced such dramatic destabilization and refocusing of power since mid-1989.

The building of a European heritage identity must give dis-proportionate emphasis to the many transnational components which exist within the continent. The Hanseatic origin of Lübeck, Rostock, Gdansk and Tallinn is still visible, and is a surer mark of European identity than their various and changing national owner-ships; similarly, Prague, Wrocław, Lvov and Trieste are united by a Habsburg identity. These underlying national identities have been contentious in this century. In the case of Gdansk and Trieste, ephemeral attempts to make them 'free cities' are testimony to their European more than their national identities. Similarly, the Celtic and Norse fringes need to emphasize a European status in place of national identities, which for the former are so highly contentious. Underpinning the heritage of the greater part of Europe is the common legacy of Rome, arguably the most powerful building-block of a European heritage, since most Euro-peans identify with it and even those that do so least (notably the Turks) realize its potential as an economic resource. These trans-national components are often the legacy of imperial conquest; but, as Western (1985) has suggested, the removal of oppression or threat facilitates identification with their heritage. This happened long ago with Rome and the empire of Charlemagne, should have happened with the Habsburg Empire, and ultimately may with respect to twentieth-century German expansionism. Certainly the shared experience of the Second World War and its memorabilia constitutes a key factor in the forging of a European heritage identity, just as it provided the initial impetus for European integration overall; we return below, however, to an important qualification to this assertion.

In the longer term, the problem for a finally united Europe will be how to give a continentalist answer to the question 'whose heritage?' without excluding the 'strangers' in its midst; whether the image-makers and heritage-shapers of the new Berlin, or any other major city, will be equal to this task remains to be seen. This brings us back to the lesson of the Jewish tragedy. Rejection of the Jewish component in the heritage of so much of Europe led to the creation of a terrible legacy of persecution and suffering; this heritage cannot be Europeanized simply because its surviving victims have been driven elsewhere. From their refuges the survivors lay claim to this heritage of suffering, sometimes disputing with other victimized groups whose heritage such an atrocity truly constitutes.

Whatever short-term nightmare and longer-term limitation may confront us in the quest for a new European heritage identity, we have no choice but to forge one if European integration is to succeed. A prerequisite for its attainment will be a sufficient harmonization of national history education to make such an identity generally intelligible – a sobering thought indeed; but a nettle that must ultimately be grasped in any case. Hovering in the background of any discussion of heritage identity is the question of the use to which the heritage will be put, it being possible to distinguish between the political/ideological role which is central here, and the tourism/commercial role which has also often surfaced above. There may be a commercial temptation to pander to partisan perspectives even when political authorities have achieved balanced European interpretations, and a free and democratic society has no choice but to tolerate deviations from official orthodoxies. But tourism agencies must be encouraged to vary their interpretations around interest emphases rather than to undermine political/ideological harmonization, if reconciled heritage identities are to play their critical role in the bonding of a new Europe.

REFERENCES

Ashworth, G.J. and Tunbridge, J.E. (1990) *The Tourist-Historic City*, London: Belhaven.

Bayer, M.E. (1991) 'Survival in a new century', *Heritage Canada Today* 2, 3, Fall.

Boyle, M. and Hughes, G. (1991) 'The politics of the representation of the real', *Area* 23, 3: 217–28.

Carter, H. (1989) 'Whose city? A view from the periphery', *Transactions of the Institute of British Geographers* NS 14, 1: 4–23.

Dalibard, J. (1991) 'Heritage is a system of values', *Heritage Canada Today*, 2, 3, Fall.

Diefendorf, J. (ed.) (1990) *Rebuilding Europe's Bombed Cities*, London: Macmillan.

Gruber, R.E. (1992) *Jewish Heritage Travel*, New York: Wiley.

Harris, R. (1992) *Fatherland*, London: Hutchinson.

Haswell, R. (1990) 'The making and remaking of Pietermaritzburg: the past, present and future morphology of a South African city', in Slater, T.R. (ed.) *The Built Form of Western Cities*, Leicester: Leicester University Press.

Martyn, P. (1990) 'Dispatch from Eastern Europe', *Urban Morphology Newsletter*, 6: 10–12.

Nelson, J.G. (1991) 'Heritage in Canada: towards a more holistic and pluralist perspective', *The Operational Geographer* 9, 2: 10–12.

Tunbridge, J.E. (1984) 'Whose heritage to conserve? Cross-cultural reflections upon political dominance and urban heritage conservation', *The Canadian Geographer* 28, 2: 171–9.

Uzell, D.L. (1989) 'The hot interpretation of war and conflict', in Uzell, D. (ed.) *Heritage Interpretation, Volume 1: The Natural and Built Environment*, London: Belhaven.

Western, J. (1985) 'Undoing the colonial city?', *Geographical Review* 75: 335–57.

Wills, T.M., Haswell, R.F. and Davies, D.H. (1987) 'The probable consequences of the repeal of the Group Areas Act for Pietermaritzburg', *Pietermaritzburg 2000*, Pietermaritzburg: City of Pietermaritzburg and Department of Geography, University of Natal.

8

HERITAGE CONSERVATION AND REVISIONIST NATIONALISM IN IRELAND

B.J. Graham

INTRODUCTION

This chapter considers the definition and uses of material heritage in contemporary Ireland. It is argued that, ultimately, the answer to the question of 'whose heritage is conserved and why?' depends upon the ideological issues which determine why certain artefacts become heritage while others are discarded. The discussion is predicated upon certain suppositions. In the first instance, it is assumed that the importance of the heritage icon does not lie in the actual artefact itself but within its interpretation. Inevitably, it follows that heritage, being ideologically defined, is value-laden. Second, heritage is seen as an essential component of the foundation myth of a nation state, a 'dreamland', part and parcel of the need to give people a dramatized sense that they belong to that state (Horne 1984). Idealized or representative heritage landscapes are an essential component of every social construction, for each 'culture weaves its world out of image and symbol' (Daniels and Cosgrove 1988: 8). Heritage landscapes are thus part of the very iconography of a region or nation (Williams 1989: 100). But, third, if that symbolism, and the identity and needs which it confers, are time-specific, then so also is the interpretation of heritage artefacts. These often sanitized and romanticized pasts are invented for ourselves (Pearce 1989: 233; Loughlin 1990). Consequently, the definition of heritage will change through time, embodying the ever-shifting balance of continuities and changes characteristic of any society. If a pre-condition for the emergence of a new Europe is a new past, Ireland as part of that Europe also requires a reconstructed myth. This is not necessarily a heritage derived from a post-nationalist past, but one emerging from, while also helping to create, revisionist nationalist interpretations which stress Ireland's cultural location in a European world. Nevertheless, this heritage must also emphasize Ireland's particularity of place, derived from the fusion of diverse, plural and external linkages from which the Irish cosmos is constructed. But patently Ireland is not a unified place. It is but one regional example among many in Europe where we can witness the dissonance between rival cultural assertions and appropriations of heritage. Thus, the present discussion must address the contrasting ideological uses of heritage between the Republic of Ireland (the twenty-six counties) and Northern Ireland (the six), the socio-political conflicts within the latter region contrasting with the relative homogeneity of the Irish nation state.

Clearly, this discussion is related to the wider heritage debate of the past decade. On the one hand, we have the argument that heritage is a conservative force, a reactionary, nostalgic pastiche which is formulated by, and used to support, the status quo (for example, Hewison 1987). On the other, there is the concept of heritage as a radical and subversive entity, defining a people's sense of cultural alienation, particularly in liberation struggles within colonial societies (Tunbridge 1984; Western 1985; Hardy 1988). However, in Ireland as elsewhere, a heritage radically defined became highly conservative once independence was achieved, demonstrating that heritage – radical in the sense that it is subversive – can be equally reactionary, nostalgic and a pastiche. In understanding the construction of what might constitute a twenty-six-county Irish heritage, the starting point must be the sense of identity which evolved into a nationalism created to underpin the drive for independence. Any nationalism is defined by continuities and, inevitably, can simultaneously embody conservative or radical ideals, the particular balance depending upon the purpose for which it has been formulated. In the two parts of Ireland, as elsewhere in Europe, ideologies continue to use material heritage as part of that iconography. Thus to formulate answers to the question, 'whose heritage is conserved and why?', we have first to examine the nature of traditional Irish nationalism and ascertain how that concept has been revised in the second half of the twentieth century.

THE NATURE OF TRADITIONAL IRISH NATIONALISM AND ITS IMPLICATIONS FOR HERITAGE

Foster (1987: 15) has described the nationalism found in late nineteenth-century Ireland as 'a curious compound of radicalism, conservatism and reaction'. It was created to underpin the demand for independence from Britain and was later incorporated into the highly conservative constitution of the twentieth-century nation state. As Boyce (1991: 385) shows, it contained at least one crucial paradox. The political theory of Irish nationalism stressed comprehensiveness, inclusiveness and non-sectarianism, but its emotional appeal was derived from the exclusive myth of an Irish nation struggling to free itself from the 'oppression' of the English and Scottish settlers, particularly those 'planted' during the sixteenth and seventeenth centuries. The crucial role for heritage in this discourse was to help forge a homogeneity, derived from the three defining characteristics of the ideology. In essence, it was Gaelic, Catholic and rural, as epitomized by the *Gaeltacht*, the scattered Irish-speaking areas in the west and south of the island which some still regard as the heartland of the language, culture and morality of the state. The form of the nationalism was dictated by its role in underpinning the exclusive nature of the evolving nation state, one from which an Anglo-Irish dimension was consciously excised. Pluralism was never a hallmark of any politically important expression of Irish nationalism after 1850, its development being directed exclusively at the attainment of a secure independent agricultural peasantry (Walker 1990: 214). The heritage landscape transmitted within such an ideological context mirrored its rurality and Gaelic provenance. To take but one example, it was argued that there was no substantive contradiction between urban and rural society in Ireland because the towns themselves were overwhelmingly rural (Lee 1973: 97–8).

Conversely, the Anglo-Irish, the Anglican propertied class of the big house and demesne, had a long tradition which dated back to the 'colonial nationalism' of the eighteenth century of perceiving themselves as being Irish. Defining nationality by Irish domicile or birth, they began to see themselves as upholders of the country's constitutional status as a kingdom against the pretensions of the British parliament and administration (Canny 1988: 135). By the late nineteenth century, however, this class had lost its Irish national function. Its presence shrank to a handful of big houses and institutions, to what MacDonagh (1983: 17) refers to as the 'ghettoes of the mind', a twilight and melancholy world best evoked in the novels of writers like Elizabeth Bowen, Molly Keane, J.G. Farrell and William Trevor. Probably the best-known embodiment of the Anglo-Irish viewpoint was in Yeats's Literary Revival, which sought to underpin the concept of a synthetic Anglo-Irish nation, presenting a distinctive Celtic contribution to European culture through the English language (Hutchinson 1987: 216). Indeed, the earliest attempts to define an Irish nationalism rested within such a cultural framework, the exclusion of the Anglo-Irish dimension being a product of the late nineteenth-century linkage of the land question to the fundamental and long-standing aspirations of the Irish people (Cullen 1980: 92), and the simultaneous creation of a Gaelic Catholic peasantry as the homogeneous embodiment of Irishness (Walker 1990: 205–6).

The radical Gaelic nationalism which evolved in the later nineteenth century and the historiography written to support it – together with the material heritage which was part of that historiography – have been variously described as chauvinistic, dogmatically certain, xenophobic and intolerant. The ideological aim – and that of the heritage which it defined and incorporated – was to create an origin-legend for the Irish state, a moral centre of Catholic social values which the then Taoiseach, Eamon de Valera, incorporated into the 1937 Constitution and thus into the everyday life of the people (Boyce 1991: 352–3). The Constitution defined the reality of de Valera's twenty-six-county state, its homogeneity more important than the lost lands of the north. Despite its contradictions, some modern commentators – the re-revisionists – would defend the Constitution (Lee 1991) but others see it as fundamentalist, a barrier to the emergence of a late-twentieth-century European state.

We can identify five characteristics of this orthodox Irish nationalism which have significant repercussions for the delineation of material heritage. In its twentieth-century form, freed from that struggle for liberty, the ideology became highly conservative and insular; the assumption was made that exogenous forces and influences – change – had become assimilated into the continuities of Gaelic life. Its origin-myth centred on pseudo-histories such as the twelfth-century *Leabhar Gabhála* (The Book of Invasions), which established a myth of national integration whereby Ireland was seen as a melting-pot of different cultures, in which the other inhabitants of the country could become Irish by Gaelicizing themselves (Morgan 1991). Second, the longevity of this Gaelic world was stressed, the justifying unity of the contemporary Irish world dating back to the pre-Viking era before AD 800. As Mac-Donagh (1983: 2) points out, this foreshortening of time – what we might call time-collapse – was crucial to Gaelic-Irish nationalism, the nature of the Celtic past being used to legitimate the exclusivity of nineteenth-century radical nationalism and, subsequently, twentieth-century social order. Somewhat ironically, the Celtic revival of the eighteenth century, which established the currency of this origin-myth, had Anglo-Irish origins. Third, the nationalism was virulently Anglophobic and, by extension, anti-Anglo-Irish, that landed class being perceived as comprising rapacious Englishmen abroad; it denied that this linkage could be anything other than a negative one. On this score, a marked ambivalence remains. Thus, the melting-pot defined by C.J. Haughey, fourth leader of Fianna Fail and then Taoiseach, in a speech in 1980, included 'Celts, Danes, Normans, Scots, Huguenots, Palatines and others', the last category presumably including the unmentionable (quoted in Morgan 1991: 15). Fourth, in the absence of a historical Gaelic-Irish polity, the Catholic church was depicted as the principal dynamic of social change and moral order, thereby embodying a continuity of authority back to the Patrician era of the fifth century. Finally, island and nation were seen as co-terminous, although a Gaelic nationalism – which defines itself by exclusivity – has always had difficulty with the essentially Anglo-Irish concept that Irish nationality emanates *per se* from Irish domicile or birth (MacDonagh 1983: 17).

Because of its exclusive nature, this nationalism defined a material heritage and representative landscapes which were interpreted as being essentially peculiar to Ireland, to the Celtic cosmos or to the Gaelic world evoked in Corkery's concept of a 'Hidden Ireland' (Cullen 1988). Further, these icons were selected to demonstrate the longevity or continuities of Irish consciousness which necessitated an undue emphasis upon the monuments of the first millennium AD and earlier. Finally, it was heritage specific to a particular origin-myth. Common artefacts thus identified included monasteries of the Early Christian church such as Clonmacnoise, Co. Offaly, and Glendalough, Co. Wicklow, Celtic Iron Age hill-forts such as the legendary crowning place of the High Kings of Ireland at Tara, Co. Meath, and megaliths of the third millennium BC, the most famous of which is Newgrange, also in County Meath. Most notably, there was no place in this heritage for towns, perceived as an alien innovation and in particular an English one. As Jones Hughes (1962: 8) once put it, 'Ireland possessed no native urban tradition. . . largely attributable, as elsewhere in the moist, cool fringe of Atlantic Europe, to the pastoral and tribal nature of society'. Again, Ireland's 'towns were of foreign origin, strung out round the coasts; in the pastoral interior a 'claustrophobic horror of towns' persisted' (O'Faolain 1960: 60). Lee (1989: 648) describes the construction of this 'symbolic universe that constituted the dominant public myth of post-Famine Ireland. . . [as] a supreme imaginative achievement'. But it was a sectarian success. The heritage defined by this nationalism – like its rhetoric – was that of 'one nation', its corollary an exclusion of northern Unionists and others from an ideology wholly Gaelic and Catholic in ethos (O'Halloran 1987: xv).

A NORTHERN HERITAGE

It is the north which has suffered the dissonance which attends rival cultural assertions and appropriations of history and heritage in Ireland. To Irish nationalists, partition meant the loss of much of Ulster, the last Gaelic area to fall to the colonists in the seventeenth century, the location of Patrick's see of Armagh and his reputed burial place at Downpatrick, and the land of the O'Neills. But the rhetoric did not include the Protestants of English or Scottish descent, nor the industrialized north-east, particularly Belfast, a heritage impossible to subsume within the ideology of the Irish Free State. As the Ulster poet Derek Mahon has put it, 'a lot of people cannot accept that the Protestant suburbs in Belfast are a part of Ireland. . . . At an aesthetic level they can't accept that' (quoted in Watson 1991: 11). In his argument for a two-nation Ireland, Pringle (1985) contends that this division was largely created by the growth and penetration of capitalism into the north-east of the island during the nineteenth century. The 1937 Irish Constitution may still lay claim to the whole of the island, but otherwise it relates to an exclusively nationalist and sectarian twenty-six-county state (O'Halloran 1987: xiii). The ideal of an agrarian, homely Catholic society could not accommodate north-east Ulster, which was simply ignored in the rhetoric of de Valera's litany of the lost lands (Boyce 1991: 352). These became no more than one further symbol, used to emphasize the homogeneity of the twenty-six-county state.

Indicative of the nebulous position of the north is the lack of a mutually agreed title. Ulster, the provincial name which extends to nine counties, three of which are in the Republic of Ireland, has been appropriated by Unionist politicians to become synonymous with Northern Ireland. The latter term, together with upper-case letters, is not regarded with approval by politicians in the Republic because it implies some form of de facto recognition. They prefer euphemisms such as 'the north', 'the north-east' – which diminishes the scale of the problem – or, particularly offensive to Unionists, the 'six counties' or the 'black north'. To quote Dervla Murphy (1978), it is 'a place apart', but crucially there is little agreement as to which cultural and material artefacts constitute its heritage or how these might relate to its definition. Yet the question of identity, and of laying claim to a representative landscape which might provide an iconography to define that consciousness, is crucial to an end to violence in the north. If we leave aside the simplistic arguments of those who demand a unified Ireland on the grounds that water defines the natural boundary of the Gaelic nation state, three responses relevant to the questions of heritage and identity can be isolated. First, there is the case that Ulster is part of Britain and therefore has no need to develop a separate heritage or place consciousness. Second, we have the argument which rejects the feasibility of Irish unity but holds that Ulster is a separate entity with its own iconography of common identity. Finally, Ulster – in this vision the nine counties (including Donegal, Cavan and Monaghan) – can be visualized as but one region in a pluralistic diversified Ireland.

Because the Unionist cause has always looked to the link with Britain as the most effective way of avoiding incorporation into a Catholic-dominated Ireland, its single most important weakness arguably lies in its failure to develop – through the creation of a specific heritage – a separate place consciousness. Neither Ulster politics nor heritage has ever been cast in a national role. No attempt has been made to produce a classical historic foundation-myth illustrating the great past of the Ulster Protestant people; the greatness of the British past was sufficient substitute (Coakley 1990: 33). Even Stormont, the neo-classical 1930s 'Protestant' House of Parliament for the 'Protestant People' of Northern Ireland, sited on a dominant hill-side location in east Belfast, was intended as a symbol of defiance of Irish Catholic nationalism, not as an icon of Ulster Protestant nationalism (Boyce 1991: 365) (Figure 8.1). The

Figure 8.1 Lord Carson, Irish Unionist Party leader from 1910 to 1920, gesticulates defiantly southwards from his plinth in front of Stormont

Source: Photograph by the author

fundamental weaknesses in this position are three-fold. In the first instance, the state to which loyalty is subscribed is largely indifferent, or even overtly hostile, to that proclamation. Second, a considerable percentage of the population of the north – not all of it Catholic – rejects the validity of the linkage with Britain. Finally, the failure to even attempt to develop a specific northern consciousness means that there is no sense of communal identity which might underpin the legitimation of the six-county state, leading C.J. Haughey, for example, to describe it as a 'failed entity' (Lee 1989: 504). British Ulster demonstrates the weakness and futility of a place in which the imaginary and symbolic world of identity is external to itself. The Unionist failure to recognize the centrality of laying claim and giving meaning to the landscape of Ulster, as distinct from grabbing territory, is part and parcel of the nationalist claim to 'the rhetorical high ground of moral advantage against the putative descendants of their oppressors' (Buckley 1991: 262).

It is precisely this Unionist failure to recognize that a claim to territory is not in itself sufficient to create a feeling of belonging to the place claimed which is addressed in the second argument that Ulster is a separate cultural entity with its own distinct cultural and material heritage and communal sense of identity. This can be regarded as a conscious attempt to lay siege to that moral high ground. We can see the converse of the Unionist stance on heritage in the development of this perspective, the essentials of which rest upon the creation of an Ulster origin-myth which establishes both a separate identity and legitimation of the claim of Ulster Protestants to their territory within the island of Ireland. In the most developed justification of this viewpoint, Adamson (1991: 104) argues that Ulster's historical and cultural heritage contains within it 'the proof of the common identity of northerners'. Somewhat ironically, he uses precisely the same sort of heritage sources and artefacts as did traditional Gaelic nationalism. Thus, his arguments are also characterized by time-collapse, the origins of Ulster identity resting in a long-past age (Adamson 1978). In this origin-myth, the earliest inhabitants of what is now Ulster were the Cruthin, who controlled a Scots-Irish cultural province prior to the arrival in Ireland of the Celts (Gaels). In this interpretation, Cú Chulainn, the hero of the Ulster Cycle, the pseudo-histories of the province, the most famous of which is the *Táin bó Cúailgne* (The Cattle Raid of Cooley), is reincarnated as the leader of the Ulster resistance against the invading Gaels who eventually pushed the Cruthin back to the extreme north-east of the region. As Buckley (1991: 269) points out, there is a wonderful irony in this, as a statue of Cú Chulainn stands in Dublin's Central Post Office to commemorate the revolutionaries of the 1916 uprising, central figures in the pantheon of martyred heroes of the new Irish nation state. But even the Gaels of Ulster, it is argued, had more in common with those of Scotland than the remainder of Ireland. Thus the Plantations of the sixteenth and seventeenth centuries, the colonization of oppressors in the Gaelic myth, can be depicted as a reconquest by a Scots-Irish people who had once been expelled from their rightful territory by the invading Gaels. Adamson (1982: 108) sets out to 'create a deeper sense of belonging to the country of our ancestors. For this Land of the Cruthin is our Homeland and we are her children.' Clearly, this is historiography to underpin an Ulster independence, which – as Aughey (1989: 14) observes – is tantamount to accepting the nationalist case that Ulster is not part of a United Kingdom.

Third, there is the argument which rejects this notion of communal Ulster separateness, in turn seeking to define a nine-county Ulster as but one region in a diversified pluralistic Ireland. Inevitably, this perspective is a rebuttal of the perceived monolithic nature of Gaelic nationalism. As Hoppen (1989) has shown in his evocation of the provincialism and localism of nineteenth-century Irish society, there was no spontaneous collective nationalist movement. Ireland was, and remains, an island of regions, a perspective which can only help deconstruct the potentially divisive nature of island-wide generalization and state-sponsored ideology (Whelan 1991). As Estyn Evans, Ulster's most influential geographer, argued, many of the nations of Europe have evolved 'through a fusion of regional loyalties' and Ireland is no different (Evans 1981: 77). He saw Ulster as one strong regional variant, part of a hybrid culture of interdependent communities forged in the seventeenth century (Canny 1987: 77). Indeed, Evans saw the conflict between native and newcomer as the dynamic in Irish society, 'the clash that struck the sparks in Irish culture' (1984: 13). It was Ireland's very insularity which attracted invaders and created the reality of its diversity (1981: xii). Given his commitment to plurality, it is again ironic that Evans saw Ulster as the most Gaelic of all the Irish provinces, an interpretation shared by irredentist Irish nationalists.

There is a curious symmetry in these latter two perspectives. As we have seen, the Unionists have made no claim to an indigenous northern heritage, but both those who seek a separate Ulster identity and those who stress its place in a diversified, pluralistic Ireland have often laid claim to the same landscape of material heritage. It is a shared vision of a rural people, succoured by a legitimation derived from prehistory. This dreamland depicts an Ulster of drumlins and hedge-girt closed landscapes, or one of naked bogs and misty hills; it is a place of small size but great distances, the foundations of its identity derived from prehistory. The irony is profound when we consider that de Valera's vision of Ulster was also shrouded in Celtic mists and populated with warrior heroes. Although there is a distinct literary commitment to a more diverse Ulster, there is often no place for Belfast, Derry and the other towns, or for industry and commerce in many of these transmitted images of a representative Ulster landscape. That rival perspectives set claim to the same material heritage icons is commonplace, but here we have conflicting ideologies sharing similar interpretations as well. Nor do they identify any icons which are specific to Ulster. The regional heritage identity derives from a specific mix of artefacts which, in almost every instance, are communal to the Irish experience as a whole. Variation stems from the particularities of their distributions. For example, Lyons (1979: 120–1) argues that Anglo-Irish culture dictated most of the appearance of Ulster. While this is a highly debatable conclusion, it would not define the province even if it could be substantiated. To varying degrees, the same transformation of landscape occurred throughout the island. The ambiguity of the north is thus underlined by the impossibility of defining a representative heritage landscape which is specific to it and might help define its separateness. But simultaneously, Gaelic historiography's definition of Irishness as an absolute quality rather than a diversity of content precludes a resolution to the crisis of ambiguity and identity which is at the heart of the north's dilemma. Clearly, the interpretation of material heritage is crucial here because, as we have seen, that is part of the symbolism of identity which underpins every state and nation.

REVISIONISM AND THE REDEFINITION OF IRISH HERITAGE

In part driven by the enduring, embittered conflict in the north, there has been an intense effort by some academics during the past twenty years to revise or reconstruct traditional Irish nationalism. By the 1950s, as Lee argues (1989: 653), the self-portrait of traditional Ireland bore only a 'tenuous relation to reality'. He depicts this vision as one which had faded away, although no alternative self-portrait has yet emerged 'to command comparable conviction'. The notion of reassessing Ireland's past – loosely known as revisionism – can best be seen as a plea for plurality, for a maturation of an Irish nationalism which no longer requires a fundamentalist and spurious homogeneity as its defining characteristic. Such an ideological transformation has profound implications for the delineation of the elements of a representative Irish heritage landscape because, inevitably, that too is being redefined. As Smyth (1993) forcefully argues, there have been and are many Irelands, crystallizing and transforming themselves within broader European, colonial, Atlantic and global frameworks. Conversely, in *Warrenpoint*, his memoirs of a south Ulster childhood, the literary critic, Denis Donoghue (1991), displays the reluctance of some northern Catholics to surrender their usurpation of the moral high ground which such re-evaluation must entail. He argues that revisionist historians are asking the Irish people to forget about nationality, seeking instead a new role in membership of the European Community (1991: 162). Largely, this is to miss the point of numerous interpretations of revisionism, itself by no means a single coherent philosophy. What is involved is a reconstitution of the idea of Irishness so that, to quote Cullen (1988: 37), it might no longer be perceived as a monolithic product 'of oppression' but as a 'rich, complex and varied stream of identity and. . . consciousness'. Two essential strands can be identified to this case. First, it is argued that the concept of a Gaelic national consciousness is an invention of the eighteenth and nineteenth centuries only, although Cullen (1980), for example, would admit to an earlier gestation of an Irish sense of identity. Second, the exclusive Gaelic world, unitary in the sense that it assimilated all exogenous influences and thereby was dominated by continuity, is replaced with a plurality of political and cultural inputs. That which is specifically Irish becomes the precise delineation of the fusion of these inputs, an Irish heritage defined not by Gaelic exclusivity but by complex diversity.

The reasons for promoting revisionism are a mixture of ideology and pragmatism. In the first instance, as we have seen, the exclusivity of Gaelic nationalism is a potent factor in the endless conflict of the north. Second, and far more important in a contemporary Republic which has largely turned its back on the north, internationalism was forced upon Ireland during the 1950s and early

1960s by the failure of de Valera's economic policies, characterized by what Brunt (1988) refers to as 'almost claustrophobic insularity'. This has taken the form of a drive to obtain external investment and a markedly positive commitment to the European Community as a source of finance. There is a parallel need to 'place' Ireland in that context, to identify components in its heritage which stress European linkages and a national self-image which no longer can seek its inspiration in negativity and insularity (Kearns 1983: 70–1). In some ways, however, the Gaelic metanarrative of assimilation can address this need. To quote C.J. Haughey again (cited in Morgan 1991: 15), 'there are few European nations which have such a rich inheritance of culture, talent and intellect. . . a great diversity of qualities and talents inherited from successive waves of immigration'. Thus Europeans are immigrants, but the English are colonizers. Finally, the *Gaeltacht* model is a failure too, and inappropriate within a materialistic and increasingly secular and urban twentieth-century world. The population of these areas is now no more than 80,000 out of the Republic's total population of around 3.7 million. Although Ireland is one of the least urbanized areas in Europe, 56 per cent of the population lived in towns of more than 1,500 people in 1981, almost one-third of the entire population being in the Greater Dublin area. The fundamentalism of a Constitution which enshrines rural Catholic values as the moral core of the nation raises numerous social and moral dilemmas in such a context, a primary source of the ambivalence which is almost a defining characteristic of contemporary Irish life. In a neat demonstration of this, Donoghue (1991: 149) writes approvingly 'of an Irish solution for an Irish problem', a euphemism for turning a 'blind eye'. Ratification of the terms of the Treaty of Maastricht may require policies rather than ambiguities.

Consequently, both the negativity of exclusive Gaelic nationalism and the inappropriateness of its values in a late twentieth-century secular world have prompted some commentators to seek a redefinition of the meaning of Irishness, a reinterpretation of the legitimating principles of Irish society. If material heritage and representative landscapes are symbolic of, and defined by, the prevailing sense of identity, two ensuing repercussions can be isolated for the question of 'whose heritage should be conserved?' First, if the meaning of heritage icons is ideologically driven, then revisionism must lead to an academic re-evaluation or even redefinition of that iconography. Its symbolism, as part of the definition of the nation state, must perforce change as the ideology of the latter is reconstructed. Second, other artefacts – formerly excluded as being of alien provenance – may now be deemed fit objects for preservation or conservation as national heritage.

An obvious example of the first point is the debate which has translated Early Christian monastic sites such as Clonmacnoise or Kildare into early medieval proto-urban settlements (the change in nomenclature is diagnostic of revisionism) (Graham 1993). The ecclesiastical buildings at Clonmacnoise, for example, are regarded by contemporary revisionists as being the core of a substantial early medieval town; the castle at the western extremity of the site, conventionally attributed to the Anglo-Normans, may have earlier origins (Figure 8.2). These sites, and their art and architecture, were formerly interpreted as symbolic of a pre-invasion 'golden age' in which Ireland was the 'isle of the saints'. Now, they are held to have functioned as political capitals and centres of economic exchange and production in what some historians see as a largely secular world (Sharpe 1984). In this re-evaluation, the monastery becomes no more than a central nucleating feature of the settlement, an urban core or burg commonplace in continental Europe, but not its diagnostic component. Consequently, it can be argued that Ireland generated its own indigenous urbanization in the early medieval period, well before the twelfth-century Anglo-Norman invasion, an argument which places it firmly within the mainstream of European urban and social development. Turning to the second point, the best-known single example of the redefinition of heritage to embrace formerly excluded objects is Georgian Dublin, the destruction of which was once presented as an act of national purification. Kearns (1983: 70–1) sees the movement to define this and similar urban areas as an Irish heritage and to conserve the buildings as evidence of the maturation of the Irish identity in its new Euro-context, an apparent willingness to accept 'variant strains of Irish nationality'.

The same point applies to the Plantation towns of the north and to the eighteenth- and nineteenth-century landscape icons of the Anglo-Irish landed élite – the big houses, demesnes and planned towns and villages. The overtly anti-urban nature of Gaelic nationalist historiography was consequent upon the equation of towns with a landscape of oppression, built through the expropriation of the production of the mass of the Gaelic peasantry. As Canny (1988: 49) remarks, 'the towns [of the Plantation] became the symbols of

Figure 8.2 Clonmacnoise, County Offaly
Source: Cambridge University Collection of Air Photographs: copyright reserved

English influence in the Irish provinces, even though they did not resemble any known English town in physical appearance'. Conversely, Canny argues that both these and the later estate towns and big houses can be seen as part of one contrasting conception of Irish nationalism. The 'environmental revolution' of the eighteenth and early nineteenth centuries, the transformation of place in a particular image, can be depicted as an element in the process through which an essentially arriviste Anglo-Irish élite set out to affirm its Irishness and claim its territory. Apart from the demesnes and big houses, almost 800 improved towns and villages emanated from this process (Graham and Proudfoot 1992). An example is the townscape at Cootehill, County Cavan, shown in Figure 8.3. Originally a Plantation settlement, the contemporary morphology and buildings of the town, which lies adjacent to the fine Palladian house of Bellamont Forest, owe much to landlord improvement in the eighteenth and early nineteenth centuries. Note the siting of the Church of Ireland to create a vista at the end of the main street. The nondescript appearance and variety in height and width of the buildings reflect the typical landlord practice of facilitating tenant construction of houses to infill a pre-existing formalized skeleton street morphology.

TOURISM AND HERITAGE REDEFINITION IN IRELAND

Arguably, however, the redefinition of the heritage which should be preserved or conserved in Ireland is being driven by factors other than academic revisionism of traditional ideological orthodoxies. There are pragmatic and economic forces at work as well, principally those of tourism. Currently, there is a major initiative, partially funded by the EC Regional Development Fund and the International Fund for Ireland, to promote and expand Irish tourism, both north and south. In this context, the constraints in heritage definition are not those of ideology but rather of practicality. As Hewison (1987: 9) points out, heritage may be a concept which nobody seems able to define, but it is one which everyone is eager to sell. During the 1980s, domestic and, principally, export tourism accounted for around 10 per cent of Ireland's GNP (Gillmor 1985). Since 1987, foreign tourism revenue has exceeded IR£1,000 million annually. The market is a curious one; on the one hand, it is dominated by the 'Visiting Friends and Relations'

Figure 8.3 A characteristic Irish townscape at Cootehill, County Cavan
Source: Photograph by the author

category, principally originating in Britain or North America. This business has been declining. On the other hand, an expanding share of the market is made up of tourists from continental Europe who tend to fall into younger age groups and higher socio-economic classifications (Gillmor 1985). In 1991, a poor year for tourism, Ireland received almost 3 million overseas visitors, of whom 840,000 were from mainland Europe. Although the statistics may not be strictly compatible, various surveys suggest that Ireland's historical and cultural heritage is a primary attraction to foreign tourists. It should be noted that this can be defined more widely than material artefacts alone, and may include literary heritage, music, theatre, crafts and summer schools. A Bord Fáilte (Irish Tourist Board) survey, carried out in 1988, showed that visiting historical/cultural heritage sites was among the most important activities indulged in by foreign tourists, 75 per cent visiting at least one site which could fall within the remit of what might be considered heritage.

However, as Ashworth and Tunbridge (1990: 259) have pointed out, there is potential for conflict between the heritage used for and defined by nationalistic purposes and that marketable to tourists. Further, both producers and consumers need to be aware of the political factor inherent in the content and goal of any heritage being presented (Ashworth 1991: 13). Much Irish heritage, as delineated within the constraints of the orthodox Gaelic tradition, is both humble and difficult to understand. For example, early medieval settlements are frequently inconspicuous earthworks or visually unimpressive ecclesiastical monuments, the interpretation of which requires specialist archaeological knowledge. Therefore, such sites may be largely invisible to both tourists and the Irish population as a whole. Even at major ecclesiastical icons such as Clonmacnoise, all extensively remodelled in the twelfth century, the visible artefacts are mostly rather later than the period to which the sites were attributed in fulfilment of their role in traditional historiography. While sites such as Clonmacnoise, Glendalough, Newgrange and Cashel, Co. Tipperary, together with their attached interpretative centres, remain significant poles of attraction, one result of the relatively humble and inconspicuous nature of much Irish landscape heritage is that the bulk of sites visited by tourists tend to be more visible and accessible monuments which include big houses, parks and castles. Obviously, these artefacts, primarily created by intrusive aristocratic élites, can be less than compatible with the Gaelic model of nationalism. Again, tourists visit and use the facilities of towns, which, as we have seen, formerly had little role to play in the traditional iconography of Irish heritage; neither urbanization nor the big house represent continuities of Gaelic life. It is this incorporation of towns, villages and stately homes – creations of the Anglo-Irish and their Stuart and Anglo-Norman precursors – within the canon of permissible icons which represents the most radical redefinition of the limits of Irish heritage, in turn demonstrating that the whole concept of time-collapse, intrinsic to Gaelic nationalism cannot be sustained. An excellent example is provided by Bord Fáilte's marketing of twenty-eight heritage towns: places which, because of their own preserved qualities, 'can be transformed' into tourist attractions in their own right. They are, to quote an undated Bord Fáilte document, 'tourism centres prioritized for marketing' and will qualify for grant aid from European Regional Development Fund sources. Although displaying a variety of origins, the contemporary built fabric of these towns is dominated by heritage icons dating from either the Anglo-Norman Middle Ages or the landlord-inspired 'environmental revolution' of the eighteenth and early nineteenth centuries. Underlining the Irish nature of Ulster's landscape, the landscape icons marketed by the Northern Ireland Tourist Board are generally indistinguishable from those in the Republic. It remains to be seen whether research can demonstrate that they fulfil different meanings to their consumers.

All in all, this pragmatic resources-oriented, tourism-driven, location-specified heritage does not necessarily fit into the traditional array of artefacts defined by the historiography of Gaelic nationalism. Indeed, nothing sums all this up better than Western's statement that, in terms of repudiating the past, 'ideology is manifestly constrained by practicality' (1985: 357). Tourism's heritage is far more at home with the general tenets of the revisionist model of nationalism; indeed the widening of Irish heritage involved is very much a vindication of Yeats's concept of an Anglo-Irish nation, one in which Irish domicile and Irish nationality are coincident. Therefore revisionism, which can be seen as ideological in perspective, and the pragmatism of the tourism industry both combine to redefine the meaning of existing heritage artefacts and also to extend their array through the absorption of artefacts, once derided, into the accepted domain of what is considered Irish.

CONCLUSIONS

But that does not quite answer the question of 'whose heritage should be conserved?' The inclusion of the heritage of the Anglo-Irish within a tourism product does not necessarily point to the reincorporation of that people or others similarly ostracized within a predominant Gaelic nationalism. To a large extent, the validity of the dominant twentieth-century discourse of Irishness as expressed within the twenty-six counties has been dependent upon its per-ceived exclusivity. Thus, in his much-lauded dissection of Irish politics and society since 1912, Lee (1989: 661) argues that the description of Irishness as a 'polyglot patchwork' constitutes 'heroic self-deception'. He regards any redefinition of consciousness along these lines as a relentless pursuit of Anglicization, a jaded alternative to an Irish identity. The argument for a plurality of influences and heritage can thus be presented as a device to recreate an English identity in Ireland. The crucial point here is the centrality of assimilation in defining Irishness and its material and indeed cultural heritage. Despite the myriad external influences involved throughout Ireland's history, apparently only the Celts and English have been able to absorb change without themselves being funda-mentally altered, thereby retaining their distinctive 'racial' identities and perpetual antagonisms.

In the context of the new Europe, this is a depressing argument because it is imbued with largely discredited notions of racial distinctiveness which further confer moral rights to territory. Although Lee – and others – may be misusing the word 'race' as a synonym for culture, wherever we look in Europe, the latter is patently a dialectic between a multiplicity of internal and external forces. Certainly, such polyglot identities may be regionally defined and particular. Nevertheless, the recognition of specific regional consciousness within Europe need not blind us to the spurious nature of the idea that Ireland's surrounding waters somehow permitted the assimilation of all external influences. In European terms, the assumption that an essential Celtic purity has survived through aeons of time would make Ireland uniquely deviant. These arguments of homogeneity are delusions and, in the context of a new Europe, dangerous ones. Equally, it can be argued that the concept of an Irish cultural uniformity is itself a modern ideological manipulation, one outcome of the forging together of a historio-graphy and heritage which had no purpose other than to create an

illusory and straightforwardly sectarian homogeneity. That ideological perspective has served successfully to provide an integrative
identity for a twenty-six-county state but equally, it has to be held
partially responsible for the prolongation of one of the most
singularly unresolved regional conflicts in Europe. The sectarian
definition of Irishness has meant that the Ulster Unionists have
been forced to define neither their identity nor claim to territory;
an essentially negative Unionism has continuously justified itself
through Gaelic exclusivity. Further, it does not say a great deal for
the maturation of the Irish state to argue that the removal of that
illusion of homogeneity would bring the whole fragile edifice
tumbling back within an English hegemony. Plurality of identity is
a prerequisite both to a successful European identity and to a
resolution of regional conflict. A new definition of Irishness need
not be built upon a post-nationalistic interpretation of the past but
upon one which stresses the distinctiveness of Ireland's hybrid
society. As the debate over a northern identity demonstrates, the
same heritage icons are open to a multiplicity of interpretations.
There is a commonality to the material artefacts which can be
defined as Ireland's heritage, north and south, but an admission of
plurality is an essential prerequisite to any resolution to the
problems posed by the rival cultural assertions and appropriations
of that heritage. In essence, therefore, the heritage of a new Ireland
in a new Europe has to be ideologically constructed to define
Ireland's heterogeneity, not homogeneity. That does not necessitate
either creeping Anglicization or a sacrifice of Ireland's identity.

However, if a historian as eminent as Lee can continue – even
inadvertently – to assume the efficacy of concepts of racial purity,
the possibility – perhaps probability – exists that revisionist ideology is an academic one, not necessarily yet relevant to the way in
which Irish heritage and history are perceived by the population at
large (Foster 1988: 595). There is no research to refer to here – nor
is there yet any on the role of interpretative centres and the myths
which they peddle – but it may be speculated that ambivalence or
even hostility to the descendants of settlers may remain (Bowman
1982). And further, some bowdlerized version of the Gaelic origin-
myth is likely to be held by many tourists, particularly North
Americans. Certainly, the revisionist argument has been a singular
failure on the streets of Belfast and Derry.

Thus, in answering the question 'whose heritage should be
conserved in Ireland?', the re-evaluation of the nation state and its

defining ideology demands that late twentieth-century Irish heritage should be a radical force, set in opposition to the antiquarian conservatism of Gaelic nationalism. Three characteristics should be reflected within it. First, it must reflect the identification of the specific fusion of all the exogenous and indigenous influences which created Ireland's history. Second, the particularity of that past and its relevance to the present must be placed within the context of a recognizable generality of European process. Finally, heritage definition must underscore the maturation of Irish identity into a plurality, central to which is the rejection of the Gaelic origin-myth and the removal of Catholicism as a defining element of nationality. This revisionist heritage is being defined by an unholy alliance, first of academics, some at least of whom are motivated by a desire to demarcate for themselves a place in the Irish nation state from which they are still partially excluded by the enduring Gaelic origin-myth with its lingering notions of Celtic 'racial' purity and assimilative assumptions, and second, by the pragmatism of a tourist business selling what is there on the ground. Ultimately, one suspects that the influence of the latter will be more enduring. As ever, a heritage is time-specific; in the strict sense it cannot be preserved but only conserved, for its meaning must alter as the definition of that which it represents changes.

REFERENCES

Adamson, I. (1978) *The Cruthin*, Belfast: Donard.

Adamson, I. (1982) *The Identity of Ulster*, Bangor: Pretani Press.

Adamson, I. (1991) *The Ulster People*, Bangor: Pretani Press.

Ashworth, G.J. (1991) *Heritage Planning: Conservation as the Management of Urban Change*, Groningen: GeoPers.

Ashworth, G.J. and Tunbridge, J.E. (1990) *The Tourist-Historic City*, London: Belhaven.

Aughey, A. (1989) *Under Siege: Ulster Unionism and the Anglo-Irish Agreement*, Belfast: Blackstaff.

Bowman, J. (1982) *De Valera and the Ulster Question, 1917–73*, Oxford: Clarendon.

Boyce, D.G. (1991) *Nationalism in Ireland* (second edition), London: Routledge.

Brunt, B. (1988) *The Republic of Ireland*, London: Paul Chapman.

Buckley, A. (1991) 'Uses of history amongst Ulster Protestants', in Dawe, G. and Foster, J.W. (eds) *The Poet's Place: Ulster Literature and Society*, Belfast: Institute of Irish Studies.

Canny, N. (1987) 'The formation of the Irish mind: religion, politics and Gaelic Irish literature, 1580–1750', in Philpin, C.H.E. (ed.)

Nationalism and Popular Protest in Ireland, Cambridge: Past and Present Publications.

Canny, N. (1988) *Kingdom and Colony: Ireland in the Atlantic World, 1560–1800*, Baltimore: Johns Hopkins University Press.

Coakley, J. (1990) 'Typical case or deviant? Nationalism in a European perspective', in Hill, M. and Barber, S. (eds) *Aspects of Irish Studies*, Belfast: Institute of Irish Studies.

Cullen, L.M. (1980) 'The cultural basis of modern Irish nationalism', in Mitchison, R. (ed.) *The Roots of Nationalism: Studies in Northern Europe*, Edinburgh: John Donald.

Cullen, L.M. (1988) *The Hidden Ireland: Reassessment of a Concept* (revised edition), Mullingar: Lilliput Press.

Daniels, S. and Cosgrove, D. (1988) 'Introduction: iconography and landscape', in Cosgrove, D. and Daniels, S. (eds) *The Iconography of Landscape*, Cambridge: Cambridge University Press.

Donoghue, D. (1991) *Warrenpoint*, London: Jonathan Cape.

Evans, E.E. (1981) *The Personality of Ireland: Habitat, Heritage and History* (revised edition), Belfast: Blackstaff.

Evans, E.E. (1984) *Ulster: The Common Ground*, Mullingar: Lilliput Press.

Foster, R.F. (1987) 'Introduction', in Philpin, C.H.E. (ed.) *Nationalism and Popular Protest in Ireland*, Cambridge: Past and Present Publications.

Foster, R.F. (1988) *Modern Ireland, 1600–1972*, London: Allen Lane.

Gillmor, D.A. (1985) *Economic Activities in the Republic of Ireland: A Geographical Perspective*, Dublin: Gill and MacMillan.

Graham, B.J. (1993) 'Early medieval Ireland: settlement as an indicator of economic and social transformation, *c.* 500–1100', in Graham, B.J. and Proudfoot, L.J. (eds) *An Historical Geography of Ireland*, London: Academic Press.

Graham, B.J. and Proudfoot, L.J. (1992) 'Landlords, planning and urban growth in eighteenth- and early nineteenth-century Ireland', *Journal of Urban History* 18: 308–29.

Hardy, D. (1988) 'Historical geography and heritage studies', *Area* 20: 333–8.

Hewison, R. (1987) *The Heritage Industry: Britain in a Climate of Decline*, London: Methuen.

Hoppen, K.T. (1989) *Ireland Since 1800: Conflict and Conformity*, London: Longman.

Horne, D. (1984) *The Great Museum: The Re-Presentation of History*, London: Pluto.

Hutchinson, J. (1987) *The Dynamics of Cultural Nationalism: The Gaelic Revival and the Creation of the Irish Nation State*, London: Allen and Unwin.

Jones Hughes, T. (1962) 'The origin and growth of towns in Ireland', *University Review* 11: 8–15.

Kearns, K.C. (1983) *Georgian Dublin: Ireland's Imperilled Architectural Heritage*, Newton Abbot: David and Charles.

Lee, J. (1973) *The Modernisation of Irish Society, 1848–1918*, Dublin: Gill and MacMillan.

Lee, J. (1989) *Ireland, 1912–1985: Politics and Society*, Cambridge: Cambridge University Press.

Lee, J. (1991) 'The Irish constitution of 1937', in Hutton, S. and Stewart, P. (eds) *Ireland's Histories: Aspects of State, Society and Ideology*, London: Routledge.

Loughlin, J. (1990) 'Some comparative aspects of Irish and English nationalism in the late nineteenth century', in Hill, M. and Barber, S. (eds) *Aspects of Irish Studies*, Belfast: Institute of Irish Studies.

Lyons, F.S.L. (1979) *Culture and Anarchy in Ireland, 1890–1939*, Oxford: Oxford University Press.

MacDonagh, O. (1983) *States of Mind: a Study of Anglo-Irish Conflict, 1780–1980*, London: Pimlico.

Morgan, H. (1991) 'Milesians, Ulstermen and Fenians', *Linen Hall Review*, December: 14–16.

Murphy, D. (1978) *A Place Apart*, Edinburgh: John Murray.

O'Faolain, S. (1960) *The Irish*, London: Penguin.

O'Halloran, C. (1987) *Partition and the Limits of Irish Nationalism*, Atlantic Highlands, NJ: Humanities Press International.

Pearce, D.G. (1989) *Conservation Today*, London: Longman.

Pringle, D.G. (1985) *One Island, Two Nations*, Letchworth: Research Studies Press.

Sharpe, R. (1984) 'Some problems concerning the organisation of the church in early medieval Ireland', *Peritia* 3: 230–70.

Smyth, W.J. (1993) 'The making of Ireland: agendas and perspectives in cultural geography', in Graham, B.J. and Proudfoot, L.J. (eds) *An Historical Geography of Ireland*, London: Academic Press.

Tunbridge, J.E. (1984) 'Whose heritage to conserve?', *Canadian Geographer* 28: 171–80.

Walker, G. (1990) 'Irish nationalism and the uses of history', *Past and Present* 126: 203–14.

Watson, G. (1991) 'Landscape in Ulster poetry', in Dawe, G. and Foster, J.W. (eds) *The Poet's Place: Ulster Literature and Society*, Belfast: Institute of Irish Studies.

Western, J. (1985) 'Undoing the colonial city?', *Geographical Review* 75: 335–57.

Whelan, K. (1991) 'Settlement and society in eighteenth-century Ireland', in Dawe, G. and Foster, J.W. (eds) *The Poet's Place: Ulster Literature and Society*, Belfast: Institute of Irish Studies.

Williams, M. (1989) 'Historical geography and the concept of landscape', *Journal of Historical Geography* 15: 92–104.

9

THE RENAISSANCE OF CULTURAL VERNACULARISM IN GERMANY

J. Soane

THE GENERAL POST-WAR SITUATION

The tourist perception of aesthetically pleasing, heritage-oriented townscapes in central Europe, now made more accessible by the ending of the cold war, must never be mistaken for the much deeper and more complex values that are associated with historic building ensembles by the indigenous inhabitants of this highly varied region. The continuing existence of a deep respect for the intangible worth of ancient physical artefacts, irrespective of any revived cultural value they may acquire for the tourist, relates directly to two conflicting factors. These are, first, the late survival there, to a considerable degree until well into the twentieth century, in comparison with the Atlantic economic world, of both the social and physical attributes of preindustrial urban lifestyles and, second, the late arrival of the disruptive impact of comprehensive industrialization. By 1900, the general desire for change and modernity within developed countries was quite widespread. However, throughout Imperial Germany and the Austro-Hungarian lands, the cultural viability of numerous surviving historic townscapes which encompassed a more corporate civic tradition than existed in western Europe and North America was threatened by a growing diversification of new social and spatial functions.

Entire medieval city centres were sometimes left undisturbed as industrialization rapidly proceeded apace in other parts of the same towns, as was the case at Nuremburg, Frankfurt and Brunswick. In other cases, considerable areas of historic townscape were swept

away by the construction of new streets lined by elaborate commercial and administrative buildings, designed in a variety of historicist
styles. At Hanover, many of the older vernacular buildings were
replaced during the 1880s by considerable numbers of larger
multipurpose structures in neo-Italianate form, a type of architecture universally popular during this epoch for the adornment of
new urban areas within expanding cities. Yet these alien intrusions
were to exist for a mere fifty years. Together with the adjacent
surviving preindustrial townscape, they were destroyed by military
action; and replaced in their turn by very different townscape
structures between 1943 and 1970 (Hammer-Schenk and Lange
1985: 139–76).

The reason for this short diversion into the recent past is to
demonstrate the exceptionally abrupt impact, and uneasy acceptance, of international economic and planning influences over the
past century within the German regions of Europe. Between the
end of the Second Reich in 1918 and German reunification in 1990,
political and military events made it difficult for a more balanced
synthesis to begin between more vernacular patterns of central
European urban culture and the very different urbanizing tradition
of the Atlantic economic world. The destruction of much of the
central European urban environment between 1939 and 1945 caused
a most severe and traumatic jolt to millions of town dwellers, who
were faced with the brutal and seemingly irredeemable loss of the
hitherto seamless and accepted background to their daily lives
(Stoilov 1987: 30–1). According to Georg Lill, the Conservator-
General of Bavaria, writing in 1946, 'Nuremburg gave the spectacle
of a huge pile of rubbish, a jumble of wires, pipes and installations
and everywhere masonry carelessly cast about giving the appearance
of disturbed mounds of earth instead of what we had hitherto
known from the drawings of Durer' (Petzet 1984: 5).

The problem of bringing together increasing social and economic
polarities, in effect matching form to function in what remained of
shattered urban environments, was a matter of exceptional concern
throughout central Europe. Many destroyed or badly damaged
regional centres having strong vernacular traditions – especially in
Western Germany – were faced with a brutal choice. For urgent
economic reasons, they could allow their commercial centres to be
reconstructed in the international, Modernist style, and risk the
steady division of formerly integrated social and economic functions in an increasingly separated, Anglo-American, urban environ-

ment. Alternatively, they could risk general political and social censure by attempting to reconstruct a facsimile of destroyed architectural and spatial structures in a pseudo-vernacular style which, immediately after 1945, had been discredited as the style had been fostered by the housing policies of the Third Reich.

Instead, under the additional influence of dominant radical Social Democratic political influences, rigid spatial planning ideas – especially in respect to new residential neighbourhoods – were now given *carte blanche* in the huge reconstruction and replanning schemes that followed. In Germany, on either side of the new Iron Curtain, whether in the name of state-directed social policies or for entirely commercial motives, Modernist concepts of design which had previously been excluded by conservative pressures and the integrated cohesiveness of hitherto undamaged urban cores, now held sway and invaded the centres of towns and cities virtually unchallenged.

The all-pervading social philosophy of universal change and renewal, which characterized parties of both Right and Left by the mid-twentieth century, ensured that there would be a natural bias against the preservation or rebuilding of integrated groups of houses, often on grounds of public health and social control. Such preservation or rebuilding had been a more usual feature of town life before the Second World War. Moreover, the conservation of surviving façades of architecturally significant buildings or streets was sometimes disregarded, as at Würzburg, on grounds of cost in the hasty scramble to reconstruct formerly prosperous commercial centres as quickly as possible (Pacykowski 1982).

Certain planning conventions began to evolve between 1945 and 1960. Apart from the reconstruction of churches and official administrative buildings, the damaged central areas were usually rebuilt in the form of large, modern commercial or service blocks, on much simplified plot plans and along existing streets and squares that were usually widened to accommodate the anticipated increase in traffic. Furthermore, many traditional residential neighbour-hoods, often consisting of numerous individual plots in the near vicinity of the central areas, were rebuilt for secondary commercial or light industrial purposes, thereby further dividing the formerly more integrated working and domestic aspects of urban life. At Cologne, not only was the medieval core rebuilt in a modern style, using much larger plot ratios, but it was also bisected by an inner relief road which, by attracting large commercial buildings to its periphery, invariably destroyed the homogeneity of the pre-war townscape. A relatively small section of the Old Town was some-what loosely rebuilt on a more traditional scale and with relatively inaccurate detailing, to show off the cathedral silhouette in relation to the river-side view of the entire city (Muuss 1972).

The radical planning priorities that dominated the rebuilding plans for the Old Town of Frankfurt, a legacy from its pre-war Modernist social housing settlements pioneered by the town planner Ernst May, are well demonstrated by the uncompromisingly rigid, if logical, proposals that were prepared in 1961 by the American architect Shadrach Woods (Woods 1975: 122–9). They would have served the same utilitarian purpose as an old medieval city, but without its evolved social and aesthetic relationships. After part of this site was used for the construction of very modern polygonal civic offices, enormous surprise was expressed by architects and conservationists alike at the reversal in public and municipal opinion in favour of reconstructing the old houses on the Römerplatz. An uneasy compromise was achieved with the Modernist faction and a so-called 'happening' complex in a plastic, post-modern style was incorporated in the vicinity of the cathedral. Moreover, houses in eclectic guise were then built round the corner in the neighbouring Saalgasse (Kiesow 1984: 2–10).

The extent of the difficulty in bridging the gulf between Modernist exclusiveness on the part of planners and architects on the one hand, and the first stirrings of a repressed vernacular instinct by particular city populations on the other, is a measure of how deep the strife over the final post-war evolution of German townscape had become by the 1970s. Indeed, the extent of these differences could be seen in the achievements of those German towns that, against all prevailing fashion, were rebuilt along more traditional lines. At Freiburg, Münster and Würzburg, a decision was consciously taken, at an early stage of rebuilding, to adhere to original medieval street structures and to ensure that the new buildings, while being fully adapted to modern urban life, adhered to the general forms and proportions of their destroyed predecessors.

In Nuremburg, which, despite intensive industrialization dur-ing the latter part of the nineteenth century, still exhibited an exceptional degree of civic solidarity, the most important priority was the recovery of the city's unique sense of identity. This was expressed by Heinz Schmeissner, the Chief Planner, as 'the preservation of the concept of Nuremburg'. There were three possible courses of action to consider; an accurate stone-by-stone reconstruction of the medieval Old Town; a modern rebuilding in the form of rectangular streets and straight, high-density blocks of commercial buildings and residential apartments; or a sensitive compromise using modern forms of construction but following, to a greater or lesser degree, the forms and proportions of the original structures, the medieval road pattern except for some essential widening, and the pre-war location of the principal retail streets.

Although extensive areas of the Old Town had been completely destroyed, after much discussion it was eventually decided to attempt the third option. One of the principal reasons for this decision, apart from the force of local tradition, was the existence of extensive remains of old structures throughout the destroyed areas. It has been calculated that 41 per cent of all new houses erected in the centre of Nuremburg since 1945 were within 25 metres of the ruins of historic structures. Another factor was the general ease by which the local building tradition could be adapted to suit the needs of modern society. The typical old Nuremburg house was a plain, unadorned structure of two to three storeys, sometimes with an oriel window, but always with a steeply pitched roof and several attics. As long as the unique roofscape was reproduced (Figure 9.1), the proportions of the replacement houses could be properly adapted to accommodate as many floors and as many domestic alterations as were deemed appropriate. The lack of much traditional ornament was also an advantage to modern, efficiency-minded building techniques. External balconies, widely used on interior façades in the 1950s, would closely resemble another well-established, medieval architectural characteristic of the Old Town if used now on exterior façades.

The chief deficiency in the reconstruction has been the considerable reduction of individual house plots (from 3,040 square metres in 1939 to 1,360 square metres by 1970) in favour of the construction of larger houses on two or more amalgamated plots. Although this change has resulted in a certain reduction of absolute visual authenticity, it does not detract from the general success of the overall appearance of the reconstruction. Even at the risk of a certain degree of monotony in respect of the façades of individual buildings, in general terms the four major aims of the rebuilding of the Old Town – the preservation of major monuments, their integration into a sympathetic urban environment, the preservation of the essential layout and social structure of the medieval centre and the effective isolation of the latter from the rest of the city

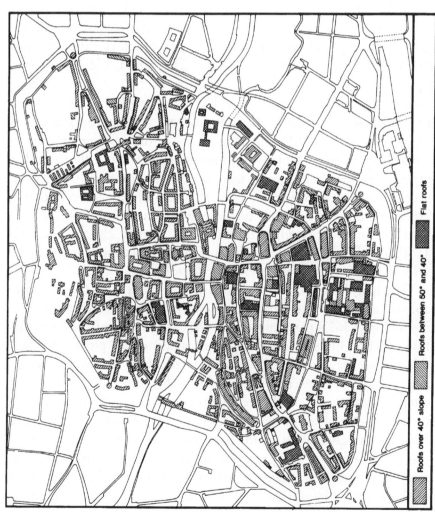

Figure 9.1 Nuremburg, roof structure
Source: Redrawn from E. Mulzer, *Der Wiederafbau der Alstadt von Nürmburg*, University of Erlangen, 1972

Roofs over 40° slope   Roofs between 50° and 40°   Flat roofs

– have been achieved (Görl 1978; Mulzer 1972; Fallstudie Nürnburg 1981; Petzet 1984).

However, irrespective of the fact that conservatively rebuilt towns had, by default, anticipated planning attitudes to the built past that have now found increasing favour in Germany, less than twenty years ago they were considered to be deviant manifestations of urban communities that still wished to identify themselves strongly with the social and spatial attributes of the preindustrial urban environment. Indeed, strong contemporary planning pressures in Nuremburg during the 1960s ensured that a portion of the Old Town was rebuilt in a somewhat freer Modernistic style.

By the early 1970s, communities could still be divided over the extent to which their built form was meant to be an integrating and stabilizing influence in an unpredictable social world. In Mainz, the reconstruction of half of the Old Town in a relatively indifferent and imperfectly designed parody of what had been destroyed, in conjunction with post-war property speculation and chronic indecision with respect to a clearly defined redevelopment plan, resulted in a general lack of interest in, and subsequent neglect of, the surviving urban fabric (Jung 1987: 45–51). Although official interest in the rehabilitation of the existing historic quarters was successfully promoted, albeit at the eleventh hour, what is significant is that there was an ambivalent perception about the ultimate morphological importance of both parts of the same Old Town, which were separated only by a wide thoroughfare.

A CLASH OF PLANNING PHILOSOPHIES?

It was becoming increasingly evident by the 1970s that a much broader view should be taken with regard to the future appearance and function of the German urban environment. Those involved began to ask more fundamental questions. What part of the surviving historic infrastructure should be valued in ephemeral terms, that is, according to its varying value to the proprietor, and what proportion should be valued in absolute terms according to its accepted current or future cultural significance? How, indeed, should such priorities be identified and how should natural economic and political pressures affect enduring folk-vernacular traditions? Other considerations that had, and still have, to be faced included the extent to which the social image of a particular place could or should be out of synchronization with the urban environment; the degree to which European towns should remain places of classical harmony or centres of dynamic innovation, and the extent to which the political, economic and technological imperatives of the modern state should be allowed to have a significant impact on the quality of life of existing townscapes.

According to Worner Durth, a leading German theoretical environmentalist, the functioning environmental spirit or *Ortgeist* of any town is a distinct and unfathomable entity which, under proper circumstances, should be a humane and orderly integrator of the pluralistic chaos of modern society. In order to achieve this aim, it would be necessary for town planners and their political masters to respect the distinctive morphological characteristics of particular urban environments which operate independently of perceived theoretical planning conceptions (Durth 1977: 163–7). Unfortunately, attempts to achieve a more balanced perception of the relationship between the aesthetic character and the appropriate social and economic activities of particular urban environments were further complicated by philosophical differences towards urban planning in the Anglo-American and central European worlds.

The Atlanticist school of thought is mainly, although not exclusively, associated with a tradition of academic urban research stretching back to the Chicago School and beyond. It has tended to focus more on the interaction of relatively unchanging, legalistic, administrative, economic and utilitarian influences within a horizontally segregated concept of space in shaping the physical and social environment of cities. This approach is well illustrated by diagrams illustrating patterns of urban function in a recent American work on urban planning (Stearns and Montag 1981). Here, irrespective of specific issues, there is a general tendency to use the physical and social structure of the city as a sounding-board for the utilization of a premeditated ecosystem. By contrast, a diagrammatic illustration from a recent publication on the history of Berlin shows contrasting visual elements of part of the townscape of the inner city (Kleihues 1987). The assumption here is that the aesthetic and social relationships, as defined by the street itself, and not merely its wider relationships with more structural, fiscal and utilitarian considerations, are what also define the sense of place of large urban areas. This approach to the urban environment, more typical of the nineteenth-century Austrian town planning theorist Camillo Sitte, gives equal importance to the essential aesthetic, social and functional elements within a more integrated townscape that should bridge the cultural and spatial disparities between medieval and early-modern, and industrial and Modernist, planning imperatives.

By the mid-1970s, the continuing confusion of these two points of view in the achievement of an equitable relationship between form and function within newly emerging German townscapes was still evident. In particular, Atlanticist concepts of urban zoning continued to exert, in indirect ways, a negative morphological impact on the more integrationist susceptibility of the German world. Quite apart from the poor rebuilding and continuing unimaginative use of considerable areas of some cities, the fiscal importance of land, as against its equitable disposition for both private and public use, still appeared to be the guiding principle of town planning strategies. This not only prevented poorer people from remaining in older-established residential districts adjacent to town centres, but also tended to make further, apparently unnecessary, divisions between previously undivided lifestyles. On the one hand, the generally inviting appearance of new retail outlets would quite easily tend to attract ready purchasers of all classes. On the other hand, the concentration of commercial enterprises and the gentrification of centrally located residential property would reduce the socio-spatial relationship between the centre and outer city neighbourhoods (Durth 1977: 11–22).

It was, in fact, a growing re-evaluation of the hitherto generally unappreciated areas of older – or secondary – townscapes between designated commercial and outer residential areas, which had often been rebuilt or renovated in a somewhat neutral, even bland architectural form, that would help to give rise to the rebirth of cultural vernacularism in towns throughout Germany. With the completion of post-war rebuilding by 1970, and stimulated by urban conservation movements in neighbouring European countries culminating in the European Architectural Heritage Year organized in 1975, a fundamental change of German urban environmental perceptions began to take place, in conjunction with a continuing recovery of German self-esteem.

The extent to which it was necessary to have such rigidly defined functional differences of use between different parts of the same city increasingly began to be questioned. It followed from this that if different functions became more integrated, the differences of architectural spatial form which distinguished these functions from each other would also become less relevant. A popular demand grew steadily for a return to multifunctional streets, more intimate open spaces and the better provision of affordable houses built to a more human scale. This demand was not solely confined to Germany: to many, indeed, these demands offered the best prospects for the renaissance of more traditional German urban lifestyles which, for a mixture of political and aesthetic reasons, had been suppressed since 1945 (Petzet 1975: 19, 22; Appleyard 1979: 7–37).

THE RISE OF THE NEW VERNACULARISM

The detailed social and spatial implications of this new approach to urban questions were gradually accepted by a new generation of urban planners in Germany. The result was a growing participatory interest in the benefits of more integrated townscapes which developed among the public at large. This whole process involved a much greater degree of attention to the evolutionary pattern of every aspect of urban topography.

At an administrative level, it was finally conceded by many *Länder* government representatives that the hitherto unquestioned hegemony of planning and economic ideologies should give way to a greater respect for the more diverse lifestyles and more irregular spatial disposition of older existing townscapes. Architects were no longer expected to change entire neighbourhoods willy-nilly, but to make a positive contribution to the existing urban scene. Indeed, more and more cities began to appoint special officials to advise potential developers on how their projected schemes would best fit into the existing urban fabric. It was also increasingly felt that the much richer and more educated society that existed in Germany in the immediate post-war period no longer needed such close guidance towards a more perfectly regulated society. Instead, more people felt that modern industrial techniques should now be used to create in a more efficient manner the wider variety of building and decorative materials required for new buildings, now increasingly being constructed using old forms.

The desire to achieve a deeper social integration of the population by the improvement of their physical environment has been the aim of continuing restoration projects within the extensive, but formerly much decayed, craft-worker quarter of Augsburg – the

Lechviertel – since 1976. The basic impetus towards the rehabilitation of the area was to arrest the rapid depopulation and decay of these neighbourhoods – which now contained a high proportion of immigrant 'guest workers' – and to prevent them from becoming a secondary service area for the commercial sector of the city. In order to encourage a traditional mix of residents, small service crafts and retail establishments, various council departments contributed funds for the restoration of neglected properties which, in turn, stimulated private enterprise to fund further restoration (Sajons 1984, 1987, 1991). In several instances, original restored buildings would be complemented by new buildings, sympathetically blended into existing townscapes; some would be financed by the town as subsidized housing, and others built by private enterprise.

A good example of this policy in action was the rehabilitation of the St Ulrich's/Spitalgasse district in the southern part of the Old Town during the 1980s. This area, containing a number of late-medieval and later artisan houses, had become very neglected over the years, and parts were also subjected to unsuitable industrial uses. The most important aspects of the scheme were the construction of a new street – the St Ulrich's Gasse – in a very derelict area, the general visual improvement of the surrounding narrow lanes, and the reduction of traffic usage throughout the entire neighbourhood. Ninety-one social housing units were built by the City Council, and thirty-three new or renovated flats were constructed by private enterprise.

Because of the general dominance of new construction in the St Ulrich's Gasse, although the new apartment buildings were built in a generally traditional form, the design did not attempt an accurate imitation of the adjacent ancient townscape. In other places, however, for example the Peter Rotzen Gasse where elements of the surviving townscape were more dominant, new social housing replacing existing property was more respectful of the earlier built environment. Throughout the area, as for example in the Kirchgasse, the Zwerchgasse, the Spitalgasse and the Sauerngreinwinkel, public and especially private initiatives have restored a considerable number of ancient buildings – some dating back to 1500 – for residential and community use. The two main aims of the entire rehabilitation programme in Augsburg have been to preserve historic townscapes in the Old Town from further service encroachment and to restore the previously balanced social fabric of the unique sixteenth-century craft-worker districts.

The ideal of restoring the social and spatial balance of decayed urban ensembles was increasingly extended to the comprehensive improvement, and even partial reconstruction, of entire inner-city neighbourhoods. At Ulm, where 80 per cent of the Old Town was destroyed during the Second World War, the increasing need to recreate the vitality of the city centre has led not only to a more sympathetic rebuilding of destroyed areas, but also to a restructuring of surviving landscapes that had been adversely affected by wartime damage and subsequent upheavals. In three medieval streets to the north and east of the Minster, reconstruction and rehabilitation took place mainly in the 1960s, the 1970s and late 1980s. As can be clearly observed, there has been an increasing degree of vernacular sensitivity in the new buildings erected in each successive decade. This tendency reflects the increasing interest of ordinary Germans in a more integrated urban environment. In the mid-1980s, therefore, a scheme similar to that at Augsburg was launched for the general improvement of the living quality, the building structure and the appearance of the townscape in north-central Ulm.

A 15 per cent sample survey of environmental attitudes to the urban morphology of the city (Figure 9.2) showed a paradoxical clash of preindustrial and postindustrial values (Ulm 1985: 52–4). While most of the respondents were in favour of the friendly, easy-going and generally well-ordered atmosphere of neighbourhoods in the form of the traditional vernacular environments, this could only be achieved at the cost of excessive noise, high-density housing and relatively small open spaces. Irrespective of the good intentions of city and town councils to preserve the social balance and the general built intensity of many evolved or reconstructed neighbourhoods, it has become clear that most people were in favour of these initiatives, provided that the technical advantages of contemporary lifestyles were not excessively compromised. General perceptions of vernacularism could still be satisfied if buildings that proved impossible to adapt to the needs of the late twentieth century were eventually replaced by well-designed facsimiles on a somewhat larger scale which respected modernized conceptions of ancient German urban culture. Indeed, the more accurate marketing of these more popular spatial concepts has now begun to be manifest not only in residential neighbourhoods, but also in the commercial areas of the large cities.

The main eastern approach to the business centre of Augsburg

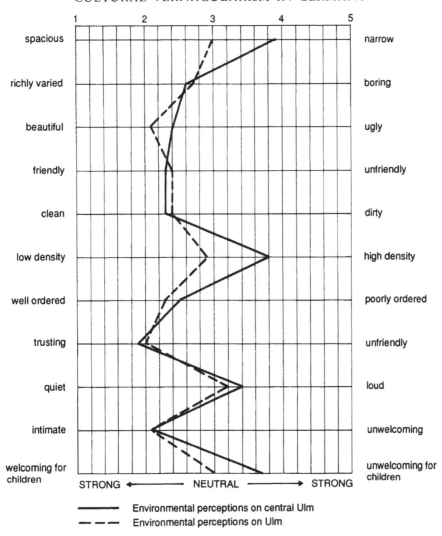

Figure 9.2 Attitudes towards the built environment
Source: Redrawn from Ulm, 1985

– the Karl Strasse – exhibits the stylistic confusion that has troubled local building entrepreneurs over the last thirty years. Only a kilometre further along the same road, at the Jakobs Platz, there is a recent, much more competent, handling of a new office and retail development which demonstrates greater respect for regional architectural susceptibilities. By the later 1980s, increasing utilization of more design-conscious layouts for important and costly redevelopment schemes had become more significant. This general trend first became manifest in southern Germany, where the increasing momentum of the international post-modernist/vernacular revival

171

began to interrelate with the existing, if still somewhat regional, neo-classical town planning tradition. It was the abiding strength of this distinctive characteristic, preserved by the relatively late arrival of industrialization in the region, which enabled the war damaged city of Munich to be rebuilt in a generally conservative fashion. The existing street layout, the general vernacular form and multifarious usage of the evolved building tradition were retained, and the introduction of inner ring roads within the ancient centre was prevented (Denkmäler 1987: 6–7).

The influence of these revived architectural and spatial priorities have now begun to create a considerable improvement in the general appearance of townscapes in the centre of larger German towns and cities. Considerable numbers of poorly designed commercial struc-tures put up between c. 1948 and 1970 have begun to be drastically remodelled. In central Munich, the ancient Sendling Strasse has been rebuilt with increasingly well styled buildings over the last twenty years, culminating in the current remodelling of the massive glass office building at the junction with Rosental.

The wider implications of the rediscovery of the physical attri-butes of German vernacularism have been considerable. Generally enhanced esteem for West German urban cultural traditions was indirectly responsible for the undermining of public support for the communist regime in the east during 1989. In the German Democratic Republic, even more than in the Federal Republic, ideological support for Modernist planning principles either had the effect of imparing the appearance of the outskirts of undamaged towns while the historic quarters were left to decay or, where ancient centres had been destroyed, the areas were usually totally rearranged with wide straight streets and monstrous slab-like structures of unbelievable banality and ugliness.

In Dresden, where the incomparable high-density baroque town-scape of the eighteenth century was destroyed in 1945, apart from individually restored masterpieces such as the Zwinger and the Opera House, the complex street and plot divisions of the Old Town were completely ignored. Large, widely spaced residential blocks and shopping areas were erected in their place. Even if some deference was paid to post-modernism by the mid-1980s, newly planned projects retained significant backward-looking character-istics due to having to conform to an official ideological line on economic hegemony and Modernist town planning (Union 1985). With the fall of the East German communist regime in 1990 new, more integrative planning attitudes, which had been evolving during the later 1980s, were at last given their head.

The most important change was the replacement of socialist functionalism with aesthetic design-oriented conceptions to prepare the appearance of Dresden for its 800-year jubilee in AD 2026. According to the latest proposals, the most important priority will be the protection of the built townscape of the inner city in close association with the surrounding riverine landscape of the Elbe (*Bauwelt* 1990: 2436–41). A balanced synthesis of these two major design elements is considered absolutely essential, for both the preservation and the further enhancement of the exceptional built quality of the Saxon capital. It is therefore proposed that the eighteenth-century terracing, that still exists above the Elbe in the Old Town, should be eventually extended in somewhat simpler form on either side of the town centre, replacing existing, somewhat derelict industrial areas with new service and educational facilities.

Within the Old Town itself, there will be a comprehensive reintroduction of the wide variety of high-quality cultural, retail and tourist facilities that existed in this area before 1945. For this reason, the more intricate and irregular medieval and baroque street pattern in the vicinity of the Neu and, to a lesser extent, the Alt Markt will be re-established (Landeshauptstadt Dresden 1991: 13–35). This will entail the rehabilitation or complete re-creation of outstanding historic structures, together with a new and more sympathetic interpretation of the former townscape, now vanished, of town houses and lesser palaces. Although the final detailed architectural form of the Old Town is yet to be determined, the former spatial and monumental relationship between built and unbuilt space will be respected at all costs. For this reason, no new buildings above seven storeys in height will be allowed in the centre, and the Frauenkirke will be rebuilt, in order to complete the famous eighteenth-century silhouette of the city when viewed from the Elbe. Apart from the special treatment of the Old Town, poorly designed residential neighbourhoods beyond the inner city will be remodelled, and various sectors of the inner/outer built-up area, long divided by excessively wide roads such as the Alt-Stadt Ring, will be reconstructed by means of a more traditional, denser building pattern of mixed residential commercial and service use, and incorporating a much improved public transport system.

Perhaps in no other major city has there been such a dramatic turnaround from a rigidly imposed Modernist, anti-historicist planning philosophy to an opposite vision in which the principal functional elements of the city are integrated and subordinated to an all-embracing and integrated aesthetic ideal as is the case in Dresden. This change was, in its own way, as abrupt as was the introduction of Modernist planning practices on a large scale in Germany during the 1940s. However, in seeking to place the rise of post-modernism/vernacularism into a wider European perspective, it would be wrong to suggest that Germany is the only place where the stark dichotomy between concepts of preindustrial architectural design and space and the advent of Modernist planning principles has had to be faced.

In Great Britain, and to some extent in France, a combination of relatively severe wartime damage and the rapid spread of cost-conscious Modernist speculative development by national commercial and residential property concerns had a significant adverse effect on surviving provincial vernacular building traditions up to about 1970. Irrespective of an early trend before this date towards what is now called post-modernism/neo-vernacularism (cf. Larkham 1988) by local development agencies, a nationwide drift in this direction by large investment corporations was not noticeable until the later 1970s (Whitehand and Larkham 1989: 217–71; Larkham 1988: 148–64; Punter 1990: 119–24, 378–80). Certainly, in Britain as in Germany, the growing impact of the urban conservation lobby has considerably lessened the pace of change in the built environment; new building developments in the vicinity of preindustrial townscapes have become more design-conscious.

If, however, a more visually integrated townscape is the final result in both countries, the recent political history and continuing cultural distinctiveness of central Europe suggest that very different ethical values are still likely to be read into these achievements in Germany compared with the Atlantic world. The relatively early separation of places of residence and work in Great Britain, and to an even greater extent in North America, ensured that not only would a more devolved valuation of historic buildings become more prevalent, but that purely aesthetic factors alone would be far more likely to be decisive in conservation/planning disputes.

By contrast, in the German regions of Europe, the much later and more reluctant break-up of many hitherto socially and economically integrated communities ensured that the preservation, rehabilitation and re-creation of distinctive areas of historic townscapes would be valued as much for being representative of the highest achievements of regional folk culture as for being objects of aesthetic admiration. Under such circumstances, modern German spatial concepts have usually included an extra morphological element beyond the normative aesthetic and functional assessment of urban space. The fostering of a distinctive social consciousness which integrates planning proposals with the built reality which they create is now considered of particular significance (Durth 1977: 39–42).

Moreover, the equal importance given in Germany to the emotional and visual elements of human activity, in which ideally there should be no difference in quality between the tourist's and the inhabitant's experiences of delight at the local street scene, can be related to general morphological theories which equate the existence of the distinctive spirit of a place to everyday experiences derived from the unique structure and influence of surviving historic and later townscapes (Conzen 1975; Whitehand and Larkham 1989: 253–5). Yet within this concept, deeper and more intractable cultural influences continue to foster important differences.

Whereas there may be genuine aesthetic satisfaction at the more vernacular trend in modern design among certain more enlightened circles in Britain and North America, the resurgence of civic pride among a wide spectrum of society in certain German towns such as Hildesheim or Augsburg following the rehabilitation or reconstruction of some distinctive historic architectural or spatial feature has become quite remarkable in recent years. In the last analysis, the degree of folk-vernacular defensiveness in Germany demonstrated in the veneration or the re-creation of historic buildings can be directly related to the general morphological pressures of alien political and economic systems that became dominant there after 1945. It may now be that with the final collapse of the post-Second World War geo-political structure following the breaching of the Berlin Wall in 1989, the obligation of the German world to conform to the distinctive architectural and spatial forms of its former conquerors/liberators is no longer necessary or relevant.

The decision of the Berlin Senate to rebuild the Leipziger and Potsdamer Platz according to the older, classical nineteenth-century Berlin building traditions, in the face of intense Atlanticist and Japanese architectural and financial pressure, is a sign that perhaps, at last, the evolved townscape tradition of central Europe is now sufficiently confident and adaptable to take its place on equal terms with the built achievements of the remainder of the post-industrialized world (*Die Welt* 1991).

REFERENCES

Appleyard, D. (1979) *The Conservation of European Cities*, Cambridge, Mass.: MIT Press.

Bauwelt (1990) 48: 2436–41.

Conzen, M.R.G. (1975) 'Geography and townscape conservation', in Uhlig, H. and Lienau, C. (eds) 'Anglo-German symposium in applied geography, Giessen-Würzburg-München, 1973', *Giessener Geographische Schriften* 1975: 95–102.

Durth, W. (1977) 'Die Inzenierung der Altagswelt', *Bau Welt Fundament* 47: 9–57, 161–94.

Fallstudie Nürnburg (1981) *Stadtentwicklung und Erhaltung alter Städte in Europa*, Bonn: German UNESCO Council.

Görl, O.P. (1978) 'The reconstruction of the Old Town of Nuremburg' (translated by N. Fry), *The Connoisseur* 199: 154–63.

Hammer-Schenk, H. and Lange, D. (1985) *Alte Stadt Moderne Zeiten*, Hanover: Cord Meckseper.

Jung, W. (1987) 'Rettung im letzten Augenblick', *Mainz* 4: 45–9.

Kiesow, G. (1984) 'Die Neubebauung des Dom-Römerberg-Bereiches in Frankfurt am Main', *Deutsche Kunst und Denkmalpflege* 42, 1: 2–10.

Kleihues, J. (1987) *750 Jahr Architektur und Städtebau in Berlin*, Berlin: Gerd Hatje.

Landeshauptstadt Dresden (1991) *Planungsleitbild Innenstadt*, Dresden: City Council.

Larkham, P.J. (1988) 'Agents and types of change in the conserved townscape', *Transactions of the Institute of British Geographers* NS 13, 2: 148–64.

Mulzer, E. (1972) 'Der Wiederaufbau der Altstadt von Nürnburg', *University of Erlangen Geographical Studies Series*.

München (1985) *Denkmäler in Bayern*, Munich: Oldenburg Verlag.

Muuss, U. (1972) *Luftbildatlas, Bundesrepublik Deutschland*, Munich: Paul List Verlag.

Pacykowski, J. (1982) *Der Wiederaufbau der Stadt Würzburg nach 1945*, Munich.

Petzet, M. (1975) 'Ein Zukunft für unsere Vergangenheit', in Petzet, M. (ed.) *Ein Zukunft für unsere Vergangenheit*, Munich: Bayerische Landkreis für Denkmalpflege.

Petzet, M. (1984) 'Denkmalpflege in Nürnburg', *Denkmalpflege Informationen* 45: 1–16.

Punter, J.V. (1990) *Design Control in Bristol, 1940–1990*, Bristol: Redcliffe Press.

Sajons, R. (1984) *Sanierung in Augsburg*, Augsburg: Stadt Augsburg.

Sajons, R. (1987) 'Altstadtsanierung: Zum Beispeil Augsburg', *Die Alte Stadt* 3/87: 294–313.

Sajons, R. (1991) *Sanierung in Augsburg*, Augsburg: Stadt Augsburg.

Stearns, F. and Montag, T. (eds) (1981) *The Urban Ecosystem*, New York: Halstead Press.

Stoilov, G. (1987) 'Planning and conservation', in *Third International Congress on Architecture, Conservation and Town Planning*, London: Heritage Trust.

Ulm S4 (1985) Altstadtsanierung, *Stadtmitte Münster*.

Union (1985) 'Ein neues Tor zur historischen Stadt', *Union* 7 October 1985.

Die Welt (1991) 5–6 October 1991.

Whitehand, J.W.R. and Larkham, P.J. (1989) 'La morfologia urbana i la planificació dels paisatges urbans històrics a la Gran Bretanya', in Claverol, L. and Vilagrasa, J. (eds) *Història urbana i intervenció en el centre històric*, Barcelona: Institut Cartogràfic de Catalunya.

Woods, S. (1975) *The Man in the Street*, Harmondsworth: Penguin.

10

URBAN HERITAGE IN THE CZECH REPUBLIC

R. Hammersley and T. Westlake

INTRODUCTION

The disintegration of the Iron Curtain over recent years has opened up a vast tract of Europe not only to eager tourists, but also to those who are concerned for the conservation of historic townscapes. It is now much more widely realized in the 'west' that the towns of the 'east' contain a storehouse of valuable assets, with exciting prospects for the understanding, enjoyment and promotion of urban heritage (see Figure 10.1). It must also be realized that these assets, which have come to us through a strange combination of circumstances, are under threat from insensitive exploitation, the poverty of maintenance agencies and the march of unthinking commercial redevelopment. Those from both east and west concerned with urban conservation need to raise the awareness among relevant controlling authorities that underpins sensible policies for heritage protection. The worry is that the rush towards 'free markets', especially in property development, will overrun and disable conservation interests. Most of the regimes of the former Soviet bloc had building conservation organizations in place, funded and managed from the centre; these organizations are today viewed by the new entrepreneurial class with deep suspicion, and by new governments as superfluous in times of economic stringency. The task is now to re-establish the legitimacy of conservation and heritage-related policies and expenditure without falling into the trap of using urban heritage indiscriminately, as mere bait to draw in the tourists.

This chapter examines the raw material, current status and prospects for urban conservation in one of the former 'eastern' countries, namely the Czech Republic (often referred to as the Czech

Figure 10.1 Town square of Telč
Source: Photograph by T. Westlake

Lands). This country – consisting of the 'lands' of Bohemia and Moravia – lies at the heart of Europe and is likely to become a test case for the integration of former communist territories into (western) European political, economic and social traditions. After forty-one years of communist rule, in which the majority of the economy was brought into state ownership, Czechoslovakia returned to a democratic system at the end of 1989. Following the formation of a new Czechoslovak government and parliament in June 1990, the machinery was set in place for the re-creation of a free-market system. This situation was complicated in December 1992 when Czechoslovakia was divided into two republics: the Czech Lands to the west and Slovakia to the east. Although this chapter focuses specifically on the Czech Republic, it is accepted that Slovakia also contains an abundance of urban heritage which is likely to be under similar pressures.

The Czech Republic is one of the richest of the former eastern bloc countries in terms of conservation-worthy townscapes. The destructive capacities of man have fortunately bypassed a majority of historic central urban areas in the Republic. While there is a massive job of maintenance and enhancement to be tackled, at least the basic fabric remains in significant quantities – mostly in good heart and unspoiled by the destruction of war and the over-whelming vandalism of modern redevelopment. There are, of course, many towns which have not escaped – as will be emphasized – but it is contended here that the lack of 'capitalist' priorities for urban development has resulted in a widespread accumulation of heritage treasures, albeit perhaps in a decrepit state.

In Bohemia, the quality of urban development of the past half-century does not match that of previous eras. Apart from a few prestige buildings, the newer areas surrounding the historic cores – and of course the several attempts at building complete new towns and suburbs – display a marked lack of quality and sensitivity. There is a strong contrast between the evident character of the older town cores and the anonymous mega-structures which dominate the expansion areas. The environmental poverty of newer develop-ments seems only to emphasize the attraction of the older parts. This chapter will show that growing financial pressure and the demands for commercial development mean that there are no guarantees that the Czech Republic's wealth of urban heritage will remain into the next century. The urban heritage of the Czech Republic occupies a vital dimension of the totality of European heritage. The country lies at the centre of Europe – a crossroads between north and south (Germanic/Italian), and east and west (French/Slav) – and as such has absorbed into its structures the traditions and influences of Europe as a whole. It is incumbent upon the new Europe, where the post-war demarcation lines have been abandoned, to look to its historic core and to defend the Czech heritage from the unleashing of destructive forces.

THE HERITAGE

The Czech people trace their ancestry back to the Slav tribes which wandered westwards in the Dark Ages and settled in the basin of the Rivers Labe and Vltava. Substantial urban development effectively began in the fourteenth century with the activities of Charles IV, King of Bohemia but more significantly Holy Roman Emperor; he set out to build up Prague as a European city and an administrative, military, commercial and industrial centre. He also furthered the established trend of encouraging the settlement there of skilled craftsmen from Germany. Indeed, the Germanic influence is one which pervades Czech history: the wars of the Reformation marked earlier years, while the vagaries of the Austrian empires dominate the political, social and economic development of the Czech Lands through to the twentieth century.

Therefore, the character of Czech historic towns lies very much within the traditions of central Europe, reflecting Germanic styles with Italian influences. Generally, the town square occupies the heart – bordered by merchants' houses and shops, the town hall and main church – surrounded by a tight-knit cluster of streets responding to the interplay of physical landforms and through routes, focused on river bridges. Interspersed among the packed rows of houses and workshops lie the larger buildings of churches, monasteries and occasional palaces, and the whole area is often dominated by the castle and its defensive adjuncts. Architectural styles for the more grandiose buildings are a mixture of medieval and later Gothic, Renaissance, baroque and classical styles; the smaller buildings are part of a vernacular tradition showing strong allegiances to the south German/Austrian style. The result is an abundance of attractive historic and functional towns (Gotkind 1972).

Some examples of late medieval and Renaissance towns survive virtually unscathed; one is described briefly here in order to establish the nature of the raw material of urban heritage in the

Czech Republic. The small town of Telč in western Moravia represents the best of the many small towns from the Renaissance period which gained their initial significance as market and service/ defensive centres for a relatively restricted agricultural hinterland. The town was rebuilt after a fire in the sixteenth century; it consists of a large rectangular cobbled square, surrounded by arcaded Renaissance buildings extending the length of the square, their impressive façades painted in pastel shades with some exquisite wall paintings – demonstrated in Figure 10.2. At one end of the square are two churches and a superb castle. Telč remains today a perfect example of a sixteenth-century provincial town. Apart from two town gatehouses and the remains of a moat, there is little else to Telč, but the completeness and integrity of the town make it worthy of its World Heritage Site status. The town reflects its rural context and the lack of any later urban development pressure has assured its survival: Telč was, and is, a small rural centre without industry or commerce to force population increase or new development. Its survival is a result of it being an undisturbed backwater; whether that status will continue in the new open society of the Czech Republic is highly unlikely – the coachloads of tourists are already arriving.

In contrast to Telč, the advent of industrialization in the nineteenth century has undoubtedly left its mark on the larger Czech towns; while its impact does not parallel the scale of industrial Britain, companies like Škoda at Plzeň and ČKD in Prague gave towns the beginnings of industrial suburbs, jostling with the preindustrial cores. Indeed today, in towns like Plzeň and Děčín, it is clear that the historic cores have been greatly affected by continued industrial and commercial attrition in the nineteenth and twentieth centuries. Plzeň achieved early fame as a spa and brewing town which, together with new metal industries, formed the basis for rapid urban growth: parts of the historic core still survive, but the tide of industrial development – spreading into arms and power engineering – has all but swamped the former salubrious environs in a welter of pollution and dereliction.

In Prague, nineteenth-century industry certainly gave rise to rapid urban growth and several industrial suburbs displayed a familiar pattern of polluting factories serviced by poor housing and infrastructure. But the industrial landscape of Prague appears somewhat muted when compared with other centres; perhaps this is due to the sharp relief of the area beyond the core, hiding away

Figure 10.2 Examples of merchants' housing in Telč
Source: Photograph by T. Westlake

and constraining the impact of industry. In the central area of the city it was the bureaucracy of government and the commercial markets which provided some pressure to replace older buildings with 'new' offices and living quarters. Also in this era the arrival of the railways, and later trams, forced the pace of change, and because of this the bulk of nineteenth-century development took the form of lateral spread. In the main, the change was evolutionary and the era of the Austro-Hungarian Empire is marked by some fine buildings and developments generally in scale with the older buildings and extending the old street patterns.

Fortunately, redevelopment in central Prague in the nineteenth and early twentieth centuries was largely restricted to the 'Jewish Town' and the city ramparts. The Old Town, the Lesser Town and the Castle area were remarkably little changed; these areas now form a chain of spaces, narrow streets and historic buildings which make up the 'King's Way' stretching from the Castle and St Vitus' Cathedral, crossing the river by the Charles Bridge, to Old Town Square (see Figure 10.3). The mix of architectural styles, variety of monuments, aesthetic experiences and enjoyable ambience is the Prague known to the tourists and rightly attracts attention for its heritage quality. The question of why this part of Prague avoided the fate of so many cities in the nineteenth century remains; the reason must lie in the relative lack of development pressure resulting from the city not being a major European focus of government or of industrial/commercial activity. There was certainly development on a large scale but it was attracted away from the historic core to the 'newer', more open, areas of the New Town, represented today by the larger-scale avenues and axes such as Wenceslas and Charles Squares and Žitná and Sokolská Streets. Not only the medieval street network, but also the scale, character and appearance of that period have been preserved in the central core of Prague (Staňková et al. 1992; City Architect's Office of Prague 1992).

Despite – or perhaps because of – its centrality in Europe, the Czech Lands experienced little military action in the First World War. The collapse of the Austro-Hungarian Empire and the birth of the post-1918 Republic of Czechoslovakia therefore found a territory largely intact from the ravages of war, with a significant industrial base and a people wishing to enter the modern world. Throughout this era there was the inevitable lateral expansion of towns – with population and industrial growth – developing naturally away from the historic town cores. Perhaps the flowering of economic growth in the 1920s should have resulted in more commercial development in town centres, but attention seems to have been focused more on peripheral zones which received a number of salubrious suburban 'planned' housing estates along German lines – such as the Baba and Střešovice suburbs of Prague. These housing areas include many fine examples of inter-war domestic architecture – some with expressive versions of the German Bauhaus style, others reflecting the British garden city models.

The Czech Lands were greatly influenced by the European garden city movement and Ebenezer Howard's ideals as an answer to the rapid growth of a number of Czech towns and cities in the early part of this century. One of the first examples of the Czech garden city movement was a railwaymen's neighbourhood in Louny, which was designed around garden city principles in 1909. A strong link developed between the English and Czech garden city movements, with visits by Unwin to Prague and senior Czech designers to Welwyn in the 1920s (Hague and Prior 1991). Howard's book was translated into Czech in 1924, by which time a variety of garden suburbs were being developed, for example Sporilov, Ostrava and Ořechovka (Musil, Slapeta and Novak 1984). The garden city movement is also evident in Zlín, a company town based around the Bata shoe factory, which was seen as a 'town amongst gardens' (Hague and Prior 1991).

The Czech Lands were soon once more submerged in economic and political upheaval. The Depression of the 1930s culminated in the storm of the Nazi annexation in 1938 of the Sudetenland – where large numbers of German settlers had congregated over the previous centuries – and the occupation of the remainder of Czechoslovakia in 1939. In the Second World War, the Czech Lands experienced little of the mass destruction of other parts of Europe, although the obliteration of the village of Lidice touched the hearts of many. The war also witnessed the removal of virtually all the Jewish population of the country and the confiscation of their property. The liberation of the country by the Soviet and American armies was accomplished without large-scale fighting, and the restored Czechoslovak Republic had relatively little physical devastation and the essential qualities of its towns remained.

At the end of the Second World War, the German population of the former Sudetenland were systematically expelled and their property confiscated. This type of population removal was common

a

b

Figure 10.3   Views along the King's Way, Prague
Source: Sketches by R.A. Cullimore

c

in Europe at the time and passed with limited international comment. Today the rights of former Czech owners of property are being recognized, but the question of German and Jewish dispossession remains untouched. This episode of 'ethnic cleansing' – a phenomenon which has returned to haunt other parts of Europe – would seem to show that, after fifty years and with the effective dispersal of the victims, the question fades away.

In early 1948, the Czechoslovak Communist Party carried out a constitutional *coup d'état*, and the country was rapidly subsumed into the Stalinist model which had become familiar in the rest of eastern Europe. There then followed forty-one years of communist rule which wrought many changes in Czech society and its economy. The effect on new urban development was ultimately equally severe, but the result was to produce a virtual stalemate as far as most historic town cores were concerned.

URBAN HERITAGE UNDER COMMUNISM

The driving force behind communist rule was the maintenance of monolithic power by the party. The Czechoslovak Communist Party saw itself as having the dual function of achieving a 'socialist' society at home and supporting the heart of communism in the Soviet Union. In any conflict between the two objectives, the latter would be paramount. The means to achieve total political control and economic direction lay in the wholesale nationalization of virtually all production, distribution and property. All land and buildings (except for most single-family housing) eventually passed to the ownership of the state; this meant, of course, that historic buildings were then largely in the control of local bureaucrats acting under government direction.

The attitudes of the party towards urban heritage could be characterized as contradictory: on the one hand, these buildings represented the concrete expression of individualistic wealth – the result of the expropriation of labour value; on the other hand, they also represented a needed asset and an artistic expression of man's triumph over nature. Consequently, it is probably fair to say that the strongest strand of government policy towards the urban heritage was to keep it low-key – the problem of definition was best left alone.

Certainly through the 1950s and 1960s, the priorities of the Czechoslovak government lay elsewhere. The defence of the Soviet Union demanded armaments and associated engineering goods, and the survival of the Czech industrial complexes through the Second World War represented a good starting point. Urban development was seen as industrial development to the virtual exclusion of all other types (except that needed to support industry), and largely took the form of extensions to existing plants. Hence industrial towns like Kladno, Ostrava and Brno received investment which today is the cause of so much of the country's pollution problems. Indeed, the demand for energy to power industry resulted in the demolition of the town of Most in order to extract the brown coal which lay below with an opencast mine. It is interesting now to note that some things have not changed: currently three American companies are planning to demolish the historic village of Chabarovice in northern Bohemia and mine the site for over 100 million tons of brown coal (Bensman 1992). Such plans are currently being opposed by the local population and conservationists, but it is unlikely that they will be able to withstand corporate pressure and offers for the construction of a new town. Incidentally, a concern is now emerging for the industrial heritage in these areas which may appear 'lost causes' in an environmental battlefield.

The historic cores of most towns thus remained largely undisturbed by development pressures in the early years of communist rule: retailing, commercial offices and other service trades which had naturally congregated in these centres were regarded as unimportant in a socialist society; the churches and monasteries were suppressed, organizationally if not physically; and housing in these areas was regarded as too differentiated for effective social control. In other words, historic cores did not fit easily into priorities for investment and were left, almost literally, to rot. The change that did occur in these years derived almost solely from lack of maintenance and continuing decay. Only for the public buildings necessary to the organization and control of society was there any kind of respite – and even that was at a low level.

In the 1970s, following the 'Prague Spring' of dissension in 1968 and despite the repression which followed, government policy switched to a pro-active attitude towards non-industrial investment (Carter 1986). This took concrete form in a range of large-scale projects, mainly in housing and other social infrastructure, but also in commercial developments including retail stores, hotels and offices. Fortunately for the historic cores, the conventional approach to such projects was to seek economies of scale and use industrialized construction techniques. The tight-knit urban fabric of the cores was usually unsuitable for this style of building. The massive housing projects of the era were mostly built on peripheral green-field sites; even the commercial developments tended to be large scale and occupy edge-of-core sites, often where nineteenth-century slum housing had been cleared – for example, in the Žižkov district of Prague.

The results of this policy can be found throughout the Czech Republic. There are examples in Prague, at Southern and South-Western Cities, of vast suburbs built from prefabricated components, housing over 200,000 people. This type of housing – panel housing in slab blocks – is cheap to construct, extremely crude and overbearing, and dominates the skyline above Prague (see Figure 10.4). Newman and Roberts (1993: 19) state that 'the concrete finish is hard and unyielding, the spaces between the blocks untidy and ragged. There is no reference to topography or identity; instead, a

Figure 10.4 New development along the Prague skyline
Source: Photograph by T. Westlake

monotonous landscape of blocks stretches relentlessly into the distance.' What is currently more disturbing is a new 63-acre estate of panel housing, approved just before the end of the old regime, which is under construction despite vain local attempts to replace the scheme with a garden city proposal (Newman and Roberts 1993).

In the 1970s, at last, the government began to pay some attention to the needs of historic buildings. Perhaps because of a desire to match western interest in heritage issues, laws were instituted and maintenance/restoration money allocated. These efforts were largely directed at the protection of the most important and visible buildings – the Castle area of Prague is one example: the Old Town Square area received effective care, although for several of the buildings, renovation was restricted to the façade (Burkett 1992). Unfortunately, restoration efforts were usually limited to individual buildings, and did little to offset the more generalized problems of maintenance for surrounding buildings.

The creation of 'town reserve' areas, where no new development could take place without strict observance of conservation objectives, did act to prevent potential wholesale destruction of historic areas. In 1971, the Czechoslovak government proclaimed the centre of Prague a protected historic area (City Architect's Office of Prague 1992): virtually the whole of the historic core was included and new, modernistic buildings excluded. While 'town reserves' appear exemplary and parallel approaches in the west at this time (including UK conservation areas and French *secteurs sauvegardées*), the picture is far from complete. In a political economy where the demands of the party were paramount, it was always possible that the whims of party bosses might put historic buildings and areas at risk. Certainly there are several examples where the desire to project a 'modern/communist' image led to the destruction of historic buildings. In Jihlava, an otherwise excellent historic square has been ruined by the replacement of supposedly 'inappropriate' merchants' houses by a concrete supermarket with a multistorey car park above. Painted in shades of brown and white, this edifice could easily win a prize for inappropriate design.

In Teplice, the oldest spa city in the Czech Lands, the town square has been afflicted by a series of Modernist buildings which have changed its nature completely. Plans for the reconstruction of its centre were discussed from 1946 to 1977, during which time historic buildings suffered from lack of maintenance and investment.

A decision was made in 1977 to opt for demolition and rebuilding rather than restoration (Starčevič 1992). The sad result is that not only has a historic core been lost, but plans are already under way to redesign the centre in a less brutalist manner (although not quite in the vernacular manner now being seen in Germany: Soane, Chapter 9, this volume).

However, cases of this type of large-scale, brutal redevelopment of historic centres are relatively rare. A more usual scenario is, first, the insertion of single replacement buildings of dubious architectural quality into otherwise graceful rows of façades and, second, but probably of greater overall significance, the imposition of large-scale, modern industrial and housing complexes on the periphery of the historic cores, affecting the setting of the historic areas.

The contrasts of Český Krumlov offer a graphic example of this latter contradiction. The historic core of Cesky Krumlov, in southern Bohemia, is a World Heritage Site amply deserving of the interest of conservationists and tourists alike. All the characteristics of the typical Czech historic town are found in abundance: a large central square surrounded by several streets of medieval and later buildings, including an ancient brewery. The central town has the dramatic feature of being contained within an incised meander of the River Vltava. The crowning glory of the town is the exquisite castle – second in size only to Prague – which perches on the opposite bank of the river with its own 'New Town' of medieval housing and extensive convents (Gutkind 1972). The contrast in the town is with the modern industrial and residential suburbs which surround and impinge upon this significant heritage asset. The river is grossly polluted by the local paper mill a few miles upstream, and standardized concrete constructions greet the visitor on all sides.

Nearby, České Budějovice is a much larger town and regional centre, and has suffered a similar fate: the historic square and few surrounding streets offer a scene of good character and heritage interest, but beyond rise grimy industrial complexes and uninspiring housing estates. Given the economic importance of the town (especially the Budvar brewery), perhaps the later ravages can be partially excused.

Whatever the impositions placed on the historic towns of the Czech Republic by new developments in the communist era, the main problem that has beset the heritage assets is that of physical maintenance. As intimated above, the investments made in historic buildings by the state have been directed at the major monuments

– most of which are in Prague itself. Maintenance of lesser buildings, and even major monuments outside Prague, has been virtually nil since the 1930s. Clearly, today's priorities must concentrate on this fact.

HERITAGE ISSUES FOLLOWING THE VELVET REVOLUTION

The communist era inadvertently protected most historic cores of Czech towns from the insensitive development which has bedevilled so many other towns in western Europe. The absence of commercial development pressures until the late 1980s has enabled many areas to escape from the destructive development pressures seen in the 1960s and 1970s in Britain. The future of Czech historic town cores will depend partly on securing renovation and maintenance, and partially on coping with commercialism; much of this may rely on the planning system. The planning systems of the former Warsaw Pact countries have been affected by the political changes since 1989. Spall (1993) identifies privatization, the restitution of land, and a new distrust of centralized state control as the keys to ever-changing planning systems – and associated policies for conservation.

The Czech government consists of a so-called centre-right coalition which is committed to wholesale and rapid privatization. Czechoslovakia embarked on a radical privatization programme by auctioning off 100,000 small state-owned businesses and selling 3,000 large state-owned firms by a voucher scheme (Hall 1992). Privatization is already having its impact on the fabric of historic cores: building uses and methods of trading are changing and there is consequent demand for physical alteration. For example, there is a trend for the establishment of sales outlets for western companies; in particular a number of car showrooms appeared in Prague – fortunately not in the heart of the historic area – and they are displaying the same brash indifference to local architectural style as is common in the west. There are large glass frontages with fascia boards giving a horizontal emphasis, implanted into the ground floors of buildings with a clear vertical emphasis and usually demonstrating some intricate detailing. In major centres, and especially Prague, commercial advertisements have been appearing everywhere with no controls. At the same time shop frontages are becoming bolder and dominating many older shopping areas.

A 1990 law allows the restitution of land to former owners whose property was nationalized between 1955 and 1962 (Hague and Prior 1991). There has been great difficulty proving ownership, as documents were often destroyed or the buildings were owned by Germans, who have no rights under the new laws. Cepl (1991) argues that the whole process of restitution will result in inevitable delays in establishing ownership and therefore maintenance responsibilities of properties. Some historic buildings have been returned to previous owners, but the outcome for conservation objectives remains uncertain (Burkett 1992). In 1992 it was obvious in Prague that many restituted owners were unable to meet the challenge of effective use and maintenance of their inheritance: many buildings were empty and falling even more rapidly into disrepair. By 1993 the number of empty buildings had been significantly reduced and it was clear that there was a rapidly growing class of small businesses willing to exploit the commercial potential as shops, restaurants and craft workshops. Whether this answers the maintenance problem remains to be seen, but it is unlikely to address the issue as far as housing units are concerned. The Czech government has not as yet bitten the ideological bullet and opened up the housing market to commercial values, but it is only a matter of time before economic pressures force them down this line. Much of this process of privatization and restitution is in a state of confusion since the split from Slovakia.

In 1990 the Mayor of the City of Prague introduced a programme of financial help for the restoration of historic buildings. As part of this programme, the Department of Care for Historic Buildings was established. It is now possible for owners who undertake renovation on their properties to apply, in retrospect, for a proportion of the costs. Thirteen million Kcs (about £300,000) have been offered by the Ministry of Finance and the City to fund this work, but there is little information available to assess how successful the programme has been. It is worth noting that the estimate for the renovation of one building in Malá Strana (the Lesser Town of Prague) would take an entire year's allocation. As a result of insufficient funding, property owners are being encouraged to find other methods of maintaining their property, for example renting out rooms or undertaking joint-venture schemes with foreign investors who convert properties into tourist accommodation or other forms of business venture (Burkett 1992). The availability of state subsidies for renovation of historic buildings is extremely limited, considering the scale of the problem, and there is little evidence of similar schemes in other historic centres.

Apart from state subsidies, other factors will influence the ability of private citizens to maintain and restore historic buildings. Unemployment has increased rapidly, with state industries being uncompetitive in the western free-market economy. The unemployment level rose from zero in April 1990 to 220,000 in February 1992 (Pilkington 1992), and went on growing rapidly – probably reflected in the crime epidemic of the early 1990s. It must also be accepted that rent levels will increase dramatically faster than wages when housing is returned to a market system (when this will occur is not yet known). The result of this is likely to be a decline in housing standards for those on low incomes. The historic housing stock, often in bad condition, has received only minimal resources for maintenance over the past fifty years. Unrealistically low housing rent levels have resulted in a scarcity of funds both to repair externally and modernize internally (Russell and Westlake 1992). The difficulties of maintenance are compounded by the concentration of high levels of low-income households in the historic cores (Musil 1987).

Within the new capitalist economy there is the eventual potential for citizens to improve their wealth and living standards. This has various implications for the maintenance and conservation of historic areas. On a positive note, some individuals and commercial businesses will have income available to invest in maintaining their property. These same economic forces will also pose negative pressures for historic areas: for example, the volume of traffic, the need to provide parking space and traffic pollution are all likely to have an adverse impact, as both private and commercial vehicle ownership rises. In Prague, the city authorities have already attempted to accommodate this growth in traffic by the design and part construction of an urban motorway system, the visual impact of which is a matter of great contention. Despite being the capital, Prague currently possesses an enviable environment, with wide transport-free areas, and only very limited levels of congestion. Bor (1992) argues that Prague is unsuited to motorization, but the high-density housing estates are already crammed with cars; and further difficulties will result from the growing pressures for an urban motorway system. It is likely that many older centres will be badly affected by rapid increases in car ownership and subsequent responses to this.

The growth in tourism in Prague has been dramatic since the Velvet Revolution; in 1991, 65 million tourists visited the city (Cooper 1992). In contrast, the historic centres outside Prague currently receive relatively few tourists. Tourist income is required to underpin maintenance and restoration programmes; the dilemma lies in responding to tourist needs without destroying the urban heritage. There are already worrying signs. In Prague, the influx of western commercial interest has expressed itself most potently in the construction of hotels; there is clearly a need for more hotel beds in the city and the market is responding. So far, developments have been concentrated on the fringe of the core area and their design has at least observed sensible building heights; but problems are evident in the observance of such factors as floor heights and building materials. But the lack of a coherent building heights policy has resulted in a number of the panoramic views from hills around the historic core being destroyed by the development of poorly located and designed high-rise hotels, offices and towers (Bor 1992). The concern must be that such unsympathetic development will soon be located in the core.

The interest of 'westerners' in the Czech heritage has placed great burdens on the tourist infrastructure of Prague; it is important to determine the reasons for this interest. Clearly the sheer volume of artefacts is important, but also it is the quality of the historic environment which attracts people: quality in terms of historic/architectural significance in the European tradition, and in terms of amenity/pleasantness of place. It is these key touchstones of attractiveness which need to be analysed in planning for a secure future. It is also interesting to speculate how much interest is generated by the curiosity of expelled Germans and/or Jews and their descendants in their own heritage.

Outside Prague the tourist boom has hardly begun, but surely places like Telč and Český Krumlov – and other places of special heritage interest like Kutná Hora and Karlovy Vary – are going to be overrun by tourists. The question of how the competent authorities will react to this potential flood remains unanswered. Telč is such a small town that any significant tourist-oriented developments, such as hotels, car parks and restaurants, will have an inordinate impact on the character of the place – not to mention the physical impact on the fabric of such development and the thousands of visitors' feet.

Of particular significance is the response of the local authority in

Český Krumlov to the maintenance/renovation problem: the town council decided in 1992 to sell the majority of its seventeenth-century properties in an attempt to attract foreign investors who would fund restoration work (Brasier 1993). As many of the property owners from pre-communist times were expelled Germans or massacred Jews, very few previous owners have come forward to reclaim their properties and they remained in the ownership of the state. The Czech government decided to pass ownership of unclaimed property to the local authority, but without giving any assistance in the costs of maintenance. The local authority has in turn decided to auction off its heritage to the highest bidders, except for certain 'gems' which will be managed by a joint public/private company. Fortunately it appears that the local authority has frozen its sales campaign until it has sorted out a strategy for conservation control of the privatized buildings – but it is still uncertain of the potential impacts of this bold move. Two further towns, Znojmo and Mikulov, are considering following the same route as Český Krumlov (Brasier 1993), and this is likely to be a disturbing precedent that could threaten hundreds of historic towns over the next decade.

At a time when major economic and demographic trends, including industrial and residential movement, are rapidly altering the character of both cities and the formerly rural areas, planning needs to be strong. It is difficult to ascertain the current state of planning but it is useful to outline the pressures which it faces (Diamant and Matouškova 1993). Planning is likely to be restricted by the prevailing political ideology within the Czech Republic. Following forty years of centralism there is vociferous support for abolishing anything associated with the socialist system, irrespective of its merits, and for introducing maximum local autonomy (Hague and Prior 1991). This current strategy of unfettered localism is unsustainable. There is a strong case for recognizing that local government is the appropriate agency for determining and implementing whatever policies local people wish to see pursued. However, individual districts do not necessarily act in ways that would safeguard their own long-term interest. The Prague master plan is being updated in 1992–3 by the city architect's department, both to rid itself of the previous administration and to respond to the changing needs of the city (Mabbitt 1992). The city architect's greatest difficulty is trying to provide a strategic planning framework and effective local policies when fighting the backlash against the old centralized planning regime.

CONCLUSIONS

The great tourist/heritage attraction of the Czech Republic lies in the fact that much of its urban form remains relatively untouched, providing a historical time capsule rare within the western world. The collapse of socialist structures, however, means that the subsidy levels previously available for historic building restoration works have been withdrawn and, without an effective system of 'listed' building control for privately owned properties, the fate of much of the historical environment lies at the mercy of unsympathetic forces.

An uphill task faces reformers in the Czech Republic, and conservation and heritage issues will not be at the forefront of their minds. As the current growth of Prague has shown, new development and infrastructure are necessary and financial investment will have to be attracted. New facilities, both private and public, must be adequately provided and appropriately sited. The clear danger is that such development will be at the expense of a vast historic heritage that must be protected.

Czech towns demonstrate a variety of responses to the development pressures of the communist and post-communist eras. The dead hand of party rule has protected many historic centres, but the uncertainties of the free market present threats which are far greater in their destructive power than the occasional forays into 'modernism' by the old-style party bosses. Development pressures on heritage assets will come from within through, on the one hand, the commercial office/retail schemes so beloved of western property developers (Cooper 1992), and on the other, from demands for 'better' infrastructure, especially roads and parking areas. An example of the former is the 40,000-square-metre Boby Centrum retail and leisure development in Brno (Ridout 1993). Pressures will also come with the burgeoning of industrial factories, service trades and possibly even housing in the central area's fringes which will erode and impinge on the historic cores.

The defence of the heritage requires a firm political commitment to protection and conservation; the Czech planning system is in the throes of change and a clear vision is needed to ensure the establishment and implementation of effective policies (Diamant and Matouškova 1993). The present Czech government needs to be reminded of the country's vital role in the defence of European heritage. This will require assistance from the 'west' both in the transfer of expertise and in money to address the real issues of restoration and enhancement. There are a number of 'aid packages' offered by the EC, among others, and heritage protection is a worthy contender for consideration.

These problems have their parallels in western Europe – the defence of the urban heritage is not an easy task. However, the crisis of the Czech Republic – and elsewhere in eastern Europe – should be a major concern of conservationists world-wide as the sheer volume of assets is so great and the threat so immediate. Cooper's comment that 'Historic Prague is ripe for development – heritage rules permitting' (Cooper 1992: 21) epitomizes the pressures that will face the Czech Republic in coming years. Eager developers are likely to try and cash in on the historic past with little thought for its future integrity. It is essential that the Czech government establishes an adequate array of 'heritage rules' and restoration initiatives to conserve the country's urban heritage: which, as has been shown, is a surviving microcosm of the urban heritage of central Europe as a whole.

ACKNOWLEDGEMENTS

This study is written by two British academics whose connections with Bohemia date only from the 'Velvet Revolution' when the country was opened up to easy access. Therefore, the work represents very much a view from the outside: westerners entering into – to use Neville Chamberlain's phrase of 1938 – 'a far-away country (of which) we know nothing'. We now know at least something and must thank our Czech colleagues – in particular, Karel Maier of the Prague Technical University and Kamila Matoušková of the Institute of Building and Architecture. We must also thank Richard Mabbitt of the Architecture and Planning Practice for alerting us to many of the examples used here. We further thank Roger Cullimore for his illustrative material.

REFERENCES

Bensman, T. (1992) 'Coal mine plan threatens Czech town', *East West Environment* 1, 3:1.

Bor, W. (1992) 'The unique townscape of Prague', *Urban Design Quarterly*, July: 14–6.

Brasier, M. (1993) 'Czech heritage under hammer', *The Times*, 5 April: 25.

Burkett, T. (1992) 'Reconstruction's crippling costs', *Prognosis*, 2–15 October: 10–11.

Carter, F.W. (1986) 'Czechoslovakia', in Dawson, A.H. (ed.) *Planning in Eastern Europe*, London: Methuen.

Cepl, V. (1991) 'A note on the restitution of property in post-communist Czechoslovakia', *The Journal of Communist Studies* 7, 3: 367–75.

City Architect's Office of Prague (1992) *Prague: Metropolitan Area Report*, Prague: City Architect's Office.

Cooper, P. (1992) 'Surveying the East', *Building*, 27 March: 20–1.

Diamant, A. and Matouškova, K. (1993) 'Structural, organizational and strategic problems of urban regeneration in the Republics of the former federation of Czechoslovakia', in Berry, J., McGreal, S. and Deddis, B. (eds) *Urban Regeneration: Property Investment and Development*, London: Spon.

Gutkind, E.A. (1972) *International History of City Development, Volume VII: Urban Development in East-Central Europe: Poland, Czechoslovakia, and Hungary*, New York: The Free Press.

Hague, C. and Prior, A. (1991) 'Planning in Czechoslovakia: retrospect and prospect', *Planning Practice and Research* 6, 2: 19–24.

Hall, D. (1992) 'Czech mates no more?', *Town and Country Planning* 61, 9: 250–1.

Mabbitt, R. (1992) 'Prague fabric threatened by new business arrivals', *Planning* 956: 15.

Musil, J. (1987) 'Housing policy and the sociospatial structure of cities in a socialist country: the example of Prague', *International Journal of Urban and Regional Research* 11, 1: 27–36.

Musil, J., Slapeta, V. and Novak, J. (1984) 'Czech mate for Letchworth', *Town and Country Planning* 53, 11: 314–15.

Newman, P. and Roberts, M. (1993) 'Czeching out old regime in favour of capitalist city', *Planning* 1003: 19.

Pilkington, E. (1992) 'Czech point', *Education Guardian*, 2 June: 1–3.

Ridout, G. (1993) 'Brno's spa-ring partner', *Building*, 23 April: 36–7.

Russell, W. and Westlake, T. (1992) 'Providing strategic vision in a separating country – a task for planning', *Town and Country Planning* 61, 7/8: 214–16.

Spall, N. (1993) 'Bulgaria faces up to image problem', *Planning* 1000: 18–19.

Staňková, J., Stursa, J. and Vodera, S. (1992) *Prague – Eleven Centuries of Architecture*, Prague: PAV Publishers.

Starčevič, P. (1992) 'Recomposition of Municipal Centre of Teplice (Czechoslovakia – Northwest Bohemia)' Unpublished paper available from BCS, Prague 6, Czech Republic.

Part IV

The achievements, hopes and limitations of heritage planning

INTRODUCTION: FROM CHOICES TO POLICIES

The key word of Part III was choice, and a wide range of choices of resources, products and goals resulted from the analyses. Part IV must begin to approach the means and limits of selection from this range, and the key word is thus policy.

The polemic by Newby (Chapter 11) indirectly raises policy issues through a series of attacks and a list of misgivings about the results of currently operating policy, especially in heritage tourism. At one level, this chapter can be read as a fundamental and complete contradiction of the argument advanced throughout this volume. Newby appeals to the ideas of 'authenticity', 'integrity', 'honesty', 'appropriateness' and the like as absolute 'cultural values', which are intrinsic qualities of history and its surviving artefacts. These he sees as being threatened by their antitheses, which are 'commercialization', 'commodification', 'distortion', 'exploitation' and 'trivialization', in the service of tourism. Clearly, the dichotomy he establishes, and the conflicts derived from it, are impossible to accommodate in the heritage argument advanced here which, by definition, assumes away any such conflict. The questions posed by Newby are, therefore, simply unposable in heritage planning.

However, this fundamentally dissenting voice is included here to fulfil two important functions. First, it is representative of a widely held view. Most of those responsible for the care and preservation of historic resources are drawn from what can be termed the professional culture lobby, who have been educated in architecture, history, archaeology or the fine arts, rather than in the social or management sciences. Therefore, they tend to be strongly oriented towards the objects of preservation rather than the purposes of preservation. In addition, much informed and articulate public opinion is uneasy with what it would see as an Orwellian tampering with the past for the purposes of political propaganda. At its simplest, therefore, this chapter introduces much of the opposition to be overcome if the aims of this volume are to be furthered.

Second, many of the actual issues raised in this chapter are relevant and important, and thus contribute towards the formulation of policy. Although tourists must not be caricatured as vandal hordes, they obviously interact with historic resources in ways that can be damaging as well as beneficial, depending upon the objective of the enterprise. The heritage argument must also recognize the existence of the 'tourism versus other uses' or 'tourists versus residents' conflicts introduced and illustrated in various guises by Newby, but these should be seen as integral parts of the multi-selling problem, to be managed by market intervention appropriate to the predetermined goals.

Morris turns firmly to practice in her examination of the problem of a capital for the new Europe, and the contribution of heritage and culture to this. Her study of what has happened, is happening and might happen in some of Europe's key cities – principally London, Paris and Berlin – draws heavily on the explicit policies of different governments. She clearly demonstrates that some administrations wish to seize the European initiative, cornering the heritage/cultural capital, if not the administrative/financial capital, while other government policy approaches ignore this question completely. Although some cities have an immense reserve of heritage/tourist-related areas and developments, others, principally Berlin, have a more chequered political and physical past. Yet some of the former cities, such as London, are resting on their laurels while Berlin is making most of the running. It is relevant in a book devoted to heritage to deal with new architecture: many of these projects are explicitly heritage-related – the Louvre and National Gallery extensions, for example – and are reinterpreting the past and creating a new heritage and new identity. Which city wins the capital race is explicitly a matter of policy and image, in which heritage and tourism play no small part.

Finally, the concluding chapter (Larkham) returns to the central theme of the volume through an assessment, based on the arguments of the preceding chapters, of the nature and scale of the problem. Is there a need for a supra-national, pan-European heritage? If so, what are the implications? What should be incorporated in such a heritage, and what omitted? The evident key to Europe's heritage is 'nastiness' (cf. Chapter 7) and diversity. Such elements cannot be conveniently omitted: what is more positive, perhaps, is to emphasize regional uniqueness and the interrelationships between regions in a new, politically (more or less) unified Europe.

11

TOURISM

Support or threat to heritage?

P.T. Newby

INTRODUCTION: A CONTEXT OF CONCERN

All European countries possess a legislative framework to protect their cultural heritage. In each, the built environment is recognized as an important cultural artefact – a framework around which to organize interpretations of social change, economic fortune, key events and personalities in a nation's past and expressions of artistic merit. For these and other reasons the countries, of western Europe at least, follow active policies to conserve the built environment. Yet the process of conservation has many intrinsic tensions, some of which are outlined in other chapters of this volume. In the most affluent areas, conservation is frequently little more than a rear-guard action against pressures for redevelopment in defence of – usually local – advantage. In less favoured areas, conservation may be a strategy to enhance an area, capitalize on its individuality and attract inward investment. Responsibility for conservation and, perhaps more importantly, the choice of what to conserve, lie in some instances with national government and in some with local.

It could be argued that the most important of these tensions is the need to act locally in the face of processes that are structural in the economy and frequently international in scale. In the UK, while the economy was buoyant during the 1980s, there were some significant attacks on the conserved environment. A well-known example is the proposal first for a Mies van der Rohe skyscraper, and then a James Stirling design, on the Mansion House site in London. The Secretary of State for the Environment, supported by a House of Lords decision, ruled that the possible quality of the Stirling design outweighed the known quality of the listed buildings on the site. In the recession of the 1990s, the collapse of private revenues and a shrinking public purse determine that the processes of ageing and decay cannot be adequately countered.

It is in this context of processes far larger in scale than a locality that this chapter looks at tourism. Tourism should be of particular concern to conservationists, though this is not always apparent. Conservation's concern with sustaining building quality and maintaining the visual environment has frequently led to disregard for the processes that shape both of these characteristics. Of all the processes at work, analysis of tourism impacts should feature highly on the conservation agenda. It was estimated in 1984/5 that 132 million people visited museums, galleries and the built heritage in Britain (Myerscough 1988: 13), and that these visitors spent £52 million on admissions. The implications for the growth in leisure time and the availability of funding from tourism in creating the market for heritage is well known (e.g. Herbert 1989). Tourism constitutes an accepted path to development, and cultural heritage constitutes an accepted tourist resource. Twenty per cent of all World Bank projects involving an impact on a country's cultural heritage are concerned with the development of a tourism economy (Goodland and Webb 1987).

As with any economic activity, tourism makes use of resources and produces an environmental impact which amounts to exploitation if the quantity and quality of those resources become degraded. The extent to which tourism could damage those very qualities which attract it would be a sufficient problem. However, from the point of view of conservation, there are two other issues which should be considered. First, what do commercialization and presentation of the past imply in terms of an expression of values? From the perspective of conservation, we should be concerned that the feedback to public attitudes may distort conservation values. Second, we should recognize that the growth and impact of tourism is a continent-wide phenomenon. Its scale will inevitably grow with the continued integration of European states. We need to identify the consequences, particularly those that appear across national boundaries as this process occurs.

This is the context of concern within which this chapter is written. It explores the ways in which tourism uses the cultural heritage and the implications of this for conservation.

THE RELATIONSHIP BETWEEN TOURISM AND CULTURAL HERITAGE

The evidence for the pursuit of cultural tourism is all around us – excursions to archaeological remains, visits to stately homes, trips to historic towns, and holidays in Egypt to see the remains of the Nile civilizations. The very act of travel, particularly in a foreign country, is a cultural experience in which differences in shopping can have an impact on us as lasting as that of a royal palace. The 'ordinariness' of a different place can be the basis for its attractiveness, as long as it is different from the 'ordinariness' of our own experiences.

However, it is not the everyday life of a host society which is of concern in this chapter but the built environment – especially the way in which it is used to support tourism and the consequences of that support. The relationship between tourism and cultural heritage can be thought of as a continuum (Figure 11.1). At one end, culture is shared between residents and the visitors; the house owner, for example, whose house and garden are open on one or two days each year, or the tourist who happens upon a fiesta or Easter procession in a Spanish or Italian town. At the other end, culture is packaged and shaped for presentation to tourists, the exact packaging being more influenced by the need to generate tourist expenditure than by the cultural element itself. Examples in Britain would include tableaux of events and stories (such as Chaucer's *Canterbury Tales*) and reconstructions of places, artefacts and lifestyles, such as Beamish Open Air Museum in north-east England or Wigan Pier Heritage Centre in north-west England. At both, there is an emphasis on the appropriateness of costume to the visitor experience, but Wigan goes further than Beamish (where it is just the attendants who dress up) and has an active programme of role

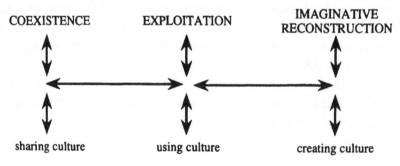

Figure 11.1 The evolution of a tourism-heritage relationship

play featuring the life (and death) and issues of the period. If Beamish lies towards the 'acceptable' limits of the conservation of cultural heritage, Wigan has well overstepped the mark, and bears the same relationship to conservation as a historical novel does to a historical treatise. But what of Hjerl Hede in Denmark or Butser in England? Do we accept these reconstructions of early dwellings because they were backed by an archaeological and sociological experiment? The issue is complex, and the answers to these questions may say more about our prejudices than anything else.

It is important, therefore, that we establish some common ground in terms of the relationship between heritage and tourism, rather than concerning ourselves merely with opinions about that relationship. As has been noted, this relationship forms a continuum along which there are three principal focuses – coexistence, exploitation and imaginative reconstruction. While there is no inevitability that a place will evolve from one state to another, from coexistence through exploitation to reconstruction, it is quite clear that the growth in tourism has been partially responsible for the extension of this continuum and the development of new forms of relationship between culture and tourism. Thus, while we find cultural heritage being increasingly exploited from the mid- to late nineteenth century onwards (e.g. Dellheim 1982), there is little widespread evidence of the use of such imaginative reconstructions as the *Canterbury Tales* and 'Wigan Pier' to serve a tourist market until after the Second World War, and the 1970s in particular. We should not imagine, though, that the position of any tourist facility on this continuum is time-bound. It would be incorrect to assume that all exploitative relationships pre-date the mid-twentieth century, just as it would be to expect that all new tourism developments would be based around an imaginative reconstruction. It is the continuum itself which is the innovation and therefore time-based, not the opportunities which are developed to satisfy tourist needs. It is important that the relationships between tourism and heritage along this continuum are understood if the pressures on the conservation environment are to be managed.

Coexistence

Tourism and heritage coexist when tourism does not dominate the local economy, even though the number of tourists may be large.

As a result, a place functions on its own terms – as a local service centre, as a centre for production or as a commuter town. The tourist experiences the cultural heritage in a setting dictated by the evolution of the settlement and its present pattern of activity. This may, of course, bring its own conservation problems but the situation is one of a modern society living in an old shell.

The 'shell' of an old built environment is frequently the cultural anchor to the tourist experience, and many cities have become tourist attractions on the basis of their buildings and townscape. Where coexistence characterizes the relationship, the number of tourists may be smaller than expected either because the built environment is a specialist interest, or because potential tourist flows are intercepted by another centre in a higher position in the tourist hierarchy. Barcelona is a good example of the first situation. Festival events such as the Olympic Games will always draw in enthusiasts, but such tourists must be distinguished from those for whom the main attraction is the city itself. In the case of Barcelona, one of the city's principal attractions is the architecture of Antonio Gaudi. His style reflected the growing self-confidence of the Catalans in the late nineteenth and early twentieth centuries. The outcome is a style that is so idiosyncratic that the buildings themselves become a destination for all those interested in the evolution of artistic style, as is now recognized by the placing of his Casa Mila on the World Heritage List.

Coexistence also occurs when the number of tourists is low relative to the potential of a place. In some instances, this may be a function of remoteness. In many cases, though, tourist numbers may be intercepted by alternative attractions. There is always a hierarchy of tourist attractions which is created by the tourist industry's need to package time. This packaging occurs at all levels. In Stratford-upon-Avon more people visit Shakespeare's birthplace than Hall's Croft, the home of Shakespeare's daughter. In Windsor, more people visit the castle, than the exhibition of 'Royalty and Empire'. Both towns receive more visitors than St Albans which, in many ways, has as much to offer the tourist (Figure 11.2). It is located about the same distance from London as Windsor. It is reached, by public transport at least, more easily than Windsor. It encapsulates, in one place, over 2,000 years of urban history with visible evidence of a large Roman city. It has played its part in England's political history, and its response to changing economic and social conditions from the late medieval period onwards is

Figure 11.2 St Albans, Hertfordshire
Source: Photograph by the author

clearly shown in its townscape. Its buildings have survived because of the operation of the property market. Long-established patterns of local ownership and sufficient revenue to adapt and to restore, but not to demolish and start anew, are prime conditions for building preservation. It has tourists but its service and commuter functions are the principal influences upon its heritage townscape. In this case, tourism and heritage coexist because the tourist industry chooses to package one set of attractions in preference to others.

Exploitation

Where tourism begins to occupy a position of importance in the local economy, the relationship ceases to be one of coexistence and becomes exploitative, and the cultural heritage becomes the basis for generating a cash flow. As a result, the impact of tourism starts to be felt. The commercial response is to seek a location in the heritage area specifically to service the tourism market. The development of a tourism economy leads to the emergence of a tourist district. A full discussion of the processes involved is given in Ashworth and Tunbridge (1990). Such districts are isolated from the local community. They are often presentations to an outside market rather than being functional for local inhabitants. This process can be observed in many of Britain's heritage towns and cities – Elm Hill in Norwich, much of the centre of Stratford-upon-Avon, and The Shambles in York. Each country has its own examples. Such areas function principally to serve the tourists who are drawn to the town because of the quality of its cultural heritage as revealed in its townscape. In these situations, the buildings, townscape and ambience are the resource which the commercial opportunities exploit. The impact, however, is not limited to buildings and economic relationships. The degradation of local cultures by tourism is a long-standing theme of social and anthropological research (see Smith 1977). This impact was noted in tourism's infancy. Ousby (1990: 133) points out that in the 1750s Castleton in the Peak District was 'a town of beggars whose chief dependence for subsistence is on every curious traveller who comes to visit'.

Imaginative reconstruction

While townscape is a physical expression of a society's culture, the final stage in the tourism–heritage continuum, imaginative reconstruction, seeks to make concrete more abstract elements of culture. It has been embraced by the tourism industry as a means of increasing the attractiveness, and thus the market potential, of heritage sites. Its object is to convert heritage into a tangible asset which can be actively marketed. The English Civil War *per se* has little general appeal as a leisure pursuit, but a re-enactment of the Battle of Naseby can constitute a full day out for all the family.

Reconstruction for the tourism market has developed from the legitimate presentation and expression of cultural heritage practised in some museums. The assembly of authentic materials to create settings and scenes appropriate to a period is practised both with interiors and exteriors. The reconstruction of Victorian and Edwardian town scenes in York's Castle Museum or in the Museum of London is little different in concept and object from the assembly of buildings from different locales and periods that we see in folk museums of the 'skansen' movement. These developed in the inter-war period and take their name from the Swedish example, but are found also at Hjerl Hede (Denmark), St Fagans (Wales), Budapest, Bucharest and others. Their purpose is to conserve an aspect of cultural heritage in a representative collection. This type of museum has proved its popularity – and, by implication, its commercial viability. Its popularity rests on its ability to project, through an appropriate setting, something of past lifestyles. The scale of the houses and the internal arrangements of rooms convey to a general public more graphically than literature ever can the standards at which people lived, and they provide a tangible foil to our own experiences of dwelling in houses and flats. The buildings are frequently furnished to give visitors insights into living conditions. Many, such as the National Museum of Wales at St Fagans, have integrated craft activity into the museum complex. Those displays of complexes that deal with the recent past seem particularly attractive to tourists. The Avoncroft Museum of Buildings, near Bromsgrove, has recently displayed a prefabricated Second World War bungalow: designed as temporary housing, many examples still exist in the Birmingham conurbation, but this display is particularly popular. In 1991, Blists Hill at Ironbridge had 256,000 visitors, and Beamish in County Durham 432,000. In both cases, the period they represent lives in the memories and reminiscences of grandparents. Their appeal often stems from the fact that they deal with everyday ephemera rather than with high culture. Even when the two are presented together, for example in a stately home, it is not unusual to find that the kitchen and bathroom create more interest than the tapestries, or that visitors are more interested in the titles on the library shelves than with the quality of the wood panelling.

The step beyond the assembly of authentic materials is reconstruction in what is believed to be the original form. This approach has a long pedigree, including the work of Viollet-le-Duc in France and Burges in Wales, but was anathema to John Ruskin and the conservation values he espoused. It is found throughout Europe and beyond. It was actively pursued in many parts of eastern Europe in order to replace townscapes destroyed in the war (for example, see Soane, Chapter 9, this volume). The motives for this deserve further assessment but, from the viewpoint of the tourist industry, the communist regimes responsible should perhaps be thanked for the resources which they have created. Reconstruction is a particularly common strategy in the presentation of archaeological sites to tourists. This has occurred at Knossos since its excavation by Arthur Evans, while the reconstruction of Ephesus (a convenient day trip from coastal resorts) is proceeding apace.

However, these reconstructions at least have foundations on which they can be based. The same is not true of the St Nicholas quarter in what was East Berlin. It looks and feels authentically medieval, not only in building terms but also in the grouping of buildings and the creation of urban spaces. It should feel authentic – the buildings are replicas of others. It is, however, all false. Berlin, as a city, is largely a nineteenth-century creation. What was not destroyed by war was razed by the communists to create Alexanderplatz. The quarter was created out of recognition of the failings of central planning, to become a leisure enclave: sheer fiction in historical terms but a pleasant and enjoyable experience for tourists and inhabitants alike (see Soane, Chapter 9, this volume for similar examples).

False though the St Nicholas quarter might be, it reveals a new stage in the tourism-heritage relationship. The reconstruction of a Viking street in the Jorvik centre in York probably falls into this stage. The presentation of the *Canterbury Tales*, the 'Oxford Story', 'A Day at the Wells' (in Tunbridge Wells) and 'Royalty and Empire' at Windsor certainly do. In order to incorporate abstract history into a marketable product, developers have to present the lifestyles and behaviours of the past by means of a tourist experience.

We should be careful, though, of the basis of criticisms of this trend. Whatever their merits or lack of them (as seen from the perspective of the educated middle classes), it is reasonable to suppose that more people know about the life of the average Viking, the story of the *Canterbury Tales* or the genteel recreations of Georgian Britain through visiting heritage centres than ever did by studying history or reading Chaucer or Jane Austen. A more valid set of criticisms concerns the impact of these tourism-led developments on the conservation of our heritage townscapes, and on our ideas about cultural heritage itself.

TOURISM – ITS CHALLENGE TO CULTURE AND TO CONSERVATION

While the environmental impact of tourism, in the context of the natural environment, is a well-researched topic (see, for example, OECD 1980; Pearce 1989: 229–43; Briassoulis and van Straaten 1992), tourism and the built environment is less well researched. There is evidence, as we have seen earlier (pp. 209–12), that tourism and townscape can coexist, and that there are situations in which tourism revenues can be used to sustain and conserve environments of heritage value. There are, however, rather more examples of situations where the growth of tourism leads steadily to the domination of conservation values by commercial values. In the natural world, it may be possible to take steps that allow natural systems and processes to re-establish themselves. This cannot be the case in the built environment, where virtually any modification constitutes the erosion of a cultural asset. Any move beyond the coexistence of tourism and culture produces a compromise in cultural values and conservation practice. The nature of the issues raised by tourism and their interrelationship is shown in Figure 11.3. We shall first consider the cultural principles at stake, before looking at the conservation problems that arise through the existence of cultural tourism.

Cultural issues

Tourism raises three cultural issues. First, there is the issue of whether it is culturally selective and, if so, whose culture is selected and why. If it is selective either in terms of ethnicity, social status or time, then this has major implications, not the least of which is that tourism is a key process in creating relative values. This theme is developed in Chapter 7 by Tunbridge.

		CONSERVATION ISSUE		
		UNIFORM CONCERN	INTEGRITY	HONESTY
CULTURAL ISSUES	CULTURAL SELECTIVITY	Distortions of conservation value; bias for periods and areas	Decline of undervalued areas	
	COMMERCIALIZATION	Economic vs cultural values	Distortion to character; appropriateness of re-use; value of form vs value of structure	Challenge of enhancement
	REPRODUCTION			Authenticity; importance of the tourist experience

Figure 11.3 Issues raised by tourism in conservation and cultural management

Second, it is not a neutral force. It is driven by commercial values which may and often do diverge from cultural values. Commercial values tend to be present values, while cultural values draw on a richer and deeper heritage. Commercial values last as long as the profit element. The tourism 'product' inevitably has a limited lifespan and this is reflected in a sequential process of change in the heritage environment as product gives way to product and initiative to initiative. Commercial values distort culture through selection, interpretation and bias. What is chosen from the past is what is expected to be profitable. But in choosing from the past commercial values effectively create a new culture which allows us to slip easily between past and present and whose values are based on the ability to be interesting rather than the need to be accurate. Commercial values force the past and history to diverge, and the past becomes a product of the present. These issues are touched on further by Corner and Harvey (1991).

The third issue concerns the relative merits of the original and the copy, and the impact of reproductions on the value we place upon the original. As an issue, this is one that the art world has confronted for many years. The knowledge that an object is not deemed authentic means that we usually hold it in less esteem. More important, though, is the impact of reproducibility upon the way in which the original is seen. There must be concern that constant copying, not just of an individual object, but of a style or a concept, must debase the original. Copying creates an immediacy of experience out of something that was much more subtle, and converts style into fashion. Tourism has the potential to do this with the very roots of our culture.

Conservation issues

It would be wrong to see the cultural and conservation issues exposed by tourism as two sets of independent variables. The cultural issues are core issues which are reflected in the principles of management and use of our heritage. In the context of the built environment, they interact with three key principles of conservation.

First, there is uniformity of concern and treatment. If there is no uniformity in our concern for and treatment of heritage environments other than on the basis of quality, then this leads to a distortion of our cultural values and conservation activity. Second, there is integrity. When we talk of 'integrity', we imply authenticity. Any change to a building or townscape which we value as an expression of our cultural roots represents a loss of historic authenticity. Third, there is honesty. The issue of 'honesty' is, in fact, to pose the questions: 'How real is the place created by heritage tourism? How honest is it in historic and conservation terms?'

Tourism, culture and conservation

The problems which tourism poses for conservation practice can now be explored within the framework of Figure 11.3. Questions of cultural selectivity are reflected as distortions of conservation value and compromises in terms of both integrity and honesty. Heritage values and tourist values coalesce around some periods and styles, and deviate around others. In general, the deviation between the two sets of values increases as we move towards the present. The strongest consensus between the two systems probably occurs

217

over the medieval period. Age and rarity underlie our conservation values; difference, ambience and the imageability of half-timbering provide the basis for tourist attraction. Many towns the length and breadth of western Europe combine these characteristics and where there is a great concentration of such towns (for example, in the Rhine and Mosel Valleys and the Black Forest) we find a significant tourist industry. As we move on in time, the consensus disappears. Bath, for example, is an important tourist destination while Blandford Forum is not; yet each is of a period, presenting similar cultural values. One has to know about Blandford in order for it to gain a place on one's itinerary. This is the feature which sets modern towns apart from medieval: specialist interest tends to be a matter for enthusiasts. One has to know and appreciate architectural history to seek out Gaudi's buildings in Barcelona or Ricardo Bofil's in Paris. One is likely to visit Saltaire, Letchworth, Welwyn or Harlow only if one has an interest in the history of planned settlement.

The danger for conservation arises because of tourism's selectivity. Particular problems arise, then, for tourist centres which have evolved through many periods and which have areas of conservation value from a sequence of periods. The heart of the danger is that commercial pressures exerted through the tourism industry may lead to public investment in conservation being directed disproportionately to support the tourism economy. This can lead not only to a time bias in conservation, but an area bias as well. Budapest provides an example of this danger. Buda stands on a bluff on the right bank of the Danube. Despite being badly damaged in the Second World War, it has been restored and renovated to give a period feel. The street plan reflects its late medieval and early modern origins, its architecture demonstrates the influence of the Gothic and baroque. It is attractive – and it is an important tourist attraction. It possesses all of the characteristics of a tourist recreation complex – from the cafes, bars and cable railway to the museums and the newly constructed Budapest Hilton. However, while Buda has been restored, on the other side of the river in Pest quality environments and buildings from the turn of the century are neglected. From the mid-nineteenth century Budapest became the economic engine of the Austro-Hungarian Empire and this was reflected in the confidence and style of its buildings. Yet many of those in Pest clearly lack the care and attention lavished on the tourist quarter of Buda.

From this and many other examples, we can see that temporal bias in conservation policy can have spatial consequences, and that this leads to compromise in the integrity of the townscape as cultural heritage. Variations in support and the prioritization of expenditure to reflect tourist potential inevitably lead to economic decay and fabric deterioration in less-favoured areas. The real danger, however, is that this clear expression of relative value on the part of the state inevitably helps to form public attitudes about which townscapes are worthwhile and which are unimportant.

The issue of the commodification of culture by the tourism industry puts the focus quite explicitly on the relative importance of economic values and cultural values. As was evident in the case of Budapest, if cultural heritage has the potential to become an economic good, then economic values predominate, and uniformity of concern suffers as a conservation principle. More than anything it is our response to economic needs that erodes the integrity of our heritage. This erosion takes many forms. The use of certain environments for 'heritage shopping' is one of these. Heritage shopping is not just the selection of a sixteenth-century building to house a top-of-the-range clothes shop. In many ways, this is acceptable to conservationists. It is not just that a building is being used, it is that it is being used to meet local needs. It is, in built environment terms, 'sustainable' in that it represents an accommodation between what we value from the past and the need to generate finance to prevent deterioration. But heritage shopping is different from this in that it implies the creation of a shopping district specifically to serve the needs of recreation and particularly the needs of tourists. This 'export' orientation undermines the notion of sustainability and leads to a spiral of rent rises which encourages a greater external orientation in order to draw more visitors which leads, as a consequence of economic success, to further rent rises. The core of heritage shopping is usually the antique and gift shops. Examples of this are widespread, and the benefits of agglomeration have led to the emergence of 'antiques centres' in 'antique towns'. Petworth, Woburn, Stow-on-the-Wold and Penzance are all examples in the UK. What is threatening the integrity of these areas, from the point of view of conservation, is not so much the appropriateness of the use of the buildings but the distortion of the character of the area and the creation of an 'outsider' zone in the heart of many of our historic districts.

The growth of a tourist district can take forms other than heritage shopping. The progressive domination of tourist service functions leads to functional conversion, particularly from retail to food service provision, and the expansion of the tourist area into surrounding craft and housing areas. In this way and through this process the character of heritage environments is being distorted. Patterns that were once confined to seaside resorts are now becoming apparent in our historic towns. However, apart from this impact on the fabric of the town and its progressive alienation from its inhabitants, there is another, more sinister problem developing. A uniformity about our heritage towns is evolving as the same types of shop selling the same types of goods appear, with the same provision of modern facilities (especially car parks) at the fringes of the core and the same enhancement of the heritage district. This uniformity in retail and service provision often represents a significant distortion of what is required to serve the local population. A high daily throughput of tourists inevitably leads to commercial opportunities responding to a different set of needs from those of the indigenous inhabitants. In Haworth, a small mill village on the edge of Bradford, famous for its association with the Brontë family, local people can choose to eat in any one of fourteen places or buy their gifts from thirty gift shops. They would, however, find difficulty buying a blouse or a pair of shoes, and many street signs are now in Japanese.

At the edge of Stratford-upon-Avon, around the walls of York and Canterbury and behind the shopping centre of Windsor lie multistorey car parks whose mass and scale fight the grain and character of the historic districts they serve. They represent not a compromise between the old and the new, but an assertion of the importance of the tourism market. The decisions of shopkeepers and planners place the interests of outsiders over those of insiders and lead, eventually, to an erosion of identity and the spread of placelessness. Italian cultural centres epitomize the problem, as Vulliamy (1992) shows with the example of Florence. The social and environmental cost of tourism in Venice, Florence, Rome, Pisa and many other centres may be in great danger of outweighing its economic benefits. Certainly, the numbers who come to 'tick the experience off their list' destroy the aesthetic enjoyment of others who value these centres and their rich heritage as cultural treasures and not tourist objects.

Enhancement is a further challenge to individuality. The installation of street furniture to support the heritage dimension of the townscape is now widespread. Throughout Britain there seems to be a feeling that 'nineteenth-century' cast iron goes with all periods of townscape. The message that this is a quality environment is expressed by having the lettering picked out in gold. The place of the pedestrian in the town scene is supported by using paved surfaces to warn off vehicles. At first this approach was individual, but its repetition throughout our historic towns serves more to destroy individuality than enhance it.

This discussion of the consequences of the emergence of a tourist district is an expression of a more general issue – how appropriate is the reuse of a conservation environment? The Castlegate area of Manchester is a case in point. Close to the city centre, the area was a mixture of small workshops, poor housing, roofed market buildings, railway arches, viaducts and a canal basin. Economic collapse led to substantial clearance, and there it stopped until the quality and potential of the industrial heritage were recognized. Now it is being redeveloped – as a museum quarter, centred around the city's industrial and engineering history, making full use of the waterfront location for a new hotel and using the pulling power of an opportunity to see *Coronation Street* while on a tour of the Granada Studios. It is the existence of *Coronation Street* which, in many ways, highlights the loss of integrity in reuse. It makes no claim to be real but its grime and appearance are more honest and representative of the situation which gave rise to the townscape than the cleaned-up and enhanced façades outside the studio walls.

There is also an issue of conservation integrity in relation to the reuse of individual buildings. Any change to a building challenges its integrity, particularly so when form and function are at variance. What is an appropriate new use for a redundant turbine hall such as AEG in Berlin? Is the functional styling of Battersea Power Station an appropriate setting for a leisure park? Is it appropriate to locate a tourist attraction based on the *Canterbury Tales* in a redundant church?

These examples raise fundamental questions about conservation values. How congruent should functional values and the values of the form be? From the perspective of conservation integrity the best function is the original one – but reuse would not be an issue if this were the case. The best alternative is to have a function whose values are sympathetic to the form. The primacy of economic forces means that this is frequently not the situation, and commercial activities, often with a leisure or tourist dimension, conflict with the form. If reuse requires structural alterations, then further questions are raised about the relative value of interior and exterior form. The issue that faces us is whether we are more concerned about preserving the building as a structure or as a shape. If, for the sake of economic viability, we allow significant structural compromise then, clearly, internal form is of little importance. From the point of view of conservation, this, however, leads us into a dangerous situation in which preservation of the external appearance lacks internal substantiation – a situation which in its way is as false as the designed townscape of the St Nicholas quarter in Berlin. Unless this situation is challenged, conservation will have few roles other than to sustain a hedonistic environment.

These examples lead to the area of honesty as a conservation principle. Issues of honesty arise because of commercial pressures to reproduce and create culture. The questions which conservationists should ask are: 'How real is the place created by heritage tourism? How honest is it in historic and conservation terms?'

Few would seriously claim that the St Nicholas quarter in Berlin was honest conservation. Similarly, while the Poble Espanyol, built for the Barcelona World Fair of 1929, represents Spanish culture, it lays no claim to be conservation. More difficult is a case such as the Parthenon whose reconstruction raises questions of authenticity. This issue is widespread (Knossos and Ephesus have already been mentioned, see p. 214) and is often associated with tourism objectives. In Bulgaria, the Greek theatre at Plovdiv and the citadel near Veliko Turnovo have been reconstructed (Figure 11.4).

The communist state in Bulgaria wished to establish its political legitimacy, and conservation was a vehicle for achieving this. Much of the conservation was of monuments and towns where there was physical or cultural resistance to the imposition of Turkish rule. The restoration of Old Plovdiv, for example, was more than a restoration of Bulgarian Renaissance architecture; it was a reaffirmation of Bulgarian identity. The restoration of Tsaravets, however, was much more than this. It was a reconstruction, more than restoration, of a citadel which represented the source of Bulgarian hegemony over the Balkans prior to the coming of the Turks. Reconstruction was a statement that the communist rulers saw themselves as the legitimate heirs of the second Bulgar state and of the struggle against the Turkish yoke. The importance of this message was reflected in the conservation investment in churches

Figure 11.4   The Greek theatre, Plovdiv
Source: Photograph by the author

and monasteries. The painted seventeenth- and eighteenth-century churches of Arbanasi, the Byzantine and tenth- and twelfth-century churches of Nessebur, and Bachkovo and Rila monasteries are but the tip of a commitment to the support of religious foundations that was extraordinary by the standards of eastern Europe. The state's purpose with all of this conservation activity was not just to create a link between the overthrow of the Turks and the overthrow of capitalism, but to demonstrate it to the Bulgarian people by creating a domestic tourist industry around the commercial exploitation of heritage and culture. Tourism was a means of spreading the message to the Bulgarian people (Newby 1984).

Whatever the motives, however, reconstruction inevitably raises issues of honesty, either in presenting the modern as authentically old or in bringing together forms that owe no allegiance to one another. In Britain, these issues of honesty are raised in a place such as Ironbridge, one of Britain's World Heritage Sites. There can be no doubt, though, that the area has been successfully conserved since the 1950s, when Darby's furnace site at Coalbrookdale was overgrown and the buildings close to failure. The principal sites have been recorded and most have been restored: the buildings are structurally sound and house information and craft functions. The issue, though, is not a simple one of accepting compromises in order to save the buildings, but rather one of whether a tourism-led strategy is the best one to sustain a heritage environment. In order to generate the revenues to conserve the buildings, the policy has been one of the progressive commercialization of activities, such as at Blists Hill, where reconstruction of the buildings has been matched by reconstruction of the past. What many visitors fail to recognize is that while the buildings are real, the settlement is not. The buildings have been 'imported'. The 'town' is no more authentic than the St Nicholas quarter in Berlin. At worst, one might argue, visitors come away with a belief that the settlement is real, thus with a false understanding of industrial history. The place exists, the lifestyles are sanitized. No amount of reconstruction can recreate the harshness of life in a nineteenth-century industrial town and, without this understanding, the presentation is a failure and the experience false. However, the issue is not just one of false understanding. For conservationists it is the compromise with honesty which is most important. The danger is that the need for revenue drives tourism and the need to create an enhanced tourist experience leads to reproduction of cultural forms and reconstruction. Reconstruction leads all too easily to compromise. Where it exists it should be argued as a means of meeting social or environmental needs, not as a key ingredient in a conservation strategy.

CONCLUSION

This chapter has explored a complex relationship between tourism and conservation. Though many of the examples have been drawn from Britain, similar ones, reflecting similar issues, can be found in any country in Europe. What is, in many respects, alarming is that the scale of this growing problem has yet to be recognized.

Tourism is not, and never has been, a neutral force. Places and peoples touched by tourism cannot remain unaffected. As individuals we may have marvelled at the cave paintings of Lascaux but, *en masse*, our breath and body heat affected the delicate microclimate that has allowed them to survive – so the caves are now closed to the public. Early in the nineteenth century, Wordsworth expressed his concerns that tourists were not necessarily people of taste (Wordsworth reported in Newby 1981). If we see ourselves as custodians of cultural heritage, we need to regard tourism not as a set of individual experiences but as an economic process which identifies resources, develops and exploits them – and, having exploited them, moves on to create the next product to meet the fashionable demands of the market. In terms of the natural environment, we accept that tourism has an impact. We need to recognize that the impact is just as great on the cultural environment. Like all processes which act at national and international scales, tourism contains within it a set of forces which lead to increasing uniformity. Whether it is the house style of an international hotel chain, or something as simple as a national market for street furniture, tourism erodes differences but markets what passes for individuality.

Although culture may be treated as the last resource in which Europe has a comparative advantage, we need to be wary of creating a product out of our cultural identities in order to generate revenue to support them. The European nations need to value their differences for their own sakes and understand the threat posed by tourism and, having understood it, begin to manage it. The solution, ultimately, is to place a higher value on cultural identity so that it is an end in itself rather than being a means to an end of economic well-being. The implication of this is that the European Commission should concern itself less with policies to promote tourism and more with the creation of a new fund whose size recognizes the importance of cultural diversity in Europe and which would be used to support and develop cultural identity. The Commission needs to address also the mechanism that would ensure that the fund's resources are directed to regions and towns which can act at a local level to conserve their cultural heritage – a real test of commitment to subsidiarity. From the point of view of conservation, tourism need not be a problem, in the same way that office development need not be a problem. Both become problems only when conservation is not the main priority but only a collateral interest. Problems arise because of the need to find an activity that will sustain the building fabric. The real villain, in these circumstances, is the under-funding of conservation. The enterprise culture of the 1980s, which saw English Heritage and similar bodies come into existence with a brief to market heritage sites, increase visitor numbers and revenues, and relieve the public purse, has to be challenged. Our culture is not something to be supported on a 'pay as you view' basis. As Hewison argues, 'museums are items of social property, and they have a value, not to the consumers, but to the community' (Hewison 1991: 176). The case he makes for the effective public funding of museums is every bit as applicable to the heritage of our built environment, and the danger of developing 'living interpretations' in order to attract 'growth in the C_2, D and E Sectors' (Carr 1989: 303) is that the success of heritage will be judged on visitor numbers. Heritage sites will be forced to develop marketing policies and the number of visitors attracted by a 'circus of reconstruction' will inevitably degrade the quality of the heritage environment. Conservation should not follow from the availability of tourist receipts – that devalues our heritage and leads to all (and more) of the compromises which were mentioned earlier.

The solution, then, is not to stop tourism but to strengthen conservation – and to recognize that, by strengthening conservation, we are sustaining individuality and creating a better resource for the tourism market. Conservation needs to be strengthened at a variety of levels. Now that in Britain we have a Minister responsible for National Heritage, we need to match this commitment with a fiscal regime that encourages owners to adopt a conservation-minded attitude. Those who own buildings which the nation wishes to conserve should not have to apply for grants on a grace-and-favour basis, but should be faced with a tax regime that encourages them to maintain them in an appropriate state and which discourages inappropriate modification. Best practice in Europe requires no less an approach in the United Kingdom. In addition the size of the National Heritage Memorial Fund needs to be increased and the scale of its area of interest and operations extended. The concept of trusts operating revolving funds to refurbish and reclaim buildings should be applied to saving and enhancing whole areas of our towns – and there is no better time to do it than in the deepest recession in the post-war period when the economy needs a boost and property prices are low. At the local level, planning control, too, needs to be strengthened to prevent the evolution of tourist enclaves with a retail and service structure unsuited to the needs of the local community.

These actions will not solve every problem of negative tourist impact. There will still be problems of managing tourist numbers. What they would indicate, though, is a strengthening of cultural, relative to economic, values. They would allow and even encourage a community to retain its individuality. They would not prevent tourism but they would assert communal values and make it clear that culture is to be shared and not used.

REFERENCES

Ashworth, G.J. and Tunbridge, J.E. (1990) *The Tourist-Historic City*, London: Belhaven.

Briassoulis, H. and van Straaten, J. (1992) *Tourism and the Environment*, Dordrecht: Kluwer.

Carr, E.A.J. (1989) 'Research and the heritage operator', in Herbert, D.T., Prentice, R.C. and Thomas, C.J. (eds) *Heritage Sites: Strategies for Marketing and Development*, Aldershot: Avebury.

Corner, J. and Harvey, B. (1991) 'Mediating tradition and modernity: the heritage/enterprise couplet', in Corner, J. and Harvey, S. (eds) *Enterprise and Heritage*, London: Routledge.

Dellheim, C. (1982) *The Face of the Past: the Preservation of the Mediaeval Inheritance in Victorian England*, Cambridge: Cambridge University Press.

Goodland, R. and Webb, M. (1987) *The Management of Cultural Property in World Bank-Assisted Projects*, Washington, DC: World Bank.

Herbert, D.T. (1989) 'Leisure trends and the heritage market', in Herbert, D.T., Prentice, R.C. and Thomas, C.J. (eds) *Heritage Sites: Strategies for Marketing and Development*, Aldershot: Avebury.

Hewison, R. (1991) 'Commerce and culture', in Corner, J. and Harvey, S. (eds) *Enterprise and Heritage*, London: Routledge.

Myerscough, J. (1988) *The Economic Importance of the Arts in Britain*, London: Policy Studies Institute.

Newby, P.T. (1981) 'Literature and the fashioning of tourist taste', in Pocock, D.C.D. (ed.) *Humanistic Geography and Literature*, London: Croom Helm.

Newby, P.T. (1984) 'Tourism in Bulgaria', in *Leisure, Tourism and Social Change*, Edinburgh: Centre for Leisure Research, University of Edinburgh.

OECD (1980) *The Impact of Tourism on the Environment*, Paris: OECD.

Ousby, I. (1990) *The Englishman's England*, Cambridge: Cambridge University Press.

Pearce, D. (1989) *Tourist Development*, Harlow: Longman.

Smith, V.L. (ed.) (1977) *Hosts and Guests: the Anthropology of Tourism*, Philadelphia: Pennsylvania Press.

Vulliamy, E. (1992) 'Sights for sour eyes', *The Guardian*, 21 October: 4–5.

12

HERITAGE AND CULTURE
A capital for the new Europe

E. Morris

INTRODUCTION – THE COMPETITIVE CONTEXT

London, Paris, Berlin, Brussels . . . the race is on as to which city will be *the* heritage/cultural capital city of the new Europe. The main contenders are London, Paris and Berlin – each has its disciples and each has its drawbacks. A closer look at major European capitals reveals that the race is not equal, although the stakes are high.

London is the cultural capital of Europe, as it is a world-class centre of culture surpassed only by New York. It has five major symphony orchestras, internationally renowned theatre, opera and ballet companies, an enormous number of museums and galleries and accompanying training schools for all the arts. Paris, with fewer advantages, is promoting its cultural magnets far harder than London. The historic heritage of Paris is on a par with London's, but London still remains the tourist capital, its tourism revenue five times higher. Berlin has a larger amount of park space per inhabitant than London, although much of this is peripheral: but London rates better than Paris in this respect. Paris and London are similarly safe and environmentally of middle rank, according to recent surveys (LPAC 1992).

Individual cities may fulfil different roles: capitals of finance, politics, manufacturing and culture are emerging from the leading cities of northern Europe. Each one is trying to capture the financial markets, the industrial market and the title of culture capital by building opera houses, art galleries and parks, and improving public transport and other facilities.

The 'European banana'

A new image to describe where political, financial and administrative power is concentrated is the 'European banana'. The centre of

229

all gross national product activity, the centre of most of the communications activity of road, rail and air, and the centre of the property market are located in a bulbous geographical area which stretches from London to Milan (Figure 12.1) (Datar 1989). The banana was identified and labelled by geographers within Datar of the French government; interestingly, two of the major capitals, Paris and Berlin, are outside the original banana. The French government was concerned to discover that France was not ideally located in economic development terms when EC policy makers endorsed the idea of the banana by designating Europe's favoured cities as those within it (Motte 1991).

A second important geographical area, the 'hot banana', sweeps westward into southern France along a southern corridor to Barcelona and Valencia, and is expected to attract more head offices and research facilities as a result of its superior transportation and

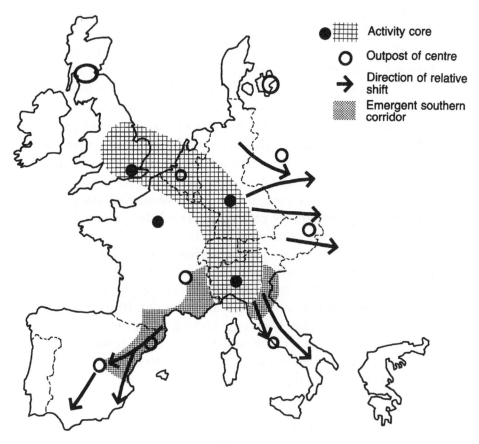

Activity core

Outpost of centre

Direction of relative shift

Emergent southern corridor

Figure 12.1 The 'European banana'
Source: Redrawn from Datar, 1989

telecommunications links. At the same time, there are counter-shifts, particularly to the German cities of Hamburg and Berlin, and the new eastern European countries which fall outside the banana (Houlder 1992). Attention here will be focused on whether Berlin, for example, can outflank the cities of 'the banana'.

THE RANKING OF EUROPEAN CITIES

Brunet (in Datar 1989) cites the relevant strengths of each European city in terms of particular characteristics which confer importance, such as the location of multinational firms, the extent of infrastructure and technology, the number of engineers and technicians, financial activity, airport traffic, high technology, etc., and then ranks the cities in order. The results confirm the importance of the banana area. The cities of first rank are London and Paris. Milan, at the opposite end of the banana, is the only European city of second rank, while Frankfurt, Madrid and Brussels are third-rank cities. Berlin, in its present form, is shown as a fourth-rank city. These rankings are based on quantitative aspects of each city's activities. For example, London is the leading financial capital, ahead of Frankfurt and Brussels. Frankfurt is its chief financial rival, and has been strengthened by German re-unification. Frankfurt made a bid as strong as London's to host the European Central Bank. Brussels is in line to be the most important political centre for the new European Community. Berlin promises to exploit the largest opportunities from reunification, both because of the decision to reinstate it as the seat of government, and also by its position as a crossroads between eastern and western Europe. However, owing to Germany's decentralized structure, Berlin may not dominate the country in the way that London dominates the UK or Paris dominates France.

There are so many 'maybes' in the economic analysis of the future of the major European cities that, in this author's opinion, the race between them will depend on the leadership of the individual countries and how they perceive the role of their capital cities. This perception will necessarily place a major emphasis on the quality of life, and it is thus important to examine the physical planning and cultural heritage of the major capital cities in order to choose the new capital of the new Europe; alternatively there may be several new capitals – a monocentric Europe or a polycentric Europe?

LONDON

Introduction

London is a world first-rank city, and its importance is growing. Its position as an international capital of finance, knowledge, the arts and tourism is said to be at its highest this century. London is the principal centre of a centralizing government, of university education, retailing, the arts, advertising, international and national communications and finance. It ranks alongside its only rivals, New York and Tokyo. It must endeavour to enhance its position in the global economy while enjoying an advantage over the latter in that English is the primary global language.

According to French research (Datar 1989), London is a first-rank city in population size, attractiveness for multinational companies (five times that of Paris), activity in advanced technologies and for research activity. It is the top financial centre in Europe; likewise, its stock exchange and commodities exchange have no rivals in Europe, and only the stock exchanges of New York and Tokyo are comparable. It is, furthermore, the seat of many of the big banks, in addition to the Bank of England.

London is of first rank in terms of volume of airport traffic, although its port is now only of second rank, having been overtaken by the European ports of Rotterdam, Hamburg and Le Havre. In terms of culture and tourist activities, conference facilities, the press and telecommunications, London is again of first rank.

Strategic planning

From 1888 to 1963, the London County Council managed the county of London, with the boroughs subordinated to it. The old LCC had a long-standing reputation for efficiency and honesty. In 1963, when the Greater London Council was created, London doubled in extent; but the GLC had difficulties working with the new boroughs, and gradually the boroughs took real control of local government. Thus a British pattern re-emerged of making piece-meal incremental adjustments that respected tradition, rather than grand schemes in the French manner (Savitch 1988).

The old LCC fulfilled many of the ideas in Abercrombie's plan for London: the population was decentralized; the Green Belt controlled the spread of Inner London, and the new towns were successful (Abercrombie 1945). But, at the same time, Abercrombie's plan caused serious problems for Greater London. The decentralization of people and industry removed jobs and left industrial buildings empty. The commuter belt meant more people entering and leaving London, clogging the motorways. In addition, the docks closed, owing to major changes in the shipping industry, and office development was restrained in the interests of keeping a more humane city.

After the Conservative government disbanded the giant Labour-controlled GLC in 1986, it substituted the new statutory body, advisory in nature, the London Planning Advisory Committee (LPAC), in accordance with the consensus that only the central government is powerful enough to force the London boroughs to work together through a commission directly responsible to it.

Now, both Labour and Conservative parties have agreed that the old centralized master planning is too inflexible for today's rapid pace of change and both are calling for a small strategic Greater London Authority. The difference in concept between the two parties is that Labour's strategic authority would have had statutory authority to plan the economic development and transport infrastructure, while the Conservatives, who will not relinquish any power to Labour-controlled boroughs, desire only an advisory strategic London body with the power to implement vested in the Department of the Environment. Instead, the Conservatives propose a Cabinet sub-committee of ministers to co-ordinate policy for the capital and promote a modernization programme designed 'to sustain into the next century London's special position as one of the world's great capital cities' (LPAC 1992).

After its re-election in 1992, the Conservative government had to face the need to integrate the management of London. Despite its liberal political structure compared to that of France, the British government needed to produce a programme to keep London a first-class European city. After its re-election in 1992, the first sign that the Conservative government was taking London's problems seriously was the publication of the LPAC's London: World City Report (1992) by the consultants Coopers and Lybrand Deloitte, but sponsored by the City of London, London Regional Transport, London Docklands Development Corporation and Westminster City Council. The major issue for the report was how to preserve London as a dominant world city. The consultants' task was to assess London's competitiveness compared to Paris, New

York, Tokyo and Frankfurt, in financial strength, infrastructure, the costs and quality of life. The criteria for financial strength, i.e. banking and financial centres, administrative headquarters, groups of think-tanks and so on, were uppermost.

The consultants found that London is reasonably competitive in terms of wealth creation and the arts, but there were grave concerns about (a) the falling standard of public transport; (b) the lack of city-wide strategic planning; (c) the lack of sufficient low-income housing; (d) failure to accommodate new business in the East End of London; and (e) the lack of self-promotion, not only in business matters but also in terms of heritage/cultural assets.

Public transport and low-income housing

The government spent £750 million on the London Underground in 1992, and will be adding the Jubilee Line extension from the City to Docklands, the Cross Rail and the additional rail link to Heathrow from Paddington Station. It is proposing to spend £750 million each year on infrastructure between 1992 and 2002. It was proposing to spend £9 billion on updating commuter services for British Rail until privatization plans intervened.

There is a need not only for extending and improving the Underground system, but also for supporting it by a rapid transit system to the outer areas. The development of a high-tech integrated public transport system could also include a series of new transport interchanges where people could leave their cars and switch to public transport, thus helping to reduce the traffic on the roads.

LPAC's own policy supports the long-held concept, so beauti- fully detailed by Rasmussen, that London is a 'city of stable and secure residential neighbourhoods capable of sustained community development' (Rasmussen 1937). The large local authority housing estates are seen as a difficulty because they restrict labour mobility. In 1993, the Conservative government is already offering greater financial incentives to transfer local authority housing into their tenants' ownership.

A programme of infill housing, of 'densification', is now neces- sary. One-fifth of London's built-up area is derelict and many houses stand empty. A programme of increasing housing densities would build houses for low rent or sale on these derelict sites, thus offering low-income families somewhere to live. The report itself promoted private rented accommodation. Dense neighbourhoods with mixed activity would save people having to commute from a dormitory suburb to a financial centre. The Docklands has been a human disaster in promoting only offices, not homes and community facilities for the office workers and their families. The lack of shops, primary schools, clinics and community centres has resulted in what has been described as a human desert (Gosling 1988).

The problem still remains of rebuilding the inner-city housing estates which have fallen into disrepair and disrepute. There will probably not be enough money for both housing rehabilitation and grand schemes such as those proposed for the Thames Embankment. It may come to a decision between maintaining London's place as a cultural and financial centre of Europe, which would benefit the whole country, and putting money into the housing and community needs of London's poorer boroughs. There is always the danger that the poor housing estates will deteriorate, becoming the ghetto of an underclass who will then turn to drugs, violence and other social crimes.

The socialist President Mitterrand in Paris has chosen the former strategy and has neglected the suburbs, where there are now considerable social and ethnic problems. Although Prime Minister Major may do the same, it is to be hoped that some money will be provided for the low-income housing estates.

Proposals for improving London's culture and heritage areas

The main heritage characteristic of a city such as London is its polycentricity, with its cultural and heritage areas concentrated in selected districts, as islands of culture (Ashworth and Tunbridge 1990). These specific clusters of historic cultural areas appeal to Londoners and tourists alike. London has five major tourist clusters which rank among the most popular in Britain with over a million visitors per year: (1) the South Kensington complex of the Science, the Natural History and the Victoria and Albert Museums; (2) the National Gallery and Trafalgar Square heritage island; (3) the Tate Gallery; (4) the British Museum; and (5) the Tower of London, Tower Bridge and HMS Belfast. Other tourist clusters exist in Westminster, the City and, on the outskirts, Greenwich and now the Docklands.

The enhancement proposals for London, or *les grands projets* in the French manner, concentrate on those selected areas, linking these islands of heritage by transport. One such proposal is for the enhancement of the Thames River. Although Michael Heseltine, then Secretary of State for the Environment, called for 'an initiative to be taken in the preparation of a coherent plan for development along the river', no action has as yet resulted. LPAC considers that the Urban Development Plan of each borough, when strung together, will produce a Thames River strategy. But this will not be enough. London needs a Thames River *grand projet* for the twenty-first century, for the people of London and for the tourist. Sir Richard Rogers (1990) has suggested the creation of a major park and pedestrian areas alongside the river, with roadways beneath the Embankment, bridges for pedestrians, the development of derelict sites, and a scheme for lighting the major buildings; eventually the banks of the Thames would become a single linear park, interconnected by new pedestrian bridges (Figure 12.2).

There is an opportunity to restore Somerset House now that the Inland Revenue have left it, and make it a lively heritage island, as proposed in the Rogers scheme (Rogers and Fisher 1992). The movement corridor of the Embankment Drive would be covered over, making it a tunnel open on the side to the river. Above would be a terrace the length of the river. The proposal would also reorganize Leicester Square and Trafalgar Square and create pedestrian links to the Embankment and the South Bank.

The National Gallery/Trafalgar Square area is one heritage island where enhancement has finally resulted in success. After various urban design battles, the National Gallery's new Sainsbury Wing, designed by Venturi and Scott-Brown, compares favourably with, and is as impressive as, the high-tech glass pyramid designed by I.M. Pei for the Louvre in Paris.

Covent Garden is both a prestige tourist island and one of the few successful *grands projets* for London. Many battles between 1968 and 1980 finally resulted in Covent Garden becoming a conservation area (Anson 1981). The final scheme included the preservation of: the market, based on Inigo Jones's arcaded square conceived in the manner of the Place du Palais Royal in Paris but only partially completed in 1630; the nineteenth-century parallel range of buildings in the middle with the space between covered over; St Paul's Church by Inigo Jones with its churchyard restored from being a car park; and the new extension to the Royal Opera House. This area now needs to be linked to other tourist islands.

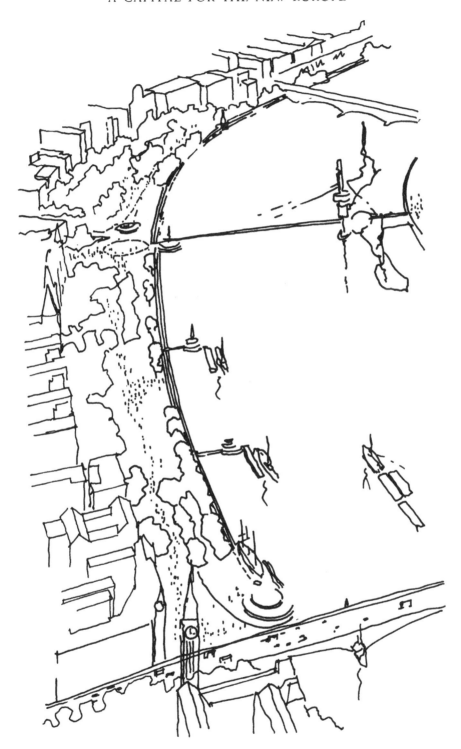

Figure 12.2   Thames Embankment pedestrianized linear path proposal
Source: Redrawn from Rogers and Fisher 1992

These heritage/tourist clusters create physical problems of traffic congestion and management and land-use conflicts between housing and tourism. For example, 4,000 tourist buses drive through London daily in the summer. A recent scheme for the rebuilding of the area around St Paul's has been completely disoriented by the demand that coaches come within five minutes' walking distance of the cathedral. As a national shrine and identity symbol, it deserves better treatment.

The Underground links these tourist clusters, with the exception of the Docklands where the new light railway is already inadequate for the task. In neighbouring clusters, the tourist corridors of movement are Oxford Street, Regent Street, the Mall and Bond Street. But it is becoming increasingly apparent that more movement possibilities are required and, in this author's opinion, more light rapid-transit railway systems should be built.

Through various urban design battles, London is revealing a reluctance to achieve grand urban schemes. This may be in the English tradition of preferring a democratic classicism in which the desire for individualism took precedence over the preference of kings and their master planners. Upon entering the new Europe, London is showing a passive sense of urbanity rather than any unified vision for the urban future.

The Conservatives pushed ahead with the Docklands as a major enterprise zone subject only to market forces, but to town planners it is a lesson in how not to redevelop the port and dock facilities of a capital city. For example, the London Docklands Development Corporation developed new streets, roads, paths and office facilities at a fast pace, without much regard to local housing or shopping or community facilities. The dearth of these facilities, the isolation of the existing dwellings, the lack of a Docklands civic centre and the total disregard of any relationship to the rest of east London have all been mistakes which will have to be expensively rectified. Now, the Docklands as a whole is in difficulty with the bankruptcy of Olympia and York, the developers of the flagship of the Docklands, Canary Wharf, with the domino effect of postponing construction of the extension of the underground line to the Docklands, signifying collapse of the private-public sector partnership.

Proposals for the East End of London are predicated on the need to shift development eastwards, away from expansion on green-field sites to the west. An excellent scheme for the East End of London known as the 'East Thames Corridor' includes extending

238

the Underground line, improving the motorway, providing a rail terminus for the end of the Channel Tunnel railway at Stratford, and a new east London river crossing; and extending the facilities of the City Airport.

Promotion of London and its urban planning

The French have a permanent exhibition in the City of Paris at the Pavillon de l'Arsenal, visited annually by thousands of people. London has no equivalent, although the Architecture Foundation is working on creating such a permanent exhibition which 'in the absence of a metropolitan authority responsible for planning will engender a comprehensive debate and increase awareness of architecture in its social, economic and cultural context' (Smith 1991).

In early 1992, the Conservatives were still only offering a London business forum and a Cabinet sub-committee to co-ordinate policy on London. But the government has proposed a new Festival of Britain to celebrate the millennium. The Festival would be held in the year 2001, fifty years after the original Festival of Britain, which symbolized the start of the 'modern' post-war era. A Millennium Fund would provide the money for the Festival, and also for cultural/heritage projects such as restoring Britain's crumbling cathedrals, historic houses and concert halls; and constructing new buildings to celebrate the millennium, such as community centres, arts centres, and other sport and trade facilities.

Although London is promoted by various different agencies, the new Festival of Britain would promote London, particularly its tourism and culture, world-wide. The new Festival could be the grand gesture to regenerate London in the way that Presidents Giscard d'Estaing and Mitterrand have used *les grands projets* to regenerate Paris.

PARIS

The historic heritage and culture of Paris

The overall impression of the city is created by its gardens, broad avenues and harmonious façades, two-thirds of which were created during the last century, first under Napoleon I and secondly under Napoleon III by the engineer Baron Haussmann. Under Haussmann, a corps of engineers devised neutral spaces punctuated by 'special monuments' such as the baroque Opera House, which constituted landmarks around which the newly created perspectives turned. Each monument was placed in the middle of a restructured setting (open avenues, crossroads with splayed corners and avenues with regulated façades) that led the eye straight to it. Space as well as volume were handled with a sense of the monumental.

After Napoleon III, totally different political regimes altered the typology of traditional monuments. The power of the trinity of church-castle-palace declined in favour of the symbols of the modern metropolis, such as town halls, court houses and libraries. Paris also indulged in a series of world fairs, the famous *Expositions Universelles*, which produced monuments such as the Eiffel Tower, dedicated to industry and technical progress.

Although the medieval city mostly disappeared in Paris, the baroque and nineteenth-century neo-classicism were carefully and beautifully integrated with the new monuments. Thus Paris had a long tradition of building monuments and preserving the urban fabric of the city long before the administrations of Presidents Giscard d'Estaing and François Mitterrand began their decades of '*les grands projets*'.

Early initiatives under Presidents de Gaulle and Pompidou

Since President de Gaulle, who authorized the extensive new town building programme, French presidents have chosen the course of integration with Europe, with the idea that France could lead the way. One of the consequences of this leadership role is that France changed the way it thought about itself in spatial terms. Previously, planning in France was inward-looking, with the biggest problem being the growth of the Paris regions. The *Aménagement du Territoire* policy was set up to control development of the Paris regions and to develop regional cities (*métropoles d'equilibre*) in order to balance and spread the benefits of French economic development. Now, the French urban system is structured by its capital city, the Paris metropolis. With 9.06 million inhabitants in 1990, a large part of the French population and economic activity is concentrated there. Investment in public infrastructure became one of the main priorities of French urban policies, particularly with respect to motorways, high-speed trains and telecommunications. Communication infrastructure is at the centre of the stakes for the European-scale development of both Paris and the French regional cities, because they are on the edge of the 'banana' (Dawson 1992).

The TGV, or *train à grande vitesse*, has given priority to routes from Paris, not only for economic reasons but also for the development of connections to the major European cities in Germany and Italy. The trains are punctual, clean and fast: the famous TGVs radiating from Paris are the world's fastest scheduled passenger trains, quicker even than those of Japan. The Paris Métro's local subsidized trains are frequent, usually every two or three minutes. The *réseau express régional* (RER) provides a new express service stopping at every fifth or sixth station, and extending well into the suburbs, a boon to commuters. Created at great expense, the RER is now showing signs of physical deterioration.

Begun during the 1970s, the first undertaking by President Pompidou, which proved to be a master stroke, was the great arts centre called the Centre Pompidou, commonly known as the Beaubourg. In opposition to post-modernism, the Pompidou Centre, by Renzo Piano and Richard Rogers, represents one of the first demonstrations of super-modernism – later called high-tech – making particular use of solar energy. The detail of the architecture is found in the technology required by the building. It must be more than coincidental that Piano has also been chosen by Daimler-Benz to design and build the first major redevelopment site in Berlin at the Potsdamerplatz.

Les grands projets of Presidents Giscard d'Estaing and Mitterrand

The history of the government of Paris is quite the opposite of that of London. Whereas London had responsible government from 1888 until the abolition of the GLC in 1986, Paris did not receive self-government until 1977, when it elected Mayor Jacques Chirac and an administration with greatly increased power which, having seen some of the problems associated with the housing estates of the 1960s Modern Movement, was anxious to maintain and enhance the traditional urban character of the city. Chirac explained that 'Not every building should be preserved. . . . Each period must be allowed to leave its mark on the city' (Davey 1989). *Quartiers*, or districts, were created which respected their contexts. Large-scale urban roadworks were cancelled and the existing Parisian street pattern was retained and enhanced. Gardens and community facilities were located in the centres of the new blocks.

Unlike those working in the spirit of Le Corbusier and the

Athens Charter of the Modern Movement, who believed in total redevelopment, Chirac and his town planners strove to retain the existing urban fabric of the city, with regard to: (a) street patterns; (b) the line of street frontages; and (c) limitations on the height of new buildings. But not everything was to be preserved. Although he was against post-war megastructures, he preferred redevelopment, if necessary, on a small scale.

Contrary to Chirac's conceptions, the next Presidents, despite being of opposing parties, accepted the challenge, so that both Giscard d'Estaing (1978–83) and François Mitterrand (1983–93) concentrated their monumental works in Paris (Ragon 1986). First, President Giscard d'Estaing commissioned Ricardo Bofill to build a large monument on the site of the old fruit and vegetable market, Les Halles, but Mayor Chirac found the design too overwhelming and stopped it. Nevertheless, at a later date, Les Halles was totally destroyed and the ground floor transformed into a shopping centre called Le Forum designed by Arch. Vasconi et Penchreach, with a socio-cultural complex underground by Arch. Chemeton. Meantime, Giscard d'Estaing and his government created the La Villette Park and science city – Cité des Sciences – designed by the architect Adrien Fausilber on the outskirts of Paris. A rehabilitation project, La Villette is a vast complex, bringing together the modernized old covered calf market, a museum of science and technology placed in a rehabilitated slaughterhouse, a geodesic dome to show films, a large park dotted with red pavilions and a rehabilitated nineteenth-century pavilion used for rock concerts, the Cité de la Musique – Music City – with auditoriums and rehearsal halls for classical music. A further *projet* was the rehabilitation of the Gare d'Orsay, a magnificent nineteenth-century railway station, into a grand museum of nineteenth-century art.

Unlike other European cities, where central sites are islands in the urban fabric, the historic heritage and culture areas of Paris are concentrated in the single centre and protected by total conservation rules first created by André Malraux. The later period of *les grands projets* was also the time of the building boom of the 1980s, during which a great deal of construction occurred and many skyscrapers were built. Also in that period, many parts of the centre of Paris were pedestrianized as the centre-city population dropped and the pressure for office space pushed the people to the suburbs and even to the new towns.

In order to ensure that the historic fabric and traditional scale

Figure 12.3   The Grand Arch at the new La Défense
Source: Photograph by the author

would not be destroyed by the large-scale requirements of corporate big business, President de Gaulle and his government decided in 1958 to create a new business centre on the fringe of Paris at La Défense. This urban planning concept has worked well, for most of the new skyscrapers are now located at La Défense and traditional Paris has been saved. La Défense is directly oriented on the east–west axis of Paris, Le Notre's great projection from the Louvre to the Tuileries to the Champs-Elysées, continued by Napoleon to the Arc de Triomphe and then westwards to La Défense, one of the great nineteenth-century defensive bastions of the city (Figure 12.3 and 12.4).

To make the progression on the east–west axis, and create a landmark which signified the business complex at La Défense, the governments of both Giscard d'Estaing and Mitterrand embraced the idea of the Grand Arch at La Défense, an open cube by the architect Johannes O. von Spreckelsen. Spreckelsen's mighty arch has simplicity and unity: an open cube – an immense 100–metre-square block of building, slightly turned on the axis. Four enormous square post-tensioned concrete frames provide the structures of the base, the two sides and the roof. The façades are sensitively detailed with squares of white Carrara marble. The 'clouds' over the central plateau are a stretched fabric tent, highlighted by the metallic gridwork of fifteen panoramic lifts, as an airy canopy of tent cloth to represent 'clouds' (Figure 12.5). The Grand Arch is a minimalist sculpture on the scale of the metropolis, and is intended to symbolize reconciliation between big corporate business, whose skyscrapers line the avenue of approach, and the bureaucratic needs of the socialist state, whose departments it houses. It sits beyond the traditional cultural heritage of Paris, thus protecting the historic buildings from invasion.

From 1981 onwards, President Mitterrand's government pursued an even more energetic architectural programme. The Ministry of Finance building by the architect Chemeton looks like an enormous rod that juts out perpendicular to the Seine, where it rests on two enormous pilings. Some people call it a lopped-off viaduct which stops in the river. It does serve as a landmark to denote the boundary of the metropolis, on the edge of the new Bercy sports arena. The Ministry is the building of the 1980s which best expresses the power wielded by the centralized state in France. Cynics have compared it to a yoke, symbolizing the heavy tax burden imposed on ordinary citizens by the Ministry of Finance.

Figure 12.4 La Défense: corporate skyscrapers seen from the roof of the Grand Arch, looking towards the
Arc de Triomphe

Source: Photograph by the author, 1992

Figure 12.5 Looking up at the offices of the Grand Arch through the canopy 'clouds'
Source: Photograph by the author

The style is neo-brutal, reminiscent of Le Corbusier and of the classical tradition in concrete as epitomized by Auguste Perret.

The new Opera House at La Bastille was intended to provide a wholly different experience from the expensive élitism of the old Opera House. It was meant to be a popular venue open to everyone, serving many operas quickly, like fast-food restaurants, and thus requiring vast areas of blind accommodation for back-stage scenery requirements. It meant too much building for a too small triangular site whose entrance had to be from the Place de la Bastille for symbolic reasons. The Opera House is a building for the masses and mass culture. The poor human being is lost. The Opera House reduces its visitors to consumers, rather than participants in the grand occasion which Garnier understood so well in his nineteenth-century opera house. Outside, the new Opera House is ill-defined on the Place de la Bastille. Its dark, foreboding grand entrance, with the high staircase, is gloomy and looks like bureaucratic Fascist architecture, out of scale, with no lightness of touch, as if the design work stopped at the diagram stages and never got down to the details.

Other *grands projets* include the Bibliothèque de France, the Institut du Monde Arabe, the rehabilitation of the Palace of the Grand Louvre and its expansion by the unique device of a high-tech glass pyramid designed by I.M. Pei to shed light on the innards of the new enlarged gallery. The pyramid is consciously designed to provide a reflected image of the old palace, and has attracted as much attention as its direct competitors in London and New York.

Les grands projets all have traits in common, as architectural symbols of the late twentieth century: (a) geometric shapes; (b) uncluttered volumes; and (c) modern materials. All of these reflect a desire on the part of France's leaders to show the dynamism and the confidence of the French in their future. Rather than falling back on the prestigious historic remains of the past, as London tends to do, the French capital is vigorously asserting its determination to hold its rank in the fast-changing landscape of contemporary international architecture. In answer to the critics of *les grands projets*, the official Strategic Plans for Paris have been devised for the eastern part of the inner city, aiming to create mixed-use and residential areas on abandoned industrial sites. This imaginative programme includes the establishment of new cultural institutions in the run-down *quartiers* to act as catalysts for further regeneration, while special attention is being paid to the creation and rehabilitation of public spaces – streets, canals, squares and parks (Davey 1989).

Effects of the transformation of Paris

Although, at first sight, it seemed that France had understood the need for an extensive amount of transformation in order to be acceptably integrated into the new Europe, it is now becoming clear that the cost has been extremely high. Paris is increasingly beset with social problems – totally unsolved by *les grands projets* – which include large areas of deteriorating housing, and overwhelming numbers of migrants flooding the suburbs and the new towns. Unlike London, which built its new towns at least 50 miles distant from the centre as part of a regional plan, Paris built its new towns rather closer to its centre and now has the acute social problems of the immigrants on its doorstep.

In addition, Mitterrand has spent a great deal, particularly in the last years of his presidency, without regard to the financial costs. He is leaving his successors with debts which they may find over-whelming. The centralized government has laid a large burden on the ordinary citizen.

THE SECOND TIER OF CONTENDERS: BERLIN

Introduction

Berlin cannot comfortably look back and celebrate a bicentennial, as could Paris in 1989. Its history has been too painful, too fraught. Berlin can only look forward, and hope that it can make a major contribution to the twenty-first century. Although Berlin was an important European city in the 1930s, today it has to be content with a fourth-rank position, making it part of the second tier of European contenders for top capital city. This second-tier position is due both to its historical heritage prior to the Second World War, and to its peculiar politico-geographical position after the war.

Berlin's historical heritage before the Second World War

Berlin's former structure contained far less of a historic urban fabric than most other European capitals. The medieval city, for example, was overlaid by developments under, first, the Prussian Friedrich I

(1657–1713) and then Friedrich Wilhelm I (1688–1740), in a series of grid-patterned new districts, laid out by surveyors for militarily controlled order and for centralized governmental power, unrelieved by open space or monuments. Friedrich Wilhelm's equestrian statue is Berlin's only elegant structure remaining from its royal past. Likewise, Frederick II 'The Great' (1712–86) added a number of new buildings, including the Opera House (of 1741) which was destroyed in the Second World War but later restored, and the Brandenburg Gate, the ceremonial Doric gateway which became the symbol of the divided Berlin. Friedrich Wilhelm II (1744–97) had schemes for the rebuilding of Berlin, but these were not implemented.

In the nineteenth century, the architect Karl Friedrich Schinkel attempted to give some form to the city following the Napoleonic Wars, but little was accomplished save the new city gates at Leipsinger Platz. Berlin's development in the nineteenth century was confronted by the demands of the expanding railway system and the ever-expanding population working in the ever-expanding industrial factories. Bismarck (1815–98) united Germany under the Prussian King as the first Kaiser in 1871, and Berlin, the Prussian capital, therefore became the national capital until 1945 (Matzerath 1984).

By the mid-twentieth century, there was little to distinguish Berlin architecturally save isolated individual buildings by architects such as Eric Mendelssohn. Therefore Hitler, through his competent architect Albert Speer, could start with a clean sheet, as there was relatively little heritage needing retention.

After building the new Chancellery (1938), Speer created a detailed master plan for a Berlin of 10 million inhabitants between 1937 and 1940, and immediately whole streets of houses were purchased and torn down to implement it. Notwithstanding Hitler's view of the plan as an instrument of political propaganda to demonstrate his immense power in architectural terms, Speer wished to design a metropolis as if it were a work of art (Balfour 1990). In this respect, Speer was in a direct line with the tradition of the Beaux Arts in Paris, the City Beautiful Movement in the United States and the ideas of Peter Behrens in Germany. The Beaux Arts effect was particularly noticeable in the planning and architecture of the main axis, which led from the southern station to Hitler's huge hall, whose dome was to be larger than that of either the Pantheon or St Peter's in Rome.

Speer's plan was based on this north–south axis, and a series of circular and square plazas, but he changed the concept of the north–south axis from being a traffic artery to evoking the new Rome. Each façade along the boulevard was separately designed to enhance the overall effect, and even skyscrapers were designed in the Roman idiom. In Hitler's eyes and by Speer's hands, 'Berlin, rebuilt as the new Rome, would be the great fruit of the war by which Hitler's presence and power would be maintained into an infinite future' (Balfour 1990: 102). The long shadow of Hitler, through Albert Speer's works, hangs over the re-creation of Berlin. That is one reason why foreign architects are being employed to rebuild the city. No one can accuse them of redoing Speer's Berlin, even though architecturally some of their answers are repeating Speer's architectural solutions.

The turbulent years 1946–90: Berlin after the Second World War

At the end of the Second World War, Allied bombing and the Russian attack left Berlin in ruins. It was then divided by the great powers into four zones, British, French, American and Russian. In 1948, the Russian Zone became part of an equally divided Germany, the German Democratic Republic, while the American, British and French Zones became one economic and governmental unit as part of the Federal Republic of Germany. Thus Berlin was located 200 kilometres inside the Soviet Zone.

The next calamity to befall Berlin was the land blockade by the Russians, successfully overcome by the Allied airlift in 1949, but the aftermath was the creation of separate municipal governments, thus splitting the city into East and West Berlin. By 1961 the East Germans stopped the flow of refugees from East to West by building the Berlin Wall, 9 feet high, topped with barbed wire, lined by wide strips of cleared ground heavily guarded and overlooked by armed guards in watchtowers. The Wall was grim and terrifying, and very few who attempted to cross it survived.

Each side attempted to rebuild its part of Berlin in its own ideological image. In West Berlin, the West built the 1957 Congress Hall, restored the Chancellery building, built the marvellous 1963 Philharmonic Concert Hall by the architect Sharoun, and a new National Gallery of Modern Art by Mies van der Rohe. In East Berlin, the communists built the prestigious television tower in 1969, rebuilt, as a vast housing project, Karl Marx Allee, and restored Unter den Linden, lining it with hotels and shops, expressing the Stalinist architectural rigidity of the 1950s. The Berlin Cathedral was not at first rebuilt (although it is now slowly being restored), Potsdamer Platz was left empty, but Schinkel's Alter Museum was restored.

In 1990, the communist regime collapsed, the German Democratic Republic ceased to exist and, in October 1990, East Germany was reunited with West Germany. In November, the Berlin Wall was opened, and by December the Brandenburg Gate had been symbolically reopened. The way was clear for the rebuilding of Berlin after forty-two years of turbulent history.

The rebuilding of Berlin: post-unification

Berlin is attempting to rebuild itself, first as the capital city of a reunified Germany and, second, as a great European capital. But both of these goals are elusive, as Berlin has hardly been either of these for very long in all its 700-year history. Berlin, an ugly city, nevertheless has a most beautiful regional setting, surrounded by enchanting forests and lakes, which have been carefully preserved and provided with recreational facilities. Berlin is in the process of transformation, trying to forget its painful past and look to a brighter future.

The municipal authorities are besieged by planning applications which cannot be referred back to a total master plan. Berlin thus has the chance to become the representative urban form of the twenty-first century, and to contemplate radical changes to suit the first decade of the new millennium. But citizens and architects alike seem to be uncertain as to the kind of Berlin they want, unlike Paris where citizens and politicians are firmly united. Any plan for Berlin must: (1) unite east and west; (2) resolve the symbolism of the Wall area; (3) provide landmarks; and also (4) provide housing, schools and community facilities for its people. The next twenty years will demonstrate whether Berliners are capable of doing this.

The shaping of Berlin as the new capital city of Germany will, it is now felt, take longer than originally conceived during the unification euphoria of 1991. The official timetable of the German federal government is to have all ready for the 1998 parliamentary session, but it now looks as if this will be in the twenty-first century. Graver still are the enormous problems created by the different levels of technological development and cultural diversity.

251

The central historic core is still compact. In East Berlin is the Unter den Linden, a great European boulevard, although not continuously linear like Haussmann's Champs Elysées in Paris, as some buildings are set back, around subsidiary spaces. Former East Germany's greatly debased neo-classical buildings and huge prefabricated blocks are visually arid, and the inhuman scale of its planning is about power rather than about people. West Berlin contains the developed part of the city, but still it is patchy and mixed. The Tiergarten is next to East Berlin, heavily forested, with architectural set-pieces. In the last thirty years, all the development out from the core has taken place along the railway lines. It is thus becoming a star-shaped city with a compact centre.

The planners have designated two sections of Berlin to accommodate the new government centres. The largest of the two is around the historic Reichstag on the banks of the Spree River. Parliament will sit in the Reichstag, and the surrounding buildings will house members of parliament and their staff. The Chancellery will be located nearby. The second centre will be a mile away, near Alexanderplatz in what was East Berlin, and will comprise the Ministries, housed in some of the former buildings of the East German parliament.

The Berlin planners are caught between the developers on the one hand, and the idealistic architects on the other. For example, the redevelopment of the Potsdamer Platz represents 'a collision between potentially conflicting forces; between the search for private profit and the making of public monuments, and between the creation of a confident contemporary architecture and the re-creation of traditional forms' (Cruickshank 1993). Potsdamer Platz has been largely bought up by Sony and Daimler-Benz, with the British architect, Sir Richard Rogers, as the original master planner; but subsequently the Munich firm of Himler and Sattler produced a conservative master plan (Cruickshank 1993). Most of the competing master plans agreed on the re-creation of the octagonal Leipsinger Platz, as one of the great urban spaces of pre-war Berlin. Hillmer and Sattler's brilliant contribution has been to break the western side of Potsdamer Platz with a new avenue which extends the vista to the west and thus makes the important visual connections between the former West and East Berlin. At the same time, twenty-five international architects were asked to prepare a new overall urban development concept for the central area between the Brandenburg Gate and Alexanderplatz and between Lustgarten and

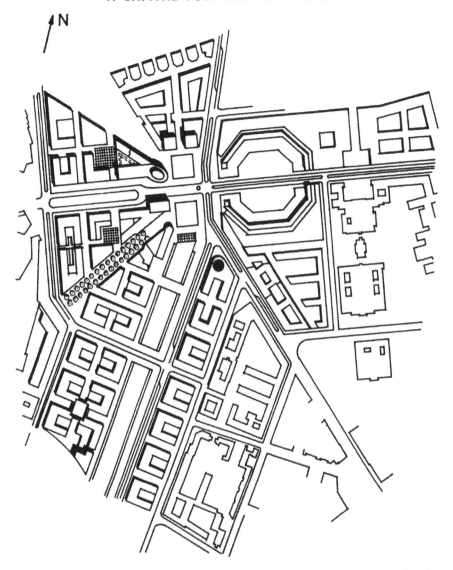

Figure 12.6 Hillmer and Sattler's competition-winning master plan for the
Potsdamer Platz
Source: Redrawn from *Architectural Review*, 1993

Mehringplatz, and also to give examples of architectural solutions for specific individual problems within the particular area
(Lampugham 1991).

Sir Norman Foster's scheme concentrated on a revitalized north–
south axis of Friedrichstrasse intersecting the refurbished area of
the Unter den Linden, reinforcing the existing street pattern and
rejoining the two halves of the city. The area of the Berlin Wall is
mostly turned into a public park to remind future generations of

its history. This is contrary to the desires of the city authorities who want to build over the entire Wall area. The Americans Venturi and Scott-Brown take the victor's attitude, as does Foster, that the Berlin Wall should be a public park to remain for ever on the consciousness of future generations, but they give it even greater emphasis by creating a Brandenburg Stair over the famous Gate as the symbolic location for commemorating the removal of the Wall (Figure 12.7).

The scheme of Giorgio Grassi is more akin to what the city authorities desire. The scheme rebuilds the western borders of the old Friedrichstadt, replicating the traditional three-storey street block buildings. Non-traditionally, the scheme rebuilds, on the derelict Wall area, an interrupted complex of buildings north–south, linking the Reichstag with the former Landtag, both functionally and visually, down to the Baroque Gardens of the former War Ministry and the ruins of the Prinz Albrecht Palais which is to be rebuilt as a memorial museum.

Aldo Rossi's scheme is similar to Grassi's in concept although its architectural form is more varied, human and historical. His plan would fill up the entire Berlin Wall area, half with traditional attractive street blocks and half with overpowering, less attractive slab blocks. Rossi's scheme includes the new Museum of German History which he won by competition in 1988, demonstrating nineteenth-century neo-classical elements.

The developers of Sony and Daimler-Benz have concluded their competitions for the development of Potsdamer Platz by respectively selecting the American architect Helmut Jahn, and the Italian architect Renzo Piano (Cruickshank 1993). The proposals represent middle-of-the-road urban development which could be found on either side of the Atlantic, as the large scale required apparently ruled out any local vernacular interpretations. Jahn's scheme centres on a swirling oval pantheon around a large atrium of public space surrounded by hotel, cinema, apartment and office space. Jahn's scheme opens on the Platz but mostly turns internally to its own private forum covered by a powerfully conceived canopy. Piano's scheme for Daimler-Benz is set back from Potsdamer Platz in a free-standing tower overlooking a new canal, with the theatre and other public buildings pushed against the State Library, and all surrounded by lakes of blue water. Piano's scheme is a further master plan within which other architects will be invited to design individual buildings. This should allow for an incremental effect,

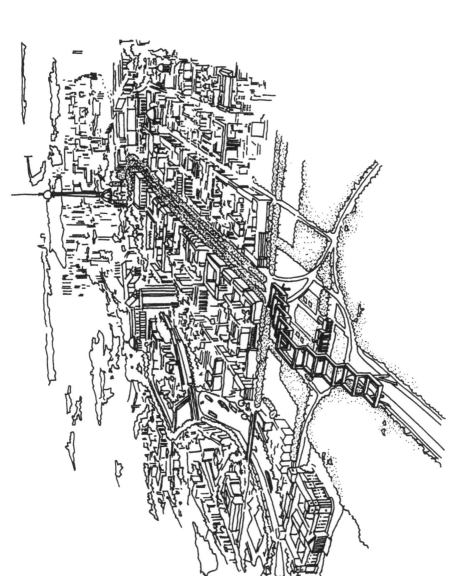

Figure 12.7 Venturi and Scott-Brown's proposal for a Berlin Wall park with a symbolic stair over the Brandenburg Gate
Source: Redrawn from *Architectural Design*, 1991

enabling the diversity and richness of a traditional city to be achieved. In this respect, the city authorities regard Piano's scheme as more in the spirit of the traditional Berlin.

Summary

In the 1920s and 1930s, Berlin was the equal of Paris and London in many fields. For example, it was an intellectual and cultural centre of European-wide stature whether in theatre, film, art, architecture or literature. Although Berlin was in area and population one of the larger cities of Europe, it is now only fourth rank, as rated by Brunet (Datar 1989). The destruction and negativism of the division of Germany into two, and the removal to Bonn of capital status, destroyed its position as a world city.

The efforts of Berlin must focus equally on trying to generate an urban character out of social housing and, equally, overcoming the disaster of their recent past. This places Berliners in a particular situation which will not allow the city to compete on an equal footing with either London or Paris. It is not the only city in a peculiar situation. If, for example, Brussels became the seat of the European Parliament, lobbyists would use it and it would be, de facto, the centre of European Community political power, although only a third-rank city and potentially more of a financial traders' jungle than a capital city (Datar 1989). This would put Brussels in an advantageous position in the competition for capital city of Europe; Berlin, which should be better placed, would be unable to compete. It has now a long task ahead if it is to climb back to its 1930s position as one of the capitals of Europe. To do this in the space of a decade is an enormous challenge, particularly as it must compete also with other German cities like Frankfurt, Munich, Hamburg and Dusseldorf.

CONCLUSION

In conclusion, no single city is likely to acquire all the characteristics needed to become what the Europeans would regard as their capital. It is not possible to say which of the front runners, London and Paris, is in the lead, as they have adopted different approaches.

London has taken the approach of making the conservation of its cultural heritage its permanent concern, with legislation to protect conservation areas, conservation grants and tourism grants focused on specific sites and events. The strategic authority has taken a conservative approach to development (with the exception of the Docklands), using, extending and adapting the buildings which exist rather than entering into expensive projects.

The French have tried to make Paris an example for Europe, providing a coherent urban structure with new architecture either carefully relating contextually to the old or standing out as monuments in carefully chosen places. The individual French achievements are based on a noble reinterpretation of the concept of the European city. But the cost of a few monuments and urban space has been high. The French government is running out of public-sector finance, and Mitterrand's administration is heavily in debt. Their Métro underground system and the RER high-speed rail system are becoming ever more run down. There are heavy commuting flows by road as the regional structure is not as good as that of London, and the new master plan for the Bassin de Paris has yet to be implemented. Social problems in Paris are on the increase.

London has avoided a great number of these problems. Paris is cleaner, but London has better environmental quality overall (LPAC 1992). On the other hand, the attitude to new buildings and new public monuments marks a difference between London and Paris. London is clearly lagging behind. Its Royal Opera House can barely manage an extension, while Paris has built a new Opera House. London's National Gallery has achieved the excellent Sainsbury Wing, but built by private money, while in Paris the Republic has paid for the massive enhancement of the Louvre and the Great Pyramid. The National Portrait Gallery cannot extend, but Paris renovates the Gare d'Orsay into a new museum. The national science museums at Kensington in London are strapped for money, but Paris builds a new science museum at La Villette.

The London Planning Advisory Committee Report clearly sets out a strategy for the twenty-first century which requires 'a clean and pleasant environment' and requires 'comprehensive information and audit' on the state of the environment, among other strategies such as improving transport and housing for lower-income households (LPAC 1992: 200).

The second- and third-rank cities will vie for various aspects of the functioning of the European Community. The French, in order to keep the European Parliament at Strasbourg, may do a deal with the Germans and, in return for their support, agree to Frankfurt as the home of the European Central Bank.

Meantime, Berlin may well become part of a group of well-balanced German cities. Bonn and Berlin would share the governmental functions, with Frankfurt acting as the financial centre and Munich and Hamburg specializing in the media and publishing. Eastern German cities like Dresden will not be contenders for decades, because of declining population owing to migration to the west, unemployment and lack of finance for rebuilding (although ambitious rebuilding plans are being devised).

Brussels will attempt to enhance its position as the political capital of the European Community; London will continue to be a world financial centre and Paris will adopt strategies to reach the same cultural levels as London, the capital city of culture and heritage in Europe. Thus Europe may end up with not a single capital, but a polycentric system of capital cities.

REFERENCES

Abercrombie, P. (1945) *Greater London Plan 1944*, London: HMSO.

Anson, B. (1981) *I'll Fight You For It! Behind the Struggle for Covent Garden*, London: Cape.

Ashworth, G.J. and Tunbridge, J.E. (1990) *The Tourist-Historic City*, London: Belhaven.

Balfour, A. (1990) *Berlin, The Politics of Order, 1737–1989*, New York: Rizzoli.

Bowen, D. (1992) 'Cost of capital punishment', *The Independent on Sunday*, 26 April: 6.

Colenutt, B. and Ellis, G. (1992) 'Squeezing Londoners into the world city mould', *Town and Country Planning*, 61, 3: 68–9.

Cruickshank, D. (1993) 'Crossroads Berlin', *Architectural Review* 1151 (January): 20–9.

Datar (1989) *Les Villes 'Européennes'*, Paris: La Documentation Française.

Davey, P. (1989) 'Paris 200', *Architectural Review*, 1110 (August): 27–74.

Dawson, J. (1992) 'European city networks: experiments in trans-national urban collaborations', *The Planner*, 78, 1: 7–9.

Gosling, D. (1988) 'Urban forms and spaces: waterfront development', *Urban Futures* 1 (1): 18–33.

Houlder, V. (1992) 'Unified market a long way off', *Financial Times*, March 13.

Kinzer, S. (1992) 'Too many capitals (and knee-deep in blueprints)', *The New York Times International*, 14 April.

Lampugham, E. (1991) *Berlin Tomorrow – International Architectural Visions*, London: Academy Editions.

London Planning Advisory Committee (LPAC) (1992) *London: World City Report*, London: HMSO.

Matzerath, H. (1984) 'Berlin, 1890–1940', in Sutcliffe, A.R. (ed.) *Metropolis 1890–1940*, London: Mansell.

Motte, A. (1991) 'The Challenges of European Integration for Urban Planning: The French Case', *The Planner*, 77, 40: 16–18.

Ragon, M. (1986) *Histoire de l'architecture et de l'urbanisme moderne*, vol. 3: *De Brazilia Au post-modernisme 1940–1991*, Paris: Castermann.

Rasmussen, S.E. (1937) *London: The Unique City*, London: Cape.

Rogers, R. and Fisher, M. (1992) *A New London*, London: Penguin.

Savitch, H.V. (1988) *Post-Industrial Cities: Politics and Planning in New York, Paris and London*, Princeton, NJ: Princeton University Press.

Smith, G. (1991) 'Architecture centres', *Architects' Journal*, 17 April, 16, 193: 54–65.

13

A NEW HERITAGE FOR A NEW EUROPE

Problem and potential

P.J. Larkham

INTRODUCTION

This deliberately diverse collection of essays has presented a wide-ranging set of views on a subject that is yet more wide-ranging, and which is subject to continuous change. This is no less than the problem of assessing, first, how the concept of heritage may be used in shaping, or reshaping, national identity, and second, how this process may be applied to the changing conception of Europe as a single supra-national unit.

The first problem has been adequately addressed above, in particular through the use of case studies such as Graham's penetrating view of heritage and Irish national identity (Chapter 8). Implicit within this problem is the question of how heritage may benefit the nation. Such benefits have recently been widely discussed, admittedly usually on the smaller scale of the city or region (Ashworth 1991; Ashworth and Tunbridge 1990). In tangible terms, benefits are often financial, with the range of heritage-related economic activities using existing urban structures and services, and thus bringing income into the system, and reusing redundant areas and relict features. Intangibly, the identification and marketing of heritage to tourists and residents alike can strengthen local identity, pride in place and confidence: 'the value of this to local creativity and enterprise, as well as to attracting investment, commercial establishments and residents from elsewhere, is incalculable' (Ashworth 1991: 124). These benefits can clearly be extrapolated to a nation state, or a supra-national new Europe. Financial benefits are, of course, advantageous; and the possible burgeoning of the tourist industry, given the changing socio-demographic structure and working conditions, easier access to previously inaccessible areas, and easier financial transactions, would lead to considerable benefits in many areas. Of possibly greater importance, however, would be the generation of a Europe-wide place-identity: a sense of belonging to Europe as much as (not instead of) to a particular country or region. Heritage, the sense of the past, is a crucial factor in the generation of a place-identity, and may thus provide a strong unifying force in a new Europe which, it would seem, is simultaneously undergoing pressures for fragmentation and unification.

But, of course, any use of heritage is fraught with problems. Although Ashworth (Chapter 2) and Newby (Chapter 11) give differing views on this, it is salutary to recall, in the context of this volume, that Canadian experience may be appropriate to parts of Europe:

> When heritage becomes linked to tourism it risks losing control of the historical message being selected and presented. If, for example, market research showed that 'ethnic' food, 'ethnic' architecture and casinos were what attracted tourists . . . then the heritage movement might find that money is only then made available for projects which enhance that image. This distorted vision then becomes adopted by the community itself, and so the creation of a 'playground' for outsiders begins to alter the historical consciousness of a community. . . . Heritage-in-the-service-of-tourism can become too closely linked to economic development . . . when the historical message offered in such projects is geared primarily to an 'outside' market or transient visitor, then it does long-term disservice to its own community members and their sense of the past.
>
> (Friesen 1990: 197)

But we are looking, in our context, at a heritage wider than a national scale. Who, then, are these 'outsiders'? Heritage production and consumption then become utilized for the European 'insiders', wherever their origins within Europe; the 'outsiders' are the tourists from outside Europe to whom Carr (Chapter 4) makes reference. Insider and outsider uses and requirements of heritage, at whatever scale, are thus different. This brings us to the second problem.

This is that of application to Europe, and is a more elusive topic.

261

There is a fundamental problem in that, over the past few years in particular, Europe has undergone radical political changes which have opened up entirely new avenues for the use, or abuse, of local, national and international heritages. No longer can Europe be seen merely as the western capitalist-centred European Community of a mere dozen states. Austria, Cyprus, Finland, Malta, Turkey and Sweden are pressing hard for admission. Profound changes in the former communist bloc necessitate a much wider view – the centre of gravity of the 'new Europe' is, for the first time in several hundred years, moving eastwards. Recent advertising material for the large Polish textile-manufacturing city of Łódź suggests that this is now the 'crossroads of the new Europe'.

Nationalism is once more a potent social force in Europe. Many of these nationalisms are, clearly, based on some form of awareness of national history; and these nationalisms are, equally clearly, coming to the fore with the removal of the threat of the Cold War and the dissolution of the Soviet bloc. Many such nationalisms are xenophobic to a greater or lesser extent. The future of a new Europe is thus problematic.

THE NEW EUROPE: UNITY OR DISUNITY?

Within this new, large-scale Europe, socio-economic and political conditions are anything but stable. The limitations of the relatively small-scale view of the EC are shown by the community's response to the initial changes in eastern Europe consequent upon Gorbachev's rise to power. De la Serre (1991: 303) noted that 'a new era has started concerning the relationships of the Community with the east that should result in the gradual setting up of a commercial and cooperation policy adjusted to the situation of each country'. The rapid fragmentation of the east renders this gradual approach of dubious value. De la Serre also showed the economic problems faced by the east, despite EC agreements to remove quantitative restrictions imposed on eastern imports, and the large sums of foreign aid being granted (for example, France granted 4 billion francs (about $800 million) to Poland for three years, and the Federal Republic of Germany granted DM 3 billion, about $1,500 million) (de la Serre 1991: 305, 312). There are major debates over the potential problems of this approach in possibly generating an aid-based economy. Moreover, the EC adjustment to the reunification of Germany has been largely a reactive process, and has revealed differences between the member states and division among EC institutions; these are significant despite the eventual possible successful adjustment of the EC to the new Germany (Feldman 1991).

Differences are clearly also evident at a popular level. In 1992, Denmark voted in a referendum to reject the Maastricht Treaty. France accepted the treaty, but by the narrowest of margins. Two public opinion polls in Britain showed a rising trend against further integration, or 'federalism', ranging from smaller – but nevertheless emotive – items such as a single currency to more fundamental issues such as the granting of more power to European political institutions. These trends were clear across the whole UK electorate and, significantly, among Conservative voters. Yet these evidences of diversity are relatively minor, albeit pervasive in several countries.

Of possibly greater concern is the rise, since the mid-1970s in particular, of political extremism in a number of countries. Such extreme parties, usually right-wing, profess an extreme nationalism often manifest in attacks upon minority groups, usually of recent migrants (Hockenos 1994). The political power of the extreme Right in France is rising. The British National Front has been implicated in attacks on Jewish cemeteries, and there have been recent attacks by young right-wingers upon refugee hostels in a number of German cities including Rostock and Magdebourg. It is worrying that these latter attacks were watched, with no evident concern but rather some implicit support, by many of the populace, and official reactions have been tardy.

Of equal significance is the conflict between ethnic and religious factions in parts of the former eastern bloc; a crisis so severe and so recent that reports are limited to those filtering into the news media. Yugoslavia has been split, and EC recognition of some of its constituents as nations has been a major setback to Yugoslavian federalism. The recognition of Slovenia and Croatia is, however, likely to be counter-productive; their sources of cheap raw materials and main markets – Bosnia-Herzegovina and Serbia – are now closed. The tourist industry, dominant on the Dalmatian coast until recently, and which brought in some 40 per cent of Yugoslavia's foreign earnings, is now virtually non-existent (West 1992). Ferocious Serbian attacks on Dubrovnik, Zadar and Sibenik have damaged or destroyed the historic monuments and much of the character which drew the tourist crowds. Even early in the attack on Dubrovnik, targets were clearly the old city and the new suburbs: neither of great military value.

> City authorities estimate that between 25 and 30 shells have landed in its centre, damaging the exterior of five important historical sites. The shells had a surprisingly low explosive charge. The damage inside the old walls is almost inconsequential compared to the destruction wrought in the suburb of Lapad where 6,000 refugees have been sheltering in modern hotels, now uninhabitable after sustained mortar attacks.
>
> (O'Kane 1991: 28)

A much greater human disaster has been the phenomenon of 'ethnic cleansing'. This has hit the world headlines, along with a graphic portrayal of death, looting, 170 detention camps filled with civilians, and wholesale population movement – ostensibly by agreement but, all interviews suggest, in practice at gunpoint. The character of the Yugoslavian landscape is changing. Entire villages have been emptied of their populations and burned; churches and mosques have been destroyed; other settlements have been repopulated by those of an 'acceptable' ethnic or religious background.

This is, admittedly, rather an extreme case, and parallels already being drawn with the Holocaust in Nazi Germany are fallacious. Analysts point to the long history of the Balkans as a racial and religious mixing-ground.

> The Croats are more politically divided than the Slovenes. They include Catholics (of various leanings) and anti-clericals, some of them liberal. Then again, different parts of the country have quite different traditions . . . Dalmatia is Italianate; the north fell under Germano-Hungarian influences; further south, Slav ways prevail. . . . The variety is such that the literary language is to some extent (opinions vary) artificial.
>
> (Stone 1992)

There are clear parallels with much of the rest of Europe, widely defined. Nationalist conflicts are occurring in parts of the former USSR; the Baltic states have become independent again; terrorist bombs explode in northern Spain, Corsica and Northern Ireland, while Welsh Nationalists have been more active in arson attacks on

English holiday homes. Even Sweden has an explicitly racist New Democratic Party, founded only in 1990 and already holding the parliamentary balance of power.

Czechoslovakia, too, is riven with discord; but the political problems evident between the Czechs and Slovaks, particularly following economic restructuring which seemed to be much more economically detrimental in Slovakia than in Czech areas, are accompanied so far by relative peace. But opinion polls in Slovakia suggest that only 13 per cent support a wholly independent Slovakia, while 60 per cent, although nationalist, wished the unitary or federal state to continue in some form. Although there is little overt conflict at present, over half of the Slovaks apparently fear ethnic violence, and feel that independence would bring territorial claims from Hungary and Ukraine.

> There are fears haunting the corridors of power in Central and Western Europe that, with turmoil in Europe's Balkan periphery and instability on the fringes of the former Soviet Union, ethnic tension, economic instability and renewed security problems could now emerge in the very heart of the continent.
>
> (Hall 1992: 251)

The largely nineteenth-century concept of the European nation state is now evidently outdated. Alone, European countries are no longer world powers; and this is becoming more the case with the trend to breaking up some of the 'artificially' created states into their constituent regions. The concept of rootedness – *enracinement* – is more clearly tied to this smaller regional scale. At a variety of scales, therefore, conflict is endemic in a Europe which has frequently been a battleground, migration and colonization route, and where nationalism rose most pointedly only in the nineteenth century. Changes in borders, political control, dominant religion and ethnic grouping are all commonplace in European history, and popular memories of previous oppression, atrocity and injustice run deep throughout the continent. England, with no successful foreign invasion since 1066, is lucky to remain in relative peace; indeed, here, tracing one's ancestry to the Norman invaders is a booming industry. Earlier ideas of integration and multiculturalism are now at risk from the rampant nationalism, intolerance and xenophobia. Opposing political groups are seeking to manipulate heritage for their own, nationalistic, ends.

265

WOUNDS AND THEIR HEALING

As this volume suggests, history as perceived is distorted, used, interpreted, rewritten (cf. Lowenthal 1985). The rewritten past is particularly problematic. It poses considerable problems for the immediate future since some of the relatively recent rewritings, particularly from the former Soviet bloc, have explicitly deleted great areas of history, razed monuments and introduced a degree of xenophobia. The case of Romania is instructive. Here, following the 1974 Urban and Rural Systematization Law, it was planned to demolish 7,000–8,000 of the 13,000 villages in the country by the year 2000, replacing them with 500 'agro/industrial centres'. The 1977 dissolution of the Directorate of Historic Buildings showed the value, or rather lack of it, placed upon the past and its heritage. By the fall of Ceausescu in late 1989, twenty-nine towns had been wholly reconstructed and thirty-seven were undergoing that process. Manifestations of the past were being comprehensively removed in favour of a very different future (Givrescu 1989). Such damage to both physical aspects of heritage and national senses of identity and belonging are difficult to repair.

Throughout much of the continent, it appears that time alone does not heal these wounds. In September 1992, two leading German aerospace companies planned a celebration of fifty years of German aerospace technology. At the last moment, however, Chancellor Kohl and the government withdrew support from this celebration, which featured the wartime V2 terror weapon; they were bowing to widespread international pressure that celebration of such a weapon was insensitive (Tomforde and Sharrock 1992). Earlier, in June 1992, the Queen Mother unveiled a statue in London to Sir Arthur Harris, leader of the wartime Bomber Command and responsible for the '1,000 bomber raids' and resulting devastation of many German cities. The occasion released controversy in Britain, and from Germany, where the event coincided with the fiftieth anniversary of the first major raid on Cologne. Joachim Becker, Lord Mayor of Pforzheim, stated that the statue was inappropriate: 'a Europe united in peace and freedom needs other symbols than the honouring of a man who is responsible for the death of 20,000 people in this city' (Victor 1992). Others, however, saw it quite differently, as part of Europe's anti-Fascist struggle of the early 1940s, which should be remembered lest collective amnesia leads to the need to repeat it.

Statues and monuments are often very powerful images evoking a particular past. The Harris statue commemorates the RAF bomber offensive during the Second World War in the same way that the Kiel U-boat monument commemorates Doenitz's naval offensive, but these monuments have a very different significance in the cities bombed or for the ships sunk. Reports of the possibility of a memorial on the site of the Berlin *Führerbunker*, made available through the fall of the Berlin Wall, similarly provoked anger in both Britain and Germany. The new statue opposite the Moscow building once occupied by the Central Committee of the Communist Party, which attracted great public interest on its unveiling, commemorates Saints Cyril and Mephody, two Bulgarian Greeks who invented the Cyrillic alphabet. Russian – or Slavic – nationalism or national culture is showing a resurgence. Russians are apparently complaining at the insidious takeover of the Latin script – a literal rewriting. As one interviewee said:

> Today there is a new form of aggression facing the Russians. It starts with our language being pushed aside. Why do you have to speak a sort of Esperanto to make yourself understood these days? Why are all the signs for western companies in Latin scripts? We are being pushed into a new world order where money governs. Russians will never join this order.
>
> (quoted in Hearst 1992)

A last statue of note is that re-erected in October 1990 in Zagreb, to Governor Jelacic, who had put down a revolution in 1848. This event prompted vast crowds to congregate, and a nostalgia for the old Austro-Hungarian Empire was widely apparent. Yet not all was happy under Imperial rule, and there was discrimination against Orthodox Serbs by Catholic Croats. 'The Croats who greeted the statue of Jelacic seem to forget, if they ever knew, that his army consisted of Serbs whose descendants are now fighting in places like Karlovac and Vukavar' (West 1992: 25).

This last example appears to show some of the popular rewriting of history, or reclaiming of heritage, which so often occurs in times of great political unrest. In the aftermath of the break-up of the USSR, when Leningrad was renamed St Petersburg, some had warned that the recent rewriting and popularizing of pre-revolutionary Russian history might lead to the invention of a 'mythical Russian golden age of benevolent autocrats, a benign aristocracy, a toothless police, indulgent censors, satisfied intellectuals and merry muzhiks' (Wood 1992). This idealized view recently emerging is contrary to the results of a 'solid body of non-partisan Western scholarship' (Wood 1992). The reclaiming, or reinterpretation, of history is, of course, important in the pacifying or subjugation of a populace. But some populations – refugees in alien countries and cultures – face the choice of whether to adapt and assimilate or to strive to preserve their cultural uniqueness. Europe's history of conflict has produced many such refugee populations, and is still doing so today. The wounds felt by such groups rarely heal fully, leading to uneasy relationships with host communities and claims and counter-claims to original territories.

WHAT HAS BEEN DONE? WHAT CAN BE DONE?

There are many socio-cultural and historical elements that are held in common throughout much of the wider Europe. The importance of ancient Greece and Rome in shaping society is acknowledged, although in Britain at least their history and languages are vanishing from our schools. Simms (1992), for example, explores the unifying features of Roman urban traditions in those countries once part of the Roman empire, and the differences with the non-Romanized part of Europe. Much of Europe shares the Christian faith, although there are many branches of Christianity and its history is riven with bloodshed and discord. But as one looks to the more recent past, large-scale unifying features become difficult to identify. Nevertheless, the continent's long and rich history provides fertile ground for exploration.

Yet relatively little has been done in this turbulent and troubled continent to weld together the disparate socio-political groups to form a coherent, continent-wide body. It is easy to point to the nature and scale of the continuing disruptions, intimating that the task is too difficult. Certainly there has been a recent trend towards the identification of smaller and smaller national units which, bolstered by often spurious tradition, have sought increasing degrees of freedom from larger national units, which were themselves often formed following conquest or dynastic marriage. Scotland, for example, using the spurious history and trappings popularized by the Victorians and the large tourist revenues thus generated, together with oil revenue, has made various moves towards greater independence throughout the late twentieth century. It is a matter of considerable concern in this respect that the Secretary-General of the United Nations, Dr Boutros Boutros Ghali, suggested in 1992 that, over the next decade, the world could splinter into some 400 economically crippled mini-states, following the example of Yugoslavia and elsewhere in eastern Europe (Leopold 1992).

It has already been shown, in several chapters of this volume, that any and all heritage planning is explicitly or implicitly political. Some features of the physical heritage are selected for re-creation or preservation; some historical incidents are emphasized, others forgotten. The process is inherently selective; what is important is the nature and number of those who are disinherited, as their heritages are not selected or are not portrayed in a favourable light. Any consideration of a supra-national European heritage must regard this as a major problem. It would be folly thus to disinherit minorities at a time when ethnic, religious and other groups are responding to pressure by attempting to create more small nation states. Instead, Europe requires a culturally and ethnically pluralist perspective.

This has been lacking, for the most part, in much of the continent. Little has been done to integrate the cultures of recent immigrants, from the Middle East, Africa and India in particular, but also increasingly from other parts of Asia. In the Netherlands, for example, the largely urban Turkish and Moroccan cultural minorities are, as yet, unrepresented in a heritage interpretation that is strongly oriented to the seventeenth-century 'Golden Age' (Ashworth and de Haan 1990). History has, as the saying goes, been written by the victors. Heritage has been decided by the powerful: the victors, the wealthy, the educated middle class. Hence the heritage guarded by Cadw (Chapter 4) is that of the conqueror, the invading Anglo-Norman, the castle and church, rather than the indigenous Celt. It has taken centuries of relative peace for the culture and history of the invading Normans to become assimilated into the history of England. In post-communist Poland, the Palace of Culture in Warsaw is a piece of typical Stalinist architecture, dominating the city by its height and scale. As a 'gift of the people of Russia' in the 1950s, this is now seen as a great symbol of cultural oppression, and there have been many calls for it to be demolished. Yet it clearly represents an important part of Poland's twentieth-century social history; its retention and reuse could be a much more appropriate way of coming to terms with the past than its demolition. In other contexts, the problem of differing religious heritages arises with increasing frequency as immigrant groups bring their traditions with them. Hence an eastern European church nestling in a leafy suburb of Birmingham is a surprise, as are the stranger forms of mosque minarets and domes in the city centre. The planning battles that can arise over these unusual, unfamiliar urban forms show considerable polarity of cultural groups.

This should not lead to the conclusion that heritage interpretation, generation or planning are, on balance, socially undesirable and divisive activities (as is asserted, for example, by Hardy 1989). It must, instead, be realized that the generation of a European heritage would provide no panacea, but that the distribution of social and cultural costs and benefits should form an integral part of heritage planning (Ashworth 1991).

Will there ever be a pan-European identity and culture, with all the trappings, heroes, villains and history that this would entail? Languages, currencies and other unique features of individual nation states may decline, as we have seen those nation states themselves declining, and as the advantages of a Europe-wide identity become more and more evident. However, although it is clearly in the interests of all countries or regimes to collaborate closely in a new Europe, some areas dissent, looking back, perhaps, to their histories of conflict, superiority or isolationism. Yet any new Europe will not actually require the subsuming of individual place-identities or national cultures; rather, perhaps, the acceptance of diversity and plurality.

In thematic terms, given the diversity of the continent, it would be impossible to prescribe a European heritage. The problem of the dispossessed in any such marketing is too great, as the controversies over the V2 and Sir Arthur Harris commemorations showed. In a multicultural Europe, even themes such as 'trade' or 'exploration' impinge upon the minority migrants from the countries explored and, later, exploited. But these would form powerful linking themes to a number of individual national heritages. The heritage given tangible form by the *SS Great Britain*, in her original dock in Bristol and redolent of Victorian technological innovation and trade, or the wreck of the *Amsterdam*, a Dutch East India Company vessel wrecked off Hastings in 1748, form actual and potential features for such trade-based heritage planning. Even the controversial theme of warfare is currently well represented by warships that were, in practice, complete failures: the *Mary Rose* and *Wasa*. Invaluable for archaeological study, these two vessels were national disasters, both sinking under the very eyes of their monarchs. They are difficult to market, or interpret, as nationalist heritage (although, in both cases, the attempt is made to do so).

It is this conception of nationalism, the representation of the might of the late nineteenth-century nation state, that must be overcome in a new Europe. What was good for one state had clear implications, often adverse, for others. The might of empire cannot form the basis for European heritage. What may be more appropriate, however, is the fostering of national, regional and even local diversity. In many senses, heritage has been commodified – it is now a product, marketed in the same way as any other. And, in the same way that productive industries specialize, so may the heritage product of countries and regions be specialized. The new Europe need not, despite the fears of many among the populations of the EC countries at present, lead to greater bureaucracy, standardization and sameness. This is not what harmonization of necessity implies. Neither would a continent-wide sameness to heritage be desirable. After all, it is diversity – the desire to see different places and things – which fuels tourism, particularly heritage-related tourism. Relph (1976) coined the term 'placelessness' to describe what he saw, and feared, as the loss of individual place-identity in the westernized world. The same is happening to heritage in minor ways, such as the diffusion of standardized, mass-produced 'heritage' cast-iron street furniture in the UK. Every historic street and town now has its black-painted, gold-trimmed bollards, litter bins and lamp-posts, purchased from just one or two large suppliers. In planning for a new Europe, a heritage that will reflect the diversities of local culture and history must be encouraged. There should be no *faits accomplis* or directives from any central European administration: it is difficult enough to legislate for one country's conservation areas, as current debate in England shows (Jones and Larkham 1993). There needs rather to be widespread acceptance of existing diversity in parallel with the development of linking themes of Europe-wide relevance. Some themes will, admittedly, 'disinherit' some groups; the 'nastiness' of a continent-wide history must be accepted, for it cannot be swept away. Other themes may overemphasize the history of other groups, arguably substituting hype for history: but this may be a valid way of exploring the past of minority and exploited groups, as the *Roots* phenomenon arguably did for the American slave trade in the 1970s. This, too, must be accepted both by policy-makers and by consumers.

But the exact nature of such a heritage requires further work, with detailed studies in each of the countries contributing to the new Europe. Such a Europe-wide project in itself may contribute, in some measure, to a sense of unity. Two major international projects, both related to urban history (and thus, indirectly, heritage) are currently in progress: the *Historic Towns Atlases*, a long-term project involving considerable research, but which has received criticism in terms of changing goals over the years and problems of data presentation and interpretation (Borgwik and Hall 1981; Slater and Lilley 1992) and the new *Historical Atlas of European Cities*, a ten-volume project supported by the Catalan regional and Spanish national governments, co-ordinated by the Centre de Cultura Contemporània de Barcelona. This latter project suggests a way forward for heritage studies in terms of large-scale multidisciplinary, multinational co-operation, aiming to produce a good overview (albeit of a sample of cities), using high-quality computer cartography, publishing rapidly and to an attractive standard, and aiming at a wide interested public. This project, much more than the scholarly *Historic Towns Atlases*, should bring a Europe-wide comparative urban history to public attention. It could serve as a model for studies of heritage, heritage-related tourism and the identification, and development, of key elements for a Europe-wide approach to heritage which would serve as a significant unifying factor in a continent wherein strong pressures for unity and fragmentation are currently plainly evident.

REFERENCES

Ashworth, G.J. (1991) *Heritage Planning*, Groningen: GeoPers.

Ashworth, G.J. and de Haan, T.Z. (1990) 'Van geschiedenis tot erfgoed: stedelijk verleden op de markt', *Recreatie en Toerisme* 3: 83–6.

Ashworth, G.J. and Tunbridge, J.E. (1990) *The Tourist-Historic City*, London: Belhaven.

Borgwik, L. and Hall, T. (1981) 'Urban History Atlases: a survey of recent publications', *Urban History Yearbook* 1981: 66–75.

Feldman, L.G. (1991) 'The EC and German unification', in Hurwitz, L. and Lequesne, C. (eds) *The State of the European Community: Policies, Institutions and Debates in the Transition Years*, London: Longman.

Friesen, J. (1990) 'Introduction: heritage futures', *Prairie Forum* 15, 2: 193–8.

Givrescu, D.C. (1989) *The Razing of Romania's Past*, New York: World Monuments Fund.

Hall, D. (1992) 'Czech mates no more?', *Town and Country Planning* 61, 9: 250–1.

Hardy, D. (1989) 'Historical geography and heritage studies', *Area* 20: 333–8.

Hearst, D. (1992) 'Bulgarian saints find themselves on a pedestal of Russian nationalism', *Guardian*, May.

Hockenos, P. (1994) *Free to Hate: the Rise of the Right in Post-Communist East Europe*, London: Routledge.

Jones, A.N. and Larkham, P.J. (1993) *The Character of Conservation Areas*, Research report commissioned from Plan Local, London: Royal Town Planning Institute.

Leopold, E. (1992) 'UN chief laments split of world into powerless mini-states', *The Times*, 21 September: 12.

Lowenthal, D. (1985) *The Past is a Foreign Country*, Cambridge: Cambridge University Press.

O'Kane, M. (1991) 'Pock-marked old city takes on air of large male prison', *The Guardian*, 16 September: 28.

Relph, E. (1976) *Place and Placelessness*, London: Pion.

de la Serre, F. (1991) 'The EC and Central and Eastern Europe', in Hurwitz, L. and Lequesne, C. (eds) *The State of the European Community: Policies, Institutions and Debates in the Transition Years*, London: Longman.

Simms, A. (1992) 'The early origins and morphological inheritance of European towns', in Whitehand, J.W.R. and Larkham, P.J. (eds) *Urban Landscapes: International Perspectives*, London: Routledge.

Slater, T.R. and Lilley, K.D. (1992) 'The British Historic Towns Atlas: a critique', Unpublished paper presented at the International Conference of Historical Geographers, Vancouver, August.

Stone, N. (1992) 'The unyoking of the Balkans', *Guardian*, 23 January: 25.

Tomforde, A. and Sharrock, D. (1992) 'Celebration of V2 launch called off', *The Guardian*, 29 September: 18.

Victor, P. (1992) 'Ten arrested at Harris protest', *The Times*, 1 June: 1, 18.

West, R. (1992) 'A catastrophe for Croatia', *Guardian*, 23 January: 25.

Wood, A. (1992) Letter to the editor, *Guardian*, 20 August.

GENERAL INDEX

PLACE INDEX